BOAC

AN ILLUSTRATED HISTORY

BOAC

AN ILLUSTRATED HISTORY

Charles Woodley

First published 2004

Tempus Publishing Ltd
The Mill, Brimscombe Port
Stroud, Gloucestershire GL5 2QG
www.tempus-publishing.com

British Library Cataloguing in Publication Data.
A catalogue record for this book is available from the British Library.

ISBN 0 7524 3161 7

Typesetting and origination by Tempus Publishing.
Printed and bound in Great Britain.

Contents

Acknowledgements

My thanks are due to the following people who gave so generously of their time, knowledge and resources to help me produce this book:

Campbell McCutcheon at Tempus Publishing, for commissioning this work, and for help and encouragement. Keith Hayward and his helpers at the British Airways Archives and Museum Collection, for allowing me to search through the Archives, and for also searching on my behalf. John Battersby at the Bristol Aero Collection for help with BOAC Britannia material. The late Roger Jackson, for sourcing and allowing me to reproduce images from the A.J. Jackson Photographic Collection. Derek King, for compiling a BOAC fleet list for me, and for supplying other BOAC material. Maurice J. Wickstead, for compiling a BOAC wartime fleet list for me, and for sending me copies of relevant articles. Mike Phipp, for much material on BOAC activities at Hurn and Poole. Peter Waller at Ian Allan Publishing, for granting permission to reproduce copyright material. Harro Ranter, for granting permission to reproduce material from the Aviation Safety Network website. Michael Crump, Head of Design Management, British Airways, for obtaining permission for me to use the British Airways copyrighted 'Speedbird' logo and name in the design of this book, and for permission to use British Airways copyright photographs. Paul Isherwood at Manchester Airport Archives, for unearthing photographs for me. Eric Loseby, for supplying images from his personal photograph albums. David Young, for granting permission to use material from his Comet website. Air-Britain (Historians) Ltd, for granting permission to reproduce photographs from their photo-library. Clive Dyball, for sending me a CD of images all the way from Australia. All the contributors to the Air-Britain Information Exchange, for answering my queries and supplying additional material. Mary Dixon, for repeatedly coming up with vintage photos and press cuttings. Bill Armstrong, for granting permission to use his website images. Stewart Dunlop, Philip Lamb at Presbus Publishing Services, Peter Berry MRAeS for permission to use extracts from 'Thirty West' and his Prestwick Airport book, and for supplying much Prestwick material, Peter White, Malcolm McCrow, David Ayling, Mrs Mary Smith, Mr B. Drinkwater, Ian Dobinson, Drew Craigie, Michael Harrison, Maurice Marsh, Malcolm D. Stride, W. McGill, The Ricky Shiels Collection, Michael H. Starritt, Michael Wall, The Handley Page Association, Heathrow Airport PLC Press Office, Barry Abraham, Steve Hocking, Magaret Day, Chris Dellar, Stan M. Lowery, Mr. R.W. Findlay, British Aerospace PLC, Margot Day, Julie McDonnell at Airbus UK for permission to reproduce Bristol copyright photographs, and finally, my wife Hazel, for her continuing support of my writing activities.

If I have forgotten anyone, please accept my apologies and thanks.

I hope that this work will prove a worthy record of the activities of a world-beating airline.

Introduction

For over thirty years the British Overseas Airways Corporation (BOAC for short) was Britain's state-owned flag-carrier on air routes to the farthest-flung parts of the globe, and in doing so it acted as an unofficial ambassador for the country and the products of its aircraft industry. Until the advent of Tourist Class and Economy-Class fares in the mid-1950s, international air travel was an elitist activity reserved for the wealthy or those travelling on official government business, and BOAC's pedigree was suitably refined, the company being a direct descendent of Imperial Airways, the airline that linked the mother country with its outposts of Empire. With Europe already at war, Imperial Airways was merged with the original British Airways to form BOAC, and the new airline spent its first years engaged on hazardous duties in support of the war effort. These included ferrying supplies to the British Expeditionary Force in France, crossing the North Sea in De Havilland Mosquitoes to bring back consignments of vital ball bearings from Sweden, and pioneering transatlantic air routes with flying-boats and converted Liberator bombers.

The resumption of peacetime flying saw BOAC struggling to operate scheduled services with hopelessly uneconomical conversions of Halifax and Lancaster bombers, and flying the legendary Douglas Dakota to the Middle East and West Africa, as well as on European routes until the formation of British European Airways (BEA) in August 1946. As the national airline, BOAC was also expected to be the launch customer for new British airliners, including the Avro Tudor, Handley Page Hermes, Bristol Britannia and, much later, the Vickers VC-10. Unfortunately, these designs ended up being tailored so closely to BOAC's rather unique requirements that their global sales prospects were extremely limited as a result.

The 1950s were probably BOAC's 'golden age', and the airline's prestigious reputation was showcased by two services in particular. At a time when other major carriers were operating modern American-built landplanes, BOAC's Short Solent flying-boat service to South Africa took a leisurely four and a half days.

The pace was slow but luxurious, with night stops in hotels along the way, and there was even an excursion to the Valley of the Kings included during the stopover at Luxor. Perhaps the ultimate expression of luxury air travel, however, was BOAC's 'Monarch' De Luxe service to New York. The Boeing Stratocruisers used featured the widest passenger cabin in service at the time, and passengers could descend a spiral staircase to the downstairs cocktail lounge for a nightcap before retiring for the night in their sleeper berths.

BOAC were also pioneers of the jet age. When their Comet 1 service to Johannesburg departed London on 2 May 1952, it inaugurated the world's first regular passenger service by a jet airliner. The revolutionary new design slashed flying times around the globe, and when two catastrophic and initially inexplicable disasters grounded the type, BOAC kept faith with De Havilland and ordered a fleet of the much-improved and developed Comet 4. By doing so they were able to outdo their rival Pan-American Airways and inaugurate the world's first transatlantic scheduled jet services in 1958. In later years the popularity of the Vickers VC-10 with discerning travellers would maintain BOAC's market position on the North Atlantic until the introduction of the wide-bodied Boeing 747 at the beginning of the 1970s.

Government pressure to introduce economies and improve efficiency in Britain's two state-owned airlines led to the establishment of the British Airways Board to take overall control of the activities of BOAC and BEA in 1972, and on 1 April 1974 the amalgamation of the two airlines to form British Airways was finally completed. In recent years it has been noticeable that many of British Airways' short-haul routes have been franchised out to smaller, more cost-effective carriers, so perhaps there is after all a case to be made for having two British national airlines, one long-haul and one short-haul, under the same holding company and sharing resources wherever possible to maximise their profitability. Time will tell.

1

The Birth of BOAC

The British Overseas Airways Corporation, abbreviated to BOAC, was conceived as Britain stood on the brink of the Second World War, and was formed by the merger of Britain's two major airlines of the time, Imperial Airways and the original British Airways.

Imperial Airways had been founded on 31 March 1924, and on the next day it took over the aircraft and services of Handley Page Transport Ltd., The Instone Air Line Ltd., The Daimler Airway and the British Marine Air Navigation Company Ltd. The combined fleet consisted of both seaplanes and landplanes, which were based at Croydon. The new airline was given the task of reopening British air routes to Europe, and of developing air communications linking the countries of the British Empire with each other and with the mother country. During the late 1920s and early 1930s, Imperial Airways pioneered air routes to the Middle East and Africa. In 1931 a major step forward in passenger comfort came with the introduction of Handley Page HP 42 equipment on both the European routes and on services from a base at Cairo to India and Africa. These four-engined airliners accommodated up to twenty-four passengers in Pullman-style interiors and carried a steward to attend to their comfort and provide a full meal service. On 18 January 1934 Qantas Empire Airways Ltd was formed by Imperial Airways and Qantas to provide Singapore-Australia connections with the Imperial Airways services to the Far East. The first models of the Short Bros. Empire Flying boats were introduced on 30 October 1936, and these facilitated the inauguration on 29 June 1937 of the Empire Air Mail Programme, under which all mail was carried by air at a flat rate of 1½*d*. During 1938 two new landplane types, the Armstrong Whitworth Ensign and the De Havilland Albatross, entered service. The 'Frobisher'-class Albatross was the first Imperial Airways type to carry the 'Speedbird' logo, later to be adopted by BOAC as its emblem. At this time many airlines were contemplating possible solutions to the problems posed by transatlantic air services and Imperial Airways experimented with the Short-Mayo composite aircraft system, consisting of the large four-engined 'Maia' flying-boat, similar to the Empire designs, and the smaller 'Mercury' seaplane, which was mounted on top of it. As 'Mercury' would be unable to take off unassisted with a full load of mail and fuel, it was carried aloft on top of 'Maia' and released at a favourable altitude. The first trial flight took place on 21 July 1938, when Mercury was released near Foynes in Ireland and flew the 2,930 miles to Montreal non-stop in 20hrs 20mins. In the summer of 1939 the last aircraft type to be designed specifically for Imperial Airways, the Short Bros. 'G' class flying-boat, was launched. This was a larger development of the Empire-class flying-boats, but before it could enter airline service the Second World War intervened, and the type served initially with the RAF on long-range reconnaissance duties.

British Airways was originally formed on 1 October 1935 as Allied British Airways, after the merger of Spartan Air Lines and United Airways. In November 1935 the name was shortened to British Airways Ltd. Based at Heston, the new airline competed with Imperial Airways on European routes. In 1936 the base was transferred to the new Gatwick Airport, and a mixed fleet which included Junkers Ju 52/3M freighters was operated. During the late 1930s re-equipment with modern American all-metal types took place. Amongst these were included the Lockheed L10 Electra and the Lockheed L14, later to be named the Hudson in RAF service.

In November 1938 the Secretary of State for Air announced in the House of Commons that Imperial Airways and British Airways were to be merged into a single Corporation, to be the single 'chosen instrument' of the United Kingdom Government in the skies outside the British Isles. By June 1939 the two companies, though nominally still in existence, were working together as a single Corporation. The British Overseas Airways Act received Royal Assent and became law on 4 August 1939. In November 1939 the British Overseas Airways Corporation was established, with Sir John Reith as its first chairman. On 1 April 1940 BOAC officially took over the aircraft, operations and staff of Imperial Airways and British Airways and became Britain's first state-owned airline. The Corporation issued £4.5 million of 3 per cent Airways Stock, and from the sums thus received BOAC paid out around £3.25 million to Imperial Airways and British Airways for their assets. Until the formation of BOAC the airline fleets had been under the direct control of the Air Ministry's National Air Communications scheme, an emergency organisation set up on the outbreak of war, and to be disbanded in June 1940 following the fall of France.

2

Second World War Operations

In 1940 the BOAC headquarters was at Whitchurch airfield near Bristol, which also served as the UK terminus for landplane services. Flying-boat operations were conducted from Poole Harbour in Dorset. The airfields at Croydon, Heston, Exeter and Shoreham were also used for flights to continental Europe, while Scandinavian destinations were served from Perth and Aberdeen (Dyce) until the deteriorating war situation caused their withdrawal on 9 April 1940. Similarly, the services to the Continent ceased soon after the French capitulation on 17 June 1940. The French defeat severed for a while the air routes to the 111 stations throughout the Middle East, Far East, Africa and Bermuda inherited from Imperial Airways. However, the pre-war Empire routes were still maintained, with the first BOAC service leaving Durban in South Africa on 3 April 1940. Services to neutral Sweden, Portugal, Spain and the USA were reopened in due course, and a vital re-routed service to Lagos was surveyed and opened in August 1940, using 'C' class flying-boats.

Only official government passengers were carried on the four-times-weekly Dakota services from Whitchurch to Lisbon. A steward was carried, to serve sandwiches and tea and coffee from Thermos flasks.

Shortly before the outbreak of the Second World War, British Airways Ltd had commenced a weekly service between Britain and Norway, Sweden and Finland. With the exception of the route to Paris, these were the only European air services from Britain to continue after hostilities began. The outbreak of war between Finland and Russia caused the truncation of the route at Stockholm, to where services continued using Ju 52 and Lockheed 14 aircraft, but on 9 April 1940 Germany invaded Norway and Denmark. The flights to Sweden were vital for several reasons, both political and strategic. German propaganda proclaiming Britain's imminent defeat had to be countered by supplying newspapers and magazines to neutral countries, and the urgent need for high-quality Swedish ball bearings made it imperative that Britain secured the supply of these. Two British negotiators were flown to Stockholm in the bomb bays of Mosquitoes and succeeded in purchasing Sweden's entire output of ball bearings, at the same time denying this source of supply to the Germans. After nine special flights from Perth BOAC received a high-priority request to open a regular service from RAF Leuchars, near Dundee, commencing in February 1941. At first, only the chartered Lockheed 14 G-AGBG was available for this work, but this was soon succeeded by Lockheed Hudsons and Lodestars, Armstrong Whitworth Whitleys, Dakotas and Mosquitoes. Initially the flights were only conducted at night, but with the introduction of the Mosquitoes in the summer of 1943 the route was flown in daylight, only to revert to night-time operation again when the Luftwaffe moved Focke Wulf 190s into the area and began to successfully intercept the flights. During 1944, Liberators and Avro Yorks were also used for special flights.

With the entry of Italy into the war on 10 June 1940 the Mediterranean section of the UK–Australia route was severed. Sixteen 'C' class flying-boats were south of Italy at the time, and these were used to open a new 'Horseshoe' routing from Durban to Sydney via Cairo, Karachi and Singapore from 19 June 1940. As had been the case pre-war, Qantas Empire Airways operated the Singapore-Sydney leg, and onward connections to New Zealand were available from Tasman Empire Airways Ltd (TEAL), which had been set up by BOAC, and Qantas and Union Airways of New Zealand for this purpose in early 1940. However, Japanese forces invaded the Malay Peninsular on 7 December 1941, and from 13 February 1942 the 'Horseshoe' route was terminated at Calcutta. To maintain the link with Australia, and following joint BOAC/RAF survey flights, a regular service over the 3,513 miles of Indian Ocean between Ceylon and Perth in Australia was opened by Catalina flying-boats of Qantas operating on behalf of BOAC from 10–11 July 1943. The route was extended westward to Karachi on 30 October 1943.

In June 1941 Air Chief Marshall Lord Tedder, the recently appointed AOC Middle East, identified an urgent need for increased air transport services in Africa that could connect his headquarters with Palestine, Turkey, Syria and Iraq, and could also transport ferry pilots back over the trans-African route to RAF Takoradi after they had delivered their aircraft. He suggested a joint RAF/BOAC organisation, to be formed with the new Lockheed Lodestars expected from the USA. As a result, a system of internal air communications was set up in the Middle East, with Almaza, near Cairo, as BOAC's terminus. During the siege of Malta in 1942 BOAC Lodestars flew services from Almaza to Gambut in Libya, where they refuelled and awaited the onset of darkness before making the crossing to Malta. Other types used on this run were converted Armstrong Whitworth Whitley bombers, the unique Curtiss-Wright CW 20, and Lockheed Hudsons. By the autumn of 1942 the fuel situation on Malta was so critical that the only aircraft that could be used were those that could fly from Gibraltar to Malta and back without refuelling. As the BOAC fleet did not contain sufficient aircraft of this size and range at that time, the Corporation reluctantly had to withdraw from the airlift.

With the formation of RAF Transport Command in early 1943 BOAC found its future in jeopardy as the result of an Air Ministry proposal to absorb the airline into the new RAF command. The Director General of BOAC, W.L. Runciman, its chairman, the Hon Clive Pearson and several other board members resigned in protest, leaving only Gerard d'Erlanger, who was also running the Air Transport Auxiliary at the time, at the helm. The ATA had been set up in 1939 to utilise the flying skills of pilots who were ineligible for active service on internal communications work, and was administered by BOAC. The role of its pilots was soon expanded to include the ferrying of aircraft from factories to operational bases. Viscount Knollys was appointed chairman of BOAC in May 1943, and the airline was allowed to retain its separate identity, but the Sunderland, York, Dakota, Liberator and Lancastrian aircraft loaned from the RAF, and their BOAC crews, were seconded to RAF Transport Command in October 1943. The aircraft concerned lost their civilian status and wore military markings, and the crews donned RAF Reserve uniforms when operating services for military purposes. However, aircraft engaged on flights to neutral countries retained their civil markings, as did aircraft that were actually owned by BOAC.

In March 1943 BOAC took over a hangar at RAF Lyneham for its Consolidated Liberators, as there was insufficient hangarage at Whitchurch and the runway there was rather short for their operations. Lyneham was also used for York operations. BOAC was to remain at Lyneham until April 1945, operating scheduled services and also special flights from there to the non-occupied parts of Europe and the Mediterranean before moving to its new base at Hurn, Bournemouth, on 1 November 1944.

On 21 September 1944, No.46 Group of No.110 Wing, RAF Transport Command began daily services from London to Paris, Brussels and Lyon, following the liberation of these cities. Services were later to include Marseilles and Naples, and new routes to Athens, Prague, Warsaw, Copenhagen and Oslo were inaugurated on VE Day, 8 May 1945. All of these services were taken over by the newly formed British European Airways Division of BOAC in 1946, the routes that had been operated on secondment to RAF Transport Command having been demilitarised by 4 March 1945. For the first time, BOAC was able to accept commercial fare-paying passengers.

During the Second World War BOAC had operated a total of 160 aircraft of many varying types and carried around 280,000 passengers. Eighty-one BOAC staff lost their lives during the company's wartime operations.

3

The Atlantic Ferry Organisation

In 1940 RAF Coastal Command was being supplied with Lockheed Hudsons by the neutral USA under the Lend-Lease scheme, but the process of transporting them by sea to their operational bases in the UK took up to three months from the time of their test flights in the USA. They took up valuable shipping space and some of them were lost at sea before they reached their destinations. It was calculated that ferrying them across by air would reduce the transit time to less than ten days. To make this possible the Atlantic Ferry Organisation was established, under the overall control of Canadian Pacific Railways at its Montreal headquarters, with technical assistance from BOAC. At the end of 1940 BOAC Captains A.S. Wilkinson, D.C.T. Bennett, R.H. Page and I.G. Ross arrived in Montreal, together with Squadron Leader G.J. Powell, a former Imperial Airways transatlantic Captain on loan from the Royal Canadian Air Force. As the USA was still neutral, the Hudsons were flown to Pembina, about sixty miles south of Winnipeg, which was on the US/Canadian border, and pulled across into Canada by teams of horses. The first aircraft to make the crossing was actually a Consolidated PBY named 'Guba', which flew from Botwood in Newfoundland to Stranraer in Scotland without heating or oxygen for the crew, and with a cargo of aluminium tubing. Departing on 25 October 1940, the flight under the command of Captain I.G. Ross took 16hrs 21mins. After arrival the aircraft was handed over to BOAC and placed into service on the West Africa route in March 1941. It was still in service there in 1944.

As the departure terminal for the Atlantic Ferry flights, the airfield at Gander underwent rapid expansion and development, and by the winter of 1940/41 had become one of the world's busiest airports. The first Hudson ferry flight consisted of a loose formation of seven aircraft under the leadership of Captain D.C.T. Bennett. The formation departed at 2222hrs on 10 November 1940 for Aldergrove, near Belfast, some 2,300 miles away. The first Hudson, under the command of Captain Bennett, touched down at Aldergrove, and six of the Hudsons landed there on 11 November, but the seventh, commanded by Captain

Pat Eves, strayed off course and landed at Prestwick on the same date. As Aldergrove was subject to German bombing raids, and its protective balloon barrage presented a hazard to friendly arrivals, the UK terminus for the Atlantic Ferry was transferred to Prestwick in January 1941. In the same month Bermuda began to be used as a departure point for PBYs en route to the UK. By February 1941 the facilities at Gander had been outgrown by the large-scale expansion of the air services, and a new airport was constructed at Dorval, Montreal. During March 1941 five Hudsons and one Liberator were delivered, plus fifteen PBYs from Bermuda.

In May 1941 the flights came under the control of the Ministry of Aircraft Production in Britain, and the contract with Canadian Pacific Railways was terminated. By that time thirty-three BOAC aircrew were employed on the ferry flights. In June 1941 the US President informed Winston Churchill that America was prepared to assist with the ferry flights of all aircraft destined for Britain. US service personnel would ferry them to the transatlantic departure point, and American civilian pilots would fly them across the Atlantic, thereby releasing British aircrew for operational duties. However, this was on condition that on arrival the aircraft were handed over to a British military command and not a civilian organisation. Thus, on 20 July 1941 the Atlantic Ferry Organisation became RAF Ferry Command. In March 1943 the title was again changed, to RAF Transport Command.

4

The Return Ferry Service

Initially, all Atlantic Ferry Organisation crews returned to Canada by sea after delivering their aircraft, and this took 10–14 days, so plans were drawn up to fly them back instead. At the time the only aircraft suitable for the task was the Consolidated Liberator. Seven aircraft were allocated, usually flown by BOAC crews, but sometimes by a mixed BOAC/RAF crew. The Liberators were unpressurised, and when bad weather forced them up to high altitudes their occupants had to resort to using a thirty-minute supply of oxygen, fed from a bottle via a rubber tube. The passengers were accommodated on the floor of the bomb bay, and were supplied with mattresses and sometimes sleeping bags. Gloves were a necessity. Up to eighteen passengers could be carried, and in good weather the trip could be accomplished in eighteen hours. However, strong headwinds could lengthen this considerably. Later in the service a means was found of fitting fourteen seats inside the fuselage of the Liberators, leaving the bomb bays free to carry freight in specially-fitted racks. Primitive though the services were, they did constitute the first regular, all-year-round transatlantic passenger and freight services, and the first transatlantic services by landplanes.

The first eastbound Return Ferry Service flight operated by Liberator AM259 arrived at Squires Gate, Blackpool from Gander on 14 March 1941 after a journey of 9hrs 1min. On 4 May 1941 Liberator AM258, under the command of Captain D.C.T. Bennett, carried four passengers, including Air Marshall Sir Hugh Dowding, and 200lb of diplomatic mail, into Prestwick after a 19hrs 5mins flight from St Hubert, Montreal and Gander. On the same day the first westbound service, with Captain Youell in charge, departed Squires Gate for Prestwick, Gander and Montreal with seven ferry crew members on board, the journey taking 19hrs 5mins. On 24 September 1941 the running of the Return Ferry Service was handed over in its entirety to BOAC, operating under the AOC RAF Ferry Command. Ten Liberators were provided by the RAF, but BOAC took full responsibility for their maintenance, operations and crewing. The first crossing under BOAC control took place on that date, under the command of Captain O.P. Jones, and services were operated from then on six days of each week.

In August 1942 the Chief Ferry Officer of the Air Transport Auxiliary, Francis Bradbrooke, who had volunteered for wartime service with BOAC, was killed while acting as second pilot on a Return Ferry Service Liberator under the command of Captain E.R.B. White which hit a mountain peak on the Isle of Arran after take-off from Prestwick, with the loss of all on board. During 1943 376 Return Ferry services were completed, but two Liberators were lost. A further 551 crossings were made during 1944, and by September 1945 BOAC had completed 1,750 trips since taking over the service in September 1941. During the summer of 1945 the Liberators had been supplemented by eight RAF PB2Y Coronado flying boats, flying from Boucherville, Montreal to Largs in Scotland. During October 1945 BOAC were operating the Return Ferry Service on behalf of RAF Transport Command as BOAC service 3A-4A, flying seven times weekly between Prestwick and Montreal. The Return Ferry Service continued until September 1946, when it was demilitarised. However, BOAC continued to use Liberators on transatlantic cargo flights for some time after this.

5

BOAC Wartime Usage of
Major Aircraft Types

NB: See Appendix 6 for a comprehensive list of types used

Armstrong Whitworth A.W. 15 Atlanta

Three examples were in service for the summer 1940 schedules. They were operated in conjunction with Indian Trans-Continental Airways on the Karachi–Jodpur–Delhi–Cawnpore–Allahabad–Calcutta route.

Armstrong Whitworth A.W. 27 Ensign

These were used on Heston-Paris services formerly operated under the National Air Communications scheme. When the fall of France caused the suspension of this route the Ensigns were seconded to RAF Fighter Command, who used them as squadron transports during the Battle of Britain period. They were also used on London–Lisbon services from June 1940. Early in 1941 they operated to Foynes in Ireland to connect with transatlantic flying-boat services. After modification to SRS 2 standard with Wright Cyclone engines they were ferried out to Cairo, from where they operated Cairo–Bahrein–Karachi–Calcutta from 2 March 1943, and on services to Freetown via Khartoum and Takoradi until 1944. From the summer of 1942 they also operated from Asmara to Lagos via Khartoum. The Ensigns were withdrawn in May 1945 and ferried back to Britain.

De Havilland D.H. 86A and D.H. 86B

Seven examples were utilised on services between Khartoum and Accra, and two were operated from Hong Kong to Bangkok until the cessation of services on

15 October 1940. These examples were then also operated on the Khartoum-Accra route.

De Havilland D.H. 91 Albatross

In common with the A.W. Ensigns, the D.H. 91 fleet served on the former NAC Heston-Paris route and also operated from London to Lisbon via Bordeaux, connecting with the Pan-American service from Lisbon to New York. After the fall of France the type was utilised to open Whitchurch-Dublin services from 4 July 1941. From Dublin, Aer Lingus provided connections to Shannon and Foynes. From 21 February 1942 the Albatrosses flew direct to Shannon, but the type was grounded after a crash on 16 July 1943.

Junkers Ju 52/3M

Three machines were inherited from British Airways, which had acquired them pre-war. In November 1939 they were flown to Perth and used on services to Scandinavia from 30 November until the routes were suspended on 9 April 1940. Because of the risk of being mistaken for Luftwaffe machines the type was not permitted to be used on services in the UK, and the two surviving examples were shipped by sea to the Middle East. Here they operated from Cairo to Khartoum, Takoradi and Lagos.

Lockheed 10A Electra

Two aircraft were shipped to Cairo and used on local routes and services to Kenya and West Africa.

Lockheed 14

Eight Imperial Airways machines were taken over by BOAC and used on services from Perth to Stockholm and from Shoreham to Alexandria. From 28 June 1940 four examples were based in Egypt and used on the trans-Sahara route to Lagos as well as on local services. On 26 January 1943 G-AFKE 'Lothair' was the first BOAC aircraft to land at Castel Benito airfield at Tripoli, only a few hours after the enemy forces had departed.

A BOAC Empire flying-boat undergoes maintenance at Congela, Durban. (R.W. Findlay)

Shorts S.23, S.30 and S.33 Empire flying-boats

The Empire flying-boats were originally built to operate transatlantic services and the Empire Air Mail routes to South Africa, India, Australia and New Zealand for Imperial Airways. Once taken over by BOAC they continued operating on the Empire routes until the entry of Italy into the war on 10 June 1940 severed the UK–Alexandria section of the network. The main operating base was then transferred to Durban, and from there the 'Horseshoe' route operated through East Africa, India and Malaya to Australia. On 3 August 1940 Captain J.C. Kelly Rogers made the first of four round trips from Poole in Dorset to New York via Botwood and Montreal in G-AFCZ 'Clare'. The first flight caused much excitement on its arrival in New York, as the aircraft had made the trip completely unarmed (as were all BOAC flying-boats in wartime), and the only evidence it carried of the war in Europe was the camouflage paint on its hull. This was the first BOAC transatlantic passenger-carrying service. From 19 October 1940 two examples made a series of flights at ten-day intervals between Poole and Freetown. When German paratroopers invaded Crete in 1941 two Empire flying-boats were camouflaged to resemble RAF Sunderlands and used to evacuate allied troops, making thirteen round trips between Alexandria and Crete during the period 22 April–5 May 1941. Thirteen examples survived the war and remained in BOAC service until March 1947.

Shorts S.26 flying-boats

These aircraft bore a superficial resemblance to the earlier Empire flying-boats, but were much larger. Three examples were ordered by Imperial Airways in 1938 for proposed non-stop transatlantic services. The first machine was handed over to BOAC for crew training on 24 September 1939, but within a few days all three of them were impressed into the RAF. One was lost in a landing accident in 1941, but the two survivors were handed over to BOAC, entering service on the Poole-Lisbon-Bathurst-Freetown-Accra-Lagos route on 18 July 1941 with the military equipment removed and seating for forty passengers installed. After the loss of G-AFCK 'Golden Horn' at Lisbon in January 1943 the remaining example G-AFCI 'Golden Hind' was transferred to the Poole-Foynes route for a year and then sent to Hythe for an overhaul, during which the camouflage paint was removed and the interior fully furnished to seat thirty-eight passengers and seven crew members. It was then ferried to Durban to operate services to Lourenco Marques, Beira and Mombasa. On 24 September 1944 a fortnightly service from Kisumu to the Seychelles via Mombasa, Pamanzi and Madagascar was inaugurated. This was extended to Ceylon via the Maldives on 28 November 1944, and was terminated on 30 August 1945. G-AFCI was then returned to Poole and was flown to Belfast for a major refit before entering post-war commercial operation.

Short S.23 Empire flying-boat G-ADHL 'Canopus'. (R.W. Findlay)

Boeing 314A

Three examples of this large flying-boat were purchased direct from Pan-American Airways in 1941 by the British government on behalf of BOAC Subsidiary Airways (Atlantic) Ltd. Operated by BOAC crews under the overall control of Captain J.C. Kelly Rogers, they were to come under the direct ownership of BOAC when the subsidiary company was absorbed in December 1941. They were pressed into service on the route from Foynes to Lagos via Lisbon, Las Palmas, Bathurst and Freetown, with the first service being operated by G-AGBZ 'Bristol' on 26 May 1941. Because the aircraft had to be ferried back to Baltimore for maintenance after every 120 hours of flying time, the fleet was actually based there at a terminal hired from Pan-American. The transatlantic trips alternated with the round trips to West Africa, and by the end of 1941 nineteen Atlantic crossings had been made by the Boeings. On 15–17 January 1942 Winston Churchill and his staff flew from Norfolk, Virginia, to Plymouth via Bermuda in G-AGCA 'Berwick', commanded by Captain Kelly Rogers. This was the first transatlantic flight by a British Prime Minister, and Mr Churchill also flew from Stranraer to New York and returned in July 1942 aboard G-AGBZ 'Bristol', completing the outbound leg non-stop in 27hrs with a total of ten passengers and twelve crew.

On 29 April 1944 the Boeings were withdrawn from the Lagos run and henceforth used exclusively on transatlantic services. These tended to be mainly VIP flights, carrying diplomats, King's Messengers, senior military officers and diplomatic mail, along with ordinary mail and the occasional group of ferry pilots urgently required back in the USA or Canada. The passengers were assembled at Airways House, by Victoria Station in London, from where they were transported non-stop by Pullman train to Poole. On arrival they processed through censorship and security checks and then were taken out by fast launch to the flying-boat 'Golden Hind' for the ferry flight to Foynes. As the transatlantic trips entailed very long non-stop sectors, and sometimes several weeks away from base, a crew of eleven was carried. The longest leg was from Bermuda to Lisbon, a distance of 2,730 nautical miles, taking 20hrs non-stop, at a cruising speed of 107 knots. Only thirty-seven passengers and some freight could be carried on this sector. However, on the seven-hour leg from Lisbon to Foynes the maximum load of sixty passengers could be accommodated. The Boeings were unpressurised, and flew at 10,000ft or less. During the summer months the crossings were made on the northern routing via Botwood in Newfoundland, saving some 1,620 miles, but in winter the eastbound flights went via Bermuda and Lisbon, while the westbound services routed via Bathurst, Belem, Trinidad and Bermuda.

Curtiss-Wright CW-20

The prototype of what was to become the C–46 Commando was purchased in America by the British Purchasing Commission and registered as G–AGDI in September 1941. It was ferried across the Atlantic to Prestwick, and entered BOAC service as a 24-seater, fitted with long-range tanks and bearing the name 'St Louis'. At the time it was the largest twin-engined aircraft in service. It was utilised on Leuchars-Stockholm services, and on the UK–Gibraltar run from May to September 1942, making occasional flights from Gibraltar to Malta during the seige, before being scrapped in October 1943.

De Havilland D.H. 95 Flamingo

Between September 1940 and April 1941 BOAC took delivery of seven camou-flaged D.H. Flamingos for use as transports in the Near East. Fitted with extra fuel tankage, they were flown out to Cairo during the period up to January 1942, and used on services to Jeddah, Asmara, Aden, Addis Ababa, Lydda, Adana and Tehran. By 1944 three had been lost, and the remainder were grounded through lack of spares. They were returned to the UK and never flew again.

Douglas DC-2, DC-3 and C-47 Dakota

After the German invasion of Holland in 1940, six Douglas airliners of KLM escaped to the UK. Arrangements were made for the KLM machines to be operated under charter to BOAC, and they were re-registered in the UK during July and August 1940. Based at Whitchurch, they operated services to Lisbon and Gibraltar. Two DC-3s were soon lost, one in a landing accident and one in an air raid on Whitchurch on 24 November 1940. On 1 June 1943, DC-3 G-AGBB took off from Lisbon for Whitchurch as BOAC flight 177-A, but was intercepted and shot down over the Bay of Biscay by a patrol of Ju 88s, and all thirteen passengers and the Dutch crew were lost. The German pilots later claimed that the incident was a case of mistaken identity, as they were new to the posting and had not been notified that civilian airliners would be flying in the area, so had assumed it was a military aircraft. However, one of the passengers on the flight was the film actor Leslie Howard, the star of the film *First of the Few*, which was showing in Lisbon at the time. In the film, Howard played the part of R.J. Mitchell, the designer of the Spitfire, and a theory put about at the time was that German intelligence had mistakenly assumed that Mitchell himself was aboard the flight and had ordered its destruction. However, R.J. Mitchell had actually died several years earlier. Another theory claimed that a Winston Churchill

Landing shot of camouflaged BOAC Dakota G-AGGB, with large Union Flag on its nose. (The A.J. Jackson Collection)

'double' was aboard the flight. To offset the aircraft losses the Air Ministry released three KLM Dakota IIIs, and these joined the surviving members of the first batch on services from Whitchurch to Lisbon and Gibraltar. At the end of the war the KLM aircraft reverted to their Dutch identities and returned to normal commercial operations from Holland.

On 17 December 1942 the Member of Parliament Mr W.D. Perkins had drawn the attention of the House of Commons to the plight of BOAC, whose fleet was unable to cope with the wartime demands being made on it. In March 1943 six RAF Dakota Mk 1s, acquired under the Lend-Lease scheme, were diverted to BOAC at Whitchurch. They were fitted with strengthened floors, large double freight doors, and bench seats for twenty-seven passengers along the cabin sides. Five were modified to take the British 24-volt electrical systems and became Dakota IIIs. Thirty Dakota IIIs were to be supplied to BOAC between May 1943 and October 1944, and twenty-three Dakota IVs, with two-speed superchargers for high altitude and tropical operations, were supplied between November 1944 and March 1945. Dakotas were introduced on four-times-weekly services to Lisbon on 11 May 1943, and on the route to Gibraltar on 4 August 1943. Dakotas were based in Cairo as BOAC's No.5 Line to operate services to the Middle East and Africa, including Cairo–Takoradi via Wadi Halfa, Khartoum and Kano from 20 August 1943, and Cairo–Basra from 18 February 1945. For these routes, the Dakotas were fitted with twenty-six lightweight seats. Other new routes for the

UK-based Dakotas included services to Algiers from 20 November 1943, to Lagos from 16 April 1944, to Cairo from 27 June 1944, from Leuchars to Stockholm from 1 September 1944, and from Hurn to Karachi from 3 June 1945. From 20 November 1943, certain routes were operated by Dakotas wearing military markings, but the aircraft used on services to neutral countries retained their civilian colours. By VE-Day on 8 May 1945, out of a total of fifty-nine Dakotas aquired by BOAC, no less than fifty-five had survived the war in Europe.

Airspeed A.S.10 Oxford

At least twenty examples of the Oxford were seconded to BOAC for use as crew trainers in the UK, the Middle East and South Africa from October 1942. After hostilities ceased, two machines were civilianised and used for crew training at Hurn.

Armstrong Whitworth A.W. 38 Whitley V

Fifteen Whitley Vs were delivered to BOAC, but three of these were soon returned to the RAF without being modified. The other twelve examples were converted to freighters at Bramcote in April and May of 1942. They were stripped of military equipment, long-range fuel tanks were installed in the bomb bays and the gun turrets were faired over. However, even then, their payload was only around 1,200lbs, so their usage was restricted to very high-priority light freight runs. They were initially used on the UK-Lagos services, but engine over-heating problems in tropical regions caused their withdrawal from the route. They were then deployed on night flights between Gibraltar and Malta during the siege of Malta in June 1942 , flying at overload during the seven-hour flight, with no possibility of remaining airborne should one engine fail. In August 1942 they were replaced by Lockheed Hudsons. They were then transferred to the Leuchars-Stockholm route in October 1942, but proved unable to climb high enough to evade the German anti-aircraft guns in the Skaggerak, and were withdrawn when Mosquitoes became available in early 1943. Finally they were used on services between Whitchurch and Shannon, providing connections with the Foynes flying-boat services.

Avro 685 York

The York was designed as a military transport for the RAF, and utilised the wings, Merlin engines and twin-fin tail unit of the Lancaster bomber (a third fin was added later). Five camouflaged Yorks were diverted from the RAF production run and delivered to BOAC during January–September 1944 in a passenger-cum-freighter layout, with twelve seats in the rear cabin. The first example to be granted a civilian Certificate of Airworthiness was G-AGJA, which departed Lyneham on 17 March 1944 under the command of Captain O.P. Jones for a proving flight to Lagos via Lisbon, Rabat and Bathurst, returning via Accra, Freetown, Bathurst, Dakar, Rabat and Gibraltar and arriving back on 6 April. G-AGJA also operated the first York service from Lyneham to Cairo on 22 April 1944. Initially the service operated via Gibraltar and Tripoli, but from 20 May it was re-routed via Rabat and Tripoli. On 1 January 1945 an extension to Karachi was inaugurated by G-AGJD, and from 31 December 1945 the service was extended to Calcutta. G-AGJC operated at least one special flight to Stockholm during 1944, and on 8 December 1944 it flew between Malmo and Gothenburg, importing the very first Willys Jeep into Sweden, for use by the American aircraft maintenance group at Malmo. From February 1945 all Yorks operating through Egypt and India were militarised, with RAF roundels and code letters replacing their civilian markings. The Lyneham to Karachi service was re-routed across France to Malta, North Africa and India from 15 July 1945.

Avro Lancastrian 1

The Lancastrian was a passenger-carrying conversion of the Lancaster bomber, with the gun turrets removed or faired over. The first conversion, of a Lancaster III, was carried out in Canada during 1943, and was used on the transatlantic mail and VIP passenger services of Trans-Canada Airlines. The first UK conversion was carried out by Avro on VB873, and twenty-one conversions were delivered to BOAC between January and October 1945 as a stop-gap measure until the new Avro Tudor airliner intended for BOAC was ready for service on the route to Australia. The first joint BOAC/Qantas service from Hurn to Sydney was operated by VF163 on 31 May 1945, with a Qantas crew taking over at Karachi. At the request of the British government, BOAC made the first British survey flight to South America in October 1945. Lancastrian G-AGMG, under the command of Captain O.P. Jones, flew from Hurn to Buenos Aires, Santiago and Lima.

Consolidated Liberator

Liberators were utilised on the North Atlantic Return Ferry Service as mentioned previously, and in January 1942 two examples plus a reserve were taken off this duty and used on UK–Cairo services. The first service was operated direct from Hurn to Cairo in 11hrs 15mins at the end of January. The return leg, commanded by Captain Humphrey Page, departed Cairo on 15 February. As it approached the English coastline the Liberator was shot down into the sea off Eddystone, and all the passengers and crew were lost. The flights to Cairo resumed a few weeks later with the remaining aircraft. They were suspended on 10 December 1942 after twenty-five round trips had been completed, but reinstated on 27 February 1943 using BOAC Liberators in RAF markings.

Late in 1942 the Air Ministry decided that it would be practicable to use modified Liberators to carry diplomats and other VIPs on services between Britain and the Soviet Union. The first aircraft to be modified was registered as G-AGCD. All the armament was removed, and bench seating for VIPs was installed on the starboard side of the rear of the cabin. Any other passengers that might be carried had to travel in the bomb bay with the baggage and cargo. In this configuration the Liberator had an endurance of around sixteen hours at a cruising height of 25,000ft. The first experimental Liberator service to Moscow ('X' base) was made on 21–22 October 1942 by Captain J.T. Percy, flying Prestwick-Ramenskoye, some thirty miles from Moscow, in 13hrs 9mins flying time with eight passengers and a crew of four. In order to avoid flying over hostile territory in daylight, and to comply with the strict regulations laid down by the Russians, a route was chosen which took the Liberator northwards from Prestwick to the Arctic Circle, then eastwards, then a sharp dash southwards across northern Norway and Finland and down the Gulf of Bothnia, followed by a turn to the east at Riga. The flying distance involved was about equal to that of an Atlantic crossing. Eight more flights were made on this routing between January and March 1943, and on 10 June 1943 G-AGHB inaugurated a new routing from Lyneham to Moscow, flying via Algiers, Habbaniyah, Tehran and Kuybyshev. Liberator IIIs were introduced by BOAC on routes from Lyneham to Lisbon and North Africa, and six Liberators were also operated on Lyneham-Stockholm services in the early spring of 1944. The first Liberator service to Stockholm, by G-AGFO, arrived at Bromma airport on 5 February 1944, and the last BOAC Liberator flight over the route was operated on 29 March 1944, two days before the Americans took over the services.

Consolidated PB2Y Coronado

RAF examples were transferred to Return Ferry Service to provide extra capacity during summer of 1945. They operated from Boucherville, Montreal to Largs, Scotland. The Coronados were then transferred to the South Atlantic route from September 1945, maintaining services from Bermuda to Lagos via Trinidad, Belem, Natal and Freetown.

De Havilland Mosquito

After a trial courier run to Stockholm by a Mosquito B.Mk IV of 105 Squadron on 5 August 1942, De Havilland carried out the first conversion of a Mosquito specifically for this purpose at Hatfield, and delivered the aircraft to BOAC as G-AGFV on 15 December 1942. After a short period of testing and crew training, this aircraft made its first crossing for BOAC on 4 February 1943. The success of this and subsequent flights enabled BOAC to negotiate for the loan of six Mosquito VIs. These were delivered to Bramcote and underwent conversion during April and May 1943. This entailed modifications to enable a single passenger to be accommodated in the bomb bay, which was padded with felt and equipped with a reading lamp, temperature control and an intercom for communication with the pilot. For the journey, the passenger was supplied with a flask of coffee, reading material and a supply of oxygen. As well as the passenger, the Mosquitoes carried mail, newspapers and magazines (to counter German propaganda) on the outward trip, and Swedish ball bearings on the return leg. In order to accommodate the maximum quantity of ball bearings on each trip the bomb bays of the Mosquitoes were fitted with baskets and hooks. Unlike previous types operated on the route, the BOAC Mosquitoes were initially operated at high altitude in daylight, but after Captain Gilbert Rae was intercepted and shot up by a Focke Wulf 190 and had to belly-land near Stockholm, the operations were switched to night time. Captain Rae was later to lose his life on another trip on this service. On average, the trip from Leuchars to Stockholm took about three hours, and many famous people travelled in this way, including the conductor Dr (later Sir) Malcolm Sargent. During 10 and 11 January 1944 Captain John H. White made three crossings of the North Sea, a distance of 2,400 miles, in 9.36 flying hours, with only forty-five minutes on the ground during this feat. Unhappily, Captain White was posted missing when his Mosquito G-AGKR failed to arrive at Leuchars on 29 August 1944. Five of the Mosquitoes survived to see the withdrawal of the type on 30 November 1944.

Handley Page Halifax VIII

Three examples were supplied to BOAC in September 1945 as freighters. During October and November 1945 they made a number of cargo flights to Accra to free up space on the Dakotas for passengers.

Lockheed Hudson

Hudson IIIs were utilised on the Leuchars-Stockholm run in 1941–42. They were then sent to the Middle East and used on Cairo–Takoradi services. Hudson

IVs of 163 Squadron RAF were seconded to BOAC from 12 September 1942, and helped on the emergency flights from Cairo to Malta via Gambut during the siege of Malta. They were returned to the RAF on 19 July 1943.

Lockheed 18 Lodestar.

Nine examples were purchased direct from Lockheed and delivered between March and July 1941. They were used on BOAC's No.5 Line route network, which covered over 15,000 miles. Radiating from Cairo, routes operated to India via the northern route through Iraq, to Southern Rhodesia via Sudan and Kenya, the Persian Gulf route to Karachi and Calcutta, and the southern route to Port Sudan. From Khartoum there was a route to Lagos. The Lodestars also flew on the Cairo–Takoradi route until they were pressed into service in the Western Desert, transporting petrol for fighter and bomber squadrons. They were also flown into Malta during the blockade in 1942. During the day they positioned from Cairo to Gambut in the Western Desert. After refuelling they awaited dusk before flying into and out of Malta during the hours of darkness. Four more machines were purchased by the Norwegian Purchasing Commission in 1941–42, and flown by Norwegian crews seconded to BOAC on the Leuchars-Stockholm route from 1942–1945.

Short S.25 Sunderland

To supplement their 'C' class flying-boats, BOAC requested the use of converted RAF Short Sunderlands, and from December 1942 Short Bros. converted four batches of six on their Rochester production line. They were stripped of their military equipment, the gun turrets in the nose and tail were replaced by metal fairings, bench-type seating was installed for the carriage of priority passengers, and they were allocated civil registrations. BOAC Sunderlands were introduced onto the Poole-Lagos route from March 1943, but they were withdrawn from this in order to begin a three-times-weekly service from the UK to Cairo and Karachi from 25 October 1943, operating under the control of RAF Transport Command and wearing military markings. The service was extended to Calcutta from 10 May 1944, and from 12 December 1944 the service was re-routed to fly directly across liberated France to Djerba, later changed to Augusta in Sicily from 20 February 1945. With the ending of the war in the Far East, the operations were extended to Rangoon from October 1945. The surviving examples became the 'Hythe' class in BOAC civilian operation, and Sunderland ML788 was modified at Rochester to become the prototype Short Sandringham.

Vickers 415 Wellington 1C

Four Wellingtons were loaned to BOAC by the South African Air Force from September 1942, and converted at Asmara to interim transport machines, pending the intended introduction of Vickers Warwick freighters. They were modified to carry sixteen passengers, and based at Almaza (Cairo) as part of BOAC's No.5 Line. On 26 October 1942 services commenced on three routings: Service 3E/4E operated between Cairo and Karachi, service 5E/6E flew from Cairo to Bahrain via Lydda, Habbaniyah and Shaibah, and service 7E/8E operated between Habbaniyah and Sharjah. The Wellingtons were replaced by Dakotas, and returned to the SAAF in July 1943.

Vickers Warwick

Fourteen Warwick 1s were built at Weybridge for intended use by BOAC as freighters on Middle East routes. Although the first example was modified to suit this purpose, problems with the aircraft's Pratt and Whitney Double Wasp engine installation prevented the type from gaining a civil Certificate of Airworthiness, and the machines were handed back to the RAF. A single Warwick V was loaned to the BOAC Development Flight at Hurn as a Bristol Centaurus VII test bed, and flown out to Africa in late September 1945 to assess the engine's performance on BOAC's African routes. It returned to the UK in late October.

Consolidated Catalina

Catalinas operated from the UK to Lagos from March 1941 and to Cairo from October 1941. They were withdrawn from both these routes in August 1942. On 18 July 1943, after a series of experimental flights by the RAF, a service between Perth in Australia and the RAF flying-boat station at Kegalla in Ceylon was inaugurated, under BOAC control, but with Qantas crews. This entailed a non-stop flight of more than 3,000 miles. In order to achieve this range, part of the cabin space was filled with extra fuel tanks. Into what space remained could just be fitted three chairs and two canvas bunks. 1,000kgs of payload could then be carried over the distance involved. From 31 October 1943 the route was extended to Karachi. The last Catalina service took place on 18 July 1945, and most of the surviving aircraft were scuttled in Australia in 1945–46.

6

The Immediate Post-War Period
(1945–1950)

At the end of the Second World War, BOAC was mainly equipped with transport conversions of wartime bombers and flying-boats. Its initial post-war operations were hopelessly uneconomic, and destined to be so for some years to come. Several new designs were on the manufacturers' drawing-boards, such as the Avro Tudor, which was intended for transatlantic services, and more futuristic projects such as the Princess flying-boat and the Bristol Brabazon would follow; but for the immediate future BOAC's short-haul routes would be maintained principally by Dakotas, and its long-haul services by flying-boats and Lancaster derivatives the Lancastrian and the York.

The Avro Lancastrian

On 1 February 1946 the Hurn–Sydney Lancastrian service was demilitarised as the 'Kangaroo' service and came under BOAC control as a commercial operation as far as Karachi, with Qantas operating the Karachi–Sydney portion. Along with the Avro Yorks, the Lancastrian 1 fleet formed part of BOAC's No.2 Line, based at Hurn. A major setback occurred on 23 March 1946 when BOAC Lancastrian G-AGLX, under the command of Captain O.F.Y. Thomas, disappeared over the Indian Ocean between Ceylon and the Cocas Islands with the loss of all ten occupants. As a result, the service was re-routed to operate via Singapore from 6 April 1946. The first eastbound service over the new routing was operated out

Opposite page:
Top: Liberator II G-AHYF, used on freight services to Canada. (Air-Britain)

Middle: Lancastrian G-AGMG 'Nicosia' operated BOACs first service from Hurn to Sydney on 29 November 1945. (The Ricky Shiels Collection)

Bottom: Passengers boarding Lancastrian G-AGLS on 28 May 1946 for the inaugural BOAC service from London Airport. (Heathrow Airport PLC)

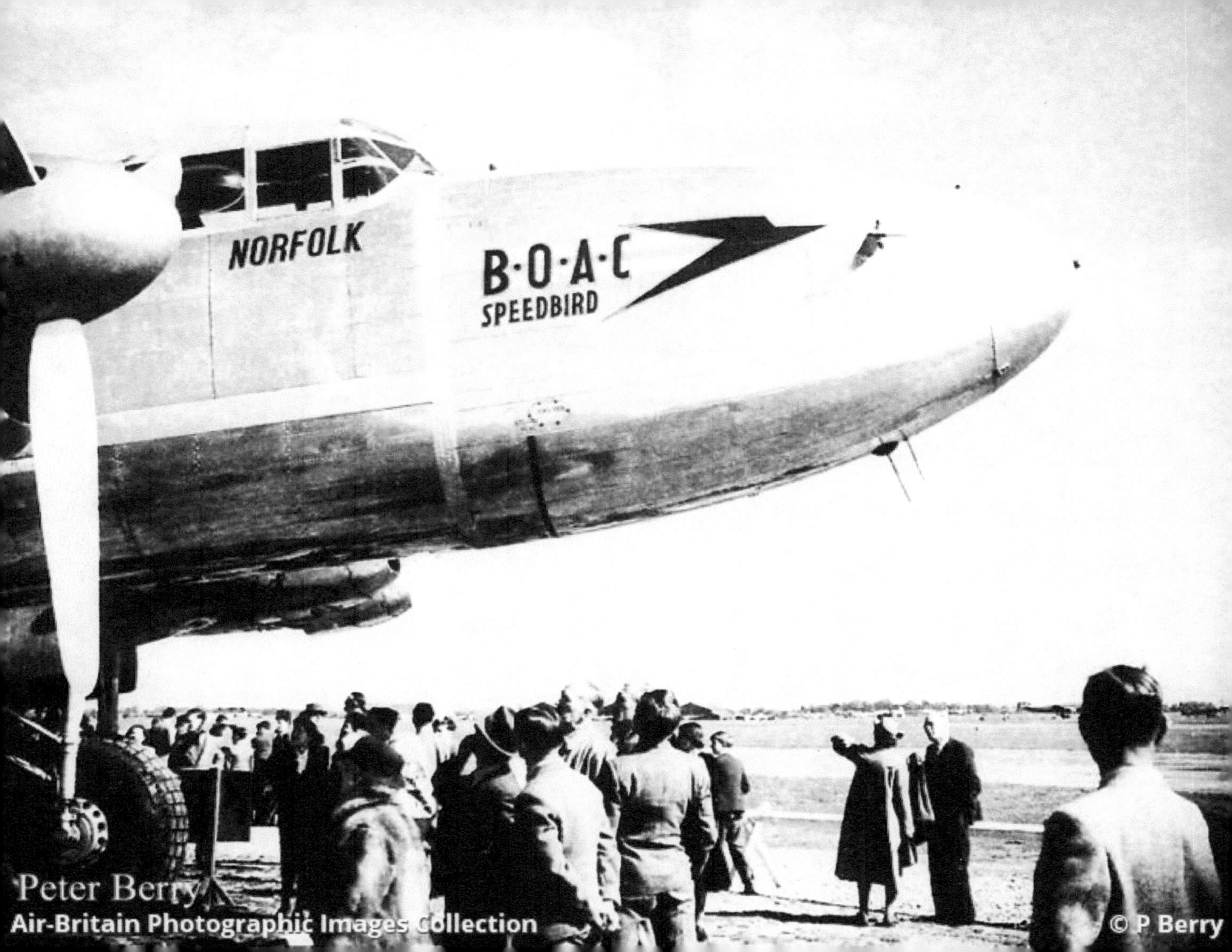
NORFOLK
B·O·A·C
SPEEDBIRD

of Hurn by G-AGME on that date, and the first revised westbound service, by G-AGMC, left Sydney on 9 April. On 12 May 1946 the 'Kangaroo' service became a joint BOAC/Qantas operation over its entire length. During May BOAC had two Lancastrians written off, fortunately without any fatalities. On the second of the month G-AGMC suffered an undercarriage collapse on landing at Sydney, and on 17 May G-AGMH was damaged beyond repair in a heavy landing at Mauripur in India. On 28 May 1946 the 'Kangaroo' service began using the newly operational London Airport instead of Hurn, with G-AGLS operating the first BOAC scheduled service out of the airport, which was not officially opened until 31 May.

The Lancastrian 1s used were hopelessly uneconomical, as they were only capable of accommodating nine passengers on daytime legs, with this figure reducing to six on overnight sleeper flights. The front part of the aircraft's interior, from the cockpit back to the main spar, remained substantially the same as the Lancaster, with a navigation table and radio operator's station on the port side, although unlike the Lancaster, the Lancastrian was fitted with dual controls. The area from the mainspar back to the end of the bomb bay was divided into the front part, containing electrical and radio equipment, and the rear portion comprising the galley working area. The long-range fuel tanks ran beneath all this, so smoking was strictly forbidden. The galley contained a sink, a two-gallon water boiler, and full-sized electric refrigerator. Even though no cooking or food reheating facilities were provided, full four-course meals were still served, the food being placed aboard in large Thermos flasks. At the top of the rear end of the bomb bay was a light bulkhead, with a door and a step down into the passenger cabin. The passenger accommodation consisted of three settee-type benches, each one being divided into three individual seats by fold-back armrests. The benches were arranged lengthwise along the port side of the cabin, with the passengers sitting facing starboard. This arrangement meant that each time the steward needed to walk the length of the cabin he had to step over the outstretched legs of the passengers. At night, the three benches, with armrests raised, served as lower sleeping berths. Positioned above them, and strapped tight against the cabin ceiling during the day, were the three upper berths, in the style of the Pullman train sleeper coaches of the period. Occupying what was originally the tail gun turret, was the faired-over tail cargo and luggage compartment. During 1946 BOAC also acquired three Lancastrian IVs, modified to seat thirteen passengers and with improved furnishings.

Two more Lancastrians were lost in August 1946. On 15 August, G-AGLU ran off the runway during take-off from Hurn. The undercarriage collapsed and the aircraft was damaged beyond repair. Then on 20 August G-AGMF crashed near Rouen during a training flight, with the loss of eight out of its nine occupants.

From 2 December 1947 the Lancastrians were displaced from the passenger services to Australia by Lockheed Constellations, but continued to operate cargo and mail services on the route. They then took over from Avro Yorks on London–Colombo passenger services from 2 February 1948, and on the onward Colombo–Singapore leg from 19 February. They were to continue to operate on this route until displaced by Canadair Argonauts on 16 November 1949. However, in the meantime, G-AGMB was lost at Tengah, Singapore, on 27 August 1948. One hour into its flight to Colombo low oil pressure on one of the engines caused a return to Singapore. On landing, the aircraft overran the runway onto rough ground, fortunately without fatalities among the nine passengers and five crew aboard. On 11 April 1948 BOAC began a weekly Lancastrian-operated freight and mail service to Johannesburg in association with South African Airways. This operated via Tripoli, Cairo, Khartoum and Nairobi, with an optional additional stop at Salisbury, and was suspended on 12 August 1949. From August 1950 the Lancastrian freight and mail service to Australia was replaced by an Avro York service as far as Singapore, with onward connections to Sydney provided by Qantas.

The Avro York

The BOAC York fleet was initially based at Hurn as part of the No.2 Line, which was also responsible for Lancastrian operations from Hurn. Hurn came under the control of the Ministry of Civil Aviation on 1 November 1944. As it was constructed as a wartime military airfield, the hangars were dispersed away from the living accommodation, an inconvenience when it came to airline operations. The BOAC terminal facilities were situated off the airfield in one of the former RAF sites at Hurn Village. Passengers travelled from London to Bournemouth by train and were taken by coach or taxi to the Long Haul Building to undergo departure formalities before being transported to the airfield to board their flight. The BOAC Catering School was also based at Hurn.

During October 1945 the following BOAC services were operated from Hurn:

Service 5F-6F. Hurn–Karachi twice weekly.
Service 5Q-6Q. Hurn–Sydney three times weekly.
Responsibility of No.2 Line, based at Hurn.
Service 7F-8F. Hurn–Karachi five times weekly.
Service 29M-30M. Hurn–Cairo fourteen times weekly.
Service 21W-22W. Hurn–Lagos three times weekly.
Responsibility of No.1 Line, based at Whitchurch.

On 10 November 1945 the joint BOAC/South African Airways 'Springbok' service from Hurn to Palmietfontein Airport, Johannesburg via Tripoli, Cairo, Khartoum and Nairobi was inaugurated, with the first flight being operated by

Avro York G-AGJC in natural metal finish, with Lancastrian in background. (Air-Britain)

York G-AGNT. Two services each week were operated, the southbound flights leaving Hurn at 1400hrs on Tuesdays and Fridays and calling at Malta, Cairo, Khartoum and Nairobi en route before arriving at Johannesburg at 1445 on Fridays and Mondays. Overnight stops were made at Cairo and Nairobi during the 6,604-statute-mile journey. South African Airways had Douglas DC-4s on order for this service, but until they were delivered nine BOAC Yorks, in full SAA livery and carrying South African registrations, were used. On 31 December 1945 the RAF-operated York service from Hurn to Karachi was extended to Calcutta, and on 1 February 1946 it reverted to BOAC operation. In February 1946 BOAC's Station Manager at Hurn was Mr G.R. Hawtin.

In March 1946 BOAC was operating Yorks in two main configurations. The standard type was the PCF (Passenger-cum-Freighter), on which the forward half of the fuselage was used as a large freight compartment, and a twelve-seat passenger cabin and galley occupied the rear half. The PCF version operated the long-haul route to Calcutta, and a stopping service to Cairo. The other main variant was known among the crews as the 'Pansy' York, and operated on the prestige 'Springbok' service to Johannesburg. Twelve passengers were carried, and this version was luxuriously appointed with polished wood panelling, thickly padded seating, and berths taking up all the available fuselage space. Large quantities of silver-plated cutlery, starched tablecloths, the finest crystal glassware and crested china were carried. On 10 April 1946 BOAC began a twice-weekly Hurn–Cairo (Almaza) York service, taking 12hrs 20mins. This spelt the end for the Armstrong Whitworth Ensign in BOAC service, and on 3 June 1946 Captain O. Pritchard departed Almaza for Hurn in G-ADSW 'Eddystone' on the last passenger flight by an Ensign. On 4 June 1946 the 'Springbok' service began using London Airport instead of Hurn, and ten days later BOAC operated its last scheduled service out of Hurn. York flight 33M/20, operated by G-AGSO, routed via Marignane, Castel Benito (Tripoli) and Almaza to Johannesburg, and after a four-day stopover returned as flight 34M/21 over the same routing, but landed at London Airport before positioning to Hurn. Although no longer on its scheduled service network, Hurn was still used by BOAC on occasions as a bad-weather alternate and for crew training. Indeed, during the period of 22 November–1 December 1948, BOAC's staff at Hurn, reinforced by personnel from London Airport and Airways Terminal, handled over 130 diversions caused by fog in the London area. 2,268 passengers were looked after, and the aircraft types handled included Constellations, DC-4s, Avro Tudors, Lancastrians, Yorks, Haltons, Dakotas and BEA Vikings.

On 22 June 1946 BOAC participated in Britain's first post-war 'Air Pageant', which was held at Eastleigh Airport, Southampton. According to reports, York G-AGNL 'showed off its paces at low altitude', and the Pageant also featured a low-level fly-past by BOAC Short Sandringham flying-boat G-AGKX. From 4 August 1946 until July 1947 the BOAC services to Karachi were operated by Yorks of Skyways Ltd, and then BOAC Handley Page Haltons took over, the same fate befalling the London–Cairo York service from 9 September 1946. On 16 July 1947 York G-AGNR was lost while on final approach to Shaibah, Iran. The aircraft was operating a scheduled service from London to Calcutta via Malta, Cairo, Basra and Delhi. Poor visibility at Basra forced a diversion to Shaibah, where the York struck the ground on the fourth attempt at a landing. The twelve passengers aboard survived the crash, but all six crew members were killed.

From 11 September the Yorks reclaimed the London–Karachi services from the Haltons, flying via Lydda and Dhahran, and on 25 November 1947 a weekly York service from London to Delhi via Tripoli, Cairo, Basra and Karachi was inaugurated. This was followed on 4 December 1947 by a weekly London–Dar Es Salaam York schedule, and a London–Nairobi York service from February

Landing shot of Avro York G-AGOE. (BOAC photograph, copyright British Airways)

1948. From then onwards the Yorks passed in and out of favour on African routes. In April 1948 Hythe flying-boats replaced them on the run to Karachi, and a weekly London–Basra service introduced on 10 April 1948 was withdrawn again a month later. At the beginning of May, Yorks replaced Haltons on the London–Accra route and on 19 September 1948 they took over from Dakotas on London–Tehran services. On 1 February 1949 another York was lost when G-AGJD swung to the right during a crosswind take-off from Castel Benito, Tripoli. The pilots overcorrected the swing and the aircraft crashed, fortunately without any fatalities among the nine passengers and six crew aboard. From 23 February 1949 the Yorks were replaced by Short Solent flying-boats on the route to Dar Es Salaam. However, on 11 April Yorks returned to the London–Cairo route on a three-times-weekly basis, and on 7 September they displaced Solents on the Karachi service, being withdrawn again on 19 November. The merger of British South American Airways into BOAC on 30 July 1949 had provided BOAC with many more Yorks, and a weekly London–Lydda service had been introduced on 21 August. However, the London–Delhi York service was withdrawn on 2 September, and on 7 October 1950 BOAC withdrew the York fleet completely from scheduled passenger services from the UK. However, a detached flight of Yorks maintained a passenger service between Nassau and Santiago, Chile, for some time afterwards, and the type was still used on charters from the UK, and on cargo flights, for which the Yorks had been fitted with large, double-freight doors. These enabled the Yorks to be utilised for the transport of large animals, as well as more conventional cargoes. On 11 November 1952 BOAC York G-AGJC, along with two BEA aircraft, was used in a demonstration of the FIDO fog-dispersal system at Blackbushe airport, members of the press being carried for the first time on this type of operation.

Avro York G-AGOA 'Montrose'. (The A.J. Jackson Collection)

The Consolidated Liberator

On 10 February 1946 BOAC reached the milestone of 2,000 transatlantic crossings on the Return Ferry Service, operated by Consolidated Liberators. The 1,000th westbound flight was under the command of Captain L.V. Messenger, and the 1,000th eastbound service was operated by Liberator AM920, from Montreal to Prestwick under the command of Captain D. Anderson. On 21 February, however G-AGEM was lost when it force-landed in icing conditions at Charlottetown, Prince Edward Island, with one fatality, the co-pilot. From 29 April 1946 BOAC began routing five of the seven Montreal–London flights each week via Shannon and Hurn, in preparation for the commencement of commercial North Atlantic passenger services. On 30 September 1946 the Return Ferry Service was demilitarised. Eight Liberators had been converted to civil standards by BOAC, but they had been granted new-category Certificates of Airworthiness which did not permit the carriage of fare-paying passengers. Thus, the first BOAC commercial service, under the command of Captain R.H. Page, carried only BOAC staff passengers, mail and freight. During the period 4 February–28 May 1948 weekly non-stop London–Montreal cargo services were operated as part of a series of in-flight refuelling trials for the Ministry of Civil Aviation. Liberator G-AHYD was used, refuelled en route by Lancastrian tankers of Flight Refuelling, which were based at Shannon and Gander. On 13 November 1948 Liberator G-AHYC sustained undercarriage damage on take-off, and landed at Heathfields with one undercarriage leg partially retracted. There were no fatalities among the nine people aboard, but the aircraft was damaged beyond repair. From 3 April 1949 Scottish Airlines crews took over the operation of the BOAC London–Montreal Liberator cargo flights (by then on a three-times-weekly basis), releasing the BOAC aircrew for training on more modern types. The service was finally withdrawn on 27 September 1949.

The Lockheed Lodestar

At the end of the Second World War extensive Lockheed Lodestar services from Cairo to Middle East points were operated by BOAC's No.5 Line on behalf of the Middle East Transport Board. In October 1945 these included:

Service 14E-13E Cairo–Wadi Halfa–Khartoum
Service 26E-25E Cairo–Wadi Halfa–Khartoum–Malakal–Juba–Nairobi
Service 37E-38E Cairo–Lydda–Baghdad–Basra
Service 3N-4N Cairo–Damascus–Baghdad–Tehran
Service 7N-8N Cairo–Nicosia–Ankara–Istanbul
Service 1R-2R Cairo–Luxor–Port Sudan–Asmara–Kamaran–Aden

Lockheed Lodestars such as G-AGBV 'Ludlow' maintained regional services in the Middle East and West Africa in the immediate post-war years. (The Ricky Shiels Collection)

Service 11R-12R Cairo–Jeddah–Port Sudan
Service 13R-14R Asmara–Aden–Hargeisa–Addis Ababa

These services were gradually phased out from 1946 onwards. On 29 and 30 January 1946 the routes to Karachi and Port Sudan were withdrawn, followed by the Khartoum route on 30 April 1946. In May 1946 the Lodestars were still providing onward connections for BOAC Dakota services to Athens. From here the Lodestars flew an Athens–Nicosia–Beirut–Lydda–Baghdad–Tehran route, with an overnight stop at Lydda, but only government priority passengers were carried. From 1 July 1947 the Lodestars still operating on the Cairo–Nairobi route were replaced by BOAC Dakotas, which had gradually been taking over the rest of the Middle East regional network.

The Douglas Dakota

During the first few months of peacetime, the UK–West Africa and the West Africa–Cairo route networks were combined. On 3 June 1945 Dakota G-AGMZ inaugurated a twice-weekly service from Hurn to Karachi via Istres, Malta, El Adem, Cairo, Baghdad and Sharjah, and from early July additional stops at Lydda and Basra were incorporated. On 24 January 1946 the five-times-weekly Dakota service to Karachi was withdrawn, but Dakotas were still in use on UK–West Africa services, and on Middle East regional routes based on Cairo. From 8 April 1946 BOAC commenced a weekly Hurn–Lydda Dakota service, which was to be suspended between 25 June 1946 and 2 May 1947 and then reinstated with an additional night stop at Malta. On 25 April that year weekly Cairo–Athens flights began, with the return leg on the following day continuing onwards to Tehran. A weekly service from Northolt to Tehran via Rome, Athens, Nicosia, Beirut, Lydda and Baghdad was inaugurated on 9 May 1946, operated by Dakotas as far as Athens, and thence onwards by Lockheed Lodestars. This was followed by a weekly London–Lydda–Beirut Dakota routing from 1 July 1946, but the London–Lagos Dakota service was withdrawn on 17 July 1947. On 25 August 1947 the Cairo-based Dakota services between Athens and Tehran were replaced by a weekly flight from London to Tehran which called at Marseilles, Rome (night stop), Athens, Nicosia, Lydda (night stop) and Baghdad.

During the period 1–15 September 1947 BOAC and three UK independent airlines participated in Operation Pakistan, the airlift of refugees between Delhi and Karachi following violent unrest after the partition of India. The operation was under the direction of Air Commodore H.G. Brackley, and the four airlines carried a total of 7,000 refugees from Delhi to Karachi, and around 1,500 in the opposite direction. Food, medicines and vaccines were also flown out to Delhi and Lahore. BOAC committed twelve Dakotas to the airlift, as well as two Yorks and a Lancastrian. Operation Pakistan was followed in October 1947 by Operation India, in which BOAC and British charter airlines transported around 35,000 people from various points in Pakistan to Delhi.

On 24 January 1948 the twice-weekly Dakota service from Lagos to Kano was taken over by the West African Airways Corporation (WAAC), and from 31 March 1948 WAAC became responsible for all the inter-colonial West Africa coastal

Dakota 3 G-AGHM in natural metal finish. (The A.J. Jackson Collection)

services. By then the Dakotas were being phased out on Middle East and African routes in favour of Avro Yorks and Handley Page Haltons, but still had a major role to play in Europe under a new owner.

The Formation of BEA

From 5 June 1945 the daytime Dakota services to Stockholm were transferred from RAF Leuchars to Croydon, and from 1 October they operated four times weekly as service 19B-20B. Service 7L-8L was also operated on a weekly basis from Croydon to Lisbon via Madrid, and service 7B-8B operated between Croydon and Helsinki via Gothenburg and Stockholm.

On 5 December the Hurn–Gibraltar services which had been operated by KLM under charter to BOAC were taken over by BOAC aircraft and crews. On 1 January 1946 the British European Airways Division of BOAC was formerly constituted, and arrangements were made for BOAC Dakotas to take over the UK–Continent services operated by No.110 Wing, 46 Group, RAF Transport Command. Accordingly, on 4 February 1946 the British European Airways Division took over the RAF-operated routes, and transferred their London terminus from Croydon to RAF Northolt, which was in temporary use for European services while London Airport was under initial development. Including new services started on that day, the list of destinations served comprised Amsterdam, Brussels, Helsinki, Lisbon, Madrid, Paris and Stockholm. At that time the Dakotas still bore RAF markings and their crews still wore RAF uniforms. It was not until 1 March that Northolt officially became a civil airport, on loan from the RAF to the Ministry of Civil Aviation. On that date the BEA Division Dakotas began to wear airline markings, and their crews BOAC uniforms. A Northolt-Gibraltar service was inaugurated on that date, and more new European routes soon followed: on 11 March a three-times-weekly service to Oslo, on the following day a four-times-weekly service to Copenhagen, and on 14 March a weekly routing Northolt–Marseilles–Rome–Athens.

On 5 April 1946 agreement was reached between the UK and Irish governments that all UK–Eire services would be operated by Aer Lingus, with the Irish government holding a 60 per cent shareholding, and BOAC 40 per cent.

BOAC lost Dakota G-AGHK on 17 April 1946 during an attempted single-engined landing at Lugo de Lanera in Spain. Fortunately, there were no fatalities among the nine passengers and four crew aboard.

On 1 August 1946 the British European Airways Corporation (generally abbreviated to BEA) was established under the provisions of the Civil Aviation Act of 1946. From that date BEA took over the routes, and twenty-one Dakotas, of the former British European Airways Division of BOAC, and worked them as a separate state-owned airline. BEA also took a 30 per cent shareholding in Aer

Lingus, reducing BOAC's financial interest to 10 per cent, which was later also acquired by BEA.

BOAC Dakotas still had one more vital role to play in Europe, as participants in the Berlin Airlift in 1948. Following the Soviet blockade of the surface routes into Berlin, the RAF and USAF aircraft used on the airlift to supply the city with food and fuel were supplemented by civil airliners from 4 August 1948. BOAC provided Dakotas G-AGIZ, G-AGNG and G-AGNK, and between 20 October and 25 November 1948 these aircraft flew eighty-one sorties out of Hamburg, carrying 294 tons in the course of 224 flying hours. The Soviet blockade was lifted on 12 May 1949, but the civil airlift continued until 15 August, to build up stocks of food and fuel in the city.

The Handley Page Halton

During October 1945 the RAF loaned BOAC three Handley Page Halifax C.VIIIs for use on a three-times-weekly mail service from Hurn to Accra via Rabat and Bathurst. An inaugural flight which set off on 13 October covered the 8,870 mile round trip in 46 flying hours. In fact, only two of the three Halifaxes supplied were used on the services to Accra, but during the first two months of operation the two aircraft flew around 1,200hrs, and the success of the operations prompted BOAC to select the type as its interim passenger type on the London–Cairo route, replacing Dakotas, until the anticipated entry into service of the forthcoming Avro Tudor airliner. The passenger conversion of the Halifax was to be known as the Halton in BOAC service, and as Handley Page was already committed to the Hastings and Hermes projects, as well as the final variants of the Halifax, the contract for the work was awarded to Short Bros at Belfast. Twelve examples of the Halifax C.VIII were purchased by BOAC and flown to Sydenham for the conversions to be carried out. The three loaned RAF Halifaxes were then transferred to BOAC's new training base at Aldermaston, to prepare crews and engineers for the introduction of the Halton.

The Halifax was not an ideal basis for a passenger aircraft, as it was never going to be spacious enough to provide real passenger comfort on long flights, and its noise level was high. However, it was faster than the Dakotas, cruising at 220mph, and Shorts and BOAC did the best they could. The glazed 'bomber' nose was replaced by a skinned solid nose in which mail could be carried, and the crew entrance door on the port side was replaced by a large entrance door on the starboard side. The fuselage portholes were replaced by 15in by 12in windows adjacent to each passenger seat. Ten comfortable seats were fitted, and the cabin furnished with blue upholstery and carpets and rust coloured curtains. A toilet was provided, and a fully equipped galley forward of the main cabin. Fitted below the fuselage was a pannier capable of carrying loads of up to 8,000lbs of baggage, freight and mail.

Handley Page Halton G-AHDU Falkirk served with BOAC from 1946 to 1948. (The Handley Page Association)

The first BOAC Halton, G-AHDU, was named 'Falkirk' by Lady Winster, the wife of the Minister of Civil Aviation, in a ceremony at Radlett on 18 July 1946. This aircraft was used initially for crew training, and then undertook a route-proving flight to Khartoum via Algiers, Castel Benito and Cairo under the command of Captain W. Buchanan. The London–Algiers leg was completed in 4hrs 50mins, and the entire 7,000-mile trip was accomplished without any major problems, the aircraft arriving back in the UK on 8 August 1946. By September six Haltons had been delivered to BOAC's No.1 Line, based at Bovingdon. None of these examples had de-icing equipment, as BOAC expected to take delivery of Avro Tudor IIs to replace them in the near future. On 9 September a six-times-weekly service to Cairo replaced the twice-weekly York service, but after just one week the lack of de-icing measures and some hydraulic systems problems caused the temporary withdrawal of the Haltons. They were returned to Handley Page for rectification and the fitting of de-icing equipment, and in the meantime the Air Ministry loaned BOAC eight standard Halifax C.VIIIs. However, none of these attained Public Transport Certificates of Airworthiness, and they were probably only used for training. The Haltons returned to the Cairo route on 2 June 1947. In the meantime a Halton proving flight to Colombo had been made in April, and from 1 July 1947 a twice-weekly Karachi service replaced the previous flights operated by Skyways on charter to BOAC. On the following day another new Halton service commenced, a three-times-weekly schedule to Lagos on the coastal routing via Casablanca, Dakar and Accra. The 4,467-mile journey took twenty-nine hours, including 24hrs 30min flying time, at an average groundspeed of 182mph. The inaugural service was operated by G-AHDT, and from 1 September the routing was changed to the trans-Sahara route via Castel Benito, Kano and Lagos to Accra, on a five-times -weekly basis.

The Haltons on the West Africa services carried ten passengers and six crew members, who appreciated the strength of the airframe when coping with the strong turbulence, towering cumulo-nimbus clouds and lightning often encountered en route, and the ruggedness of the undercarriage when landing on the unmade runways. The Haltons were not equipped with navigation aids such as Gee or LORAN, and navigation was by means of QDM fixes obtained by use of the direction-finding loop, and astro-navigation using a sextant. The fleet was achieving the low maintenance figure of 3.94 man-hours per flying hour, but since its introduction BOAC had been experiencing problems with the Bovingdon base. There was a shortage of heated hangarage and a lack of suitable local living accommodation. During 1946 the Haltons had completed only 1,000 hours of service but the Bovingdon base had incurred costs of £193,120. It was considered unproductive and was gradually run down. The Haltons were gradually transferred to London Airport, and the last BOAC staff vacated Bovingdon at the beginning of February 1948. Avro Yorks replaced the Haltons on the run to Colombo from 8 September 1947, and on the Accra services from 2 May 1948. On 3–4 May 1948 G-AHDX operated from Accra to London on BOAC's last Halton service, and almost the entire fleet including spares was then sold to Aviation Traders.

BOAC Handley Page Halton G-AHDU Falkirk in flight. (The Handley Page Association)

The rudimentary passenger facilities at London Airport in 1946 consisted mainly of marquees. (Heathrow Airport PLC)

Flying-Boat Operations

During October 1945 the Boeing 314s were still maintaining the transatlantic services from Poole to Baltimore. Twenty passengers could be carried on each service, plus eleven crew members. Most of the passengers were priority government officials, but a few seats were made available for fare-paying passengers at the rate of £142 one way or £254 round trip. The passengers travelled from London to Poole in special trains and were then transported by motor launch to the aircraft. On board the Boeing, bunks were provided for all passengers for the overnight flight to Botwood in Newfoundland, where they went ashore for breakfast. The last transatlantic service by Boeing 314 was operated from Poole to Baltimore via Bathurst on 7 March 1946 by G-AGCA 'Berwick' under the command of Captain B.C. Frost.

During overhauls at their Baltimore base in 1945 the BOAC Boeing 314s were stripped of their wartime camouflage and furnished to accommodate fifty-five passengers on three-times-weekly tourist services from Baltimore to Bermuda. BOAC's final Boeing 314 service was operated from Bermuda to Baltimore on 17 January 1948, with Captain J.W. Burgess in charge of G-AGBZ 'Bristol'. The marine base at Darnell's Island was then closed, and Lockheed Constellations opened a new landplane service over the route on the same day. In BOAC service the Boeings had flown 4,238,867 miles in 29,100 flying hours. 42,000 passengers had been carried, and 596 Atlantic crossings accomplished.

At the end of the war in Europe the BOAC-operated Sunderland IIIs were stripped of their camouflage and re-engined with more powerful Bristol Pegasus 38s. Their interiors were re-arranged to accommodate twenty-four daytime or sixteen sleeper passengers plus mail and freight in readiness for the opening of new post-war Empire routes to the Far East and Australia at the beginning of 1946. Eighteen Sunderlands were converted by BOAC at Hythe, and a further four by Shorts at Belfast. The first conversion was G-AGJM 'Hythe' and this name was also adopted by BOAC as the class name for the type. During October 1945 these aircraft were operating six services each week from Poole to Cairo, four to Calcutta, and two to Karachi. The formalities for health, customs, immigration etc were carried out at the premises of Carter's Potteries, overlooking the quay. Pilot briefings, signals services and navigation services were provided at the Harbour Yacht Club at Lilliput, and passengers were accommodated overnight at the Harbour Heights and Sandacres Hotels. They were ferried by motor launch from Salterns Pier to the aircraft at its moorings about 400 yards offshore. Night landings could be made at Poole, the landing area being marked by lighted launches and electrically illuminated pram dinghies. During 1945, 11,641 passengers arrived at Poole on 463 flights. These were all priority government passengers, no fare-paying seats were available at that time. Although the Sunderlands operated from Poole, their maintenance was still carried out at Hythe.

The interior of one of the marquees used for passenger handling at London Airport in 1946. (Heathrow Airport PLC)

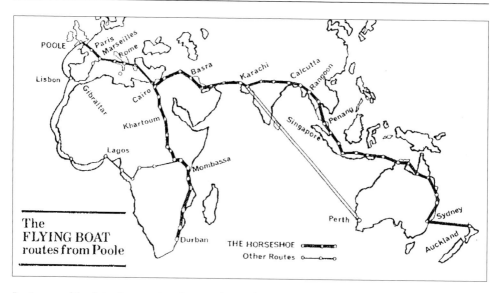

Route map of the flying-boat services from Poole. (Poole Maritime Trust)

Another adaptation of the Sunderland III was carried out by Short Bros at Rochester, the aircraft in question having its nose and tail remodelled to resemble those of the Empire flying-boats. It re-emerged on 28 November 1945 as the first Sandringham 1, G-AGKX 'Himalaya'. Both the Hythe class and the Sandringham 1 offered seating for up to twenty-four passengers, plus baggage, mail and freight stowage, and dining facilities. The Sandringham 1 also offered a cocktail bar, dressing rooms and a ladies powder room complete with hot and cold running water. This was situated amidships on the starboard side, and amidships to port were a toilet and linen locker and a cloakroom for outer garments. On the upper deck, and reached by a staircase athwartships to starboard, were bar and buffet facilities and an adjoining dining saloon which could accommodate eight passengers at each sitting. The settee-type seating could be transformed into four sleeping berths if necessary. The seven-man crew was provided with its own rest room, and immediately behind the dual-control positions for the pilots was the Flight Engineer's compartment. Shorts were hopeful that BOAC would adopt the Sandringham as its standard type for the Empire routes, but the Corporation declined to place an order at that stage, preferring to wait for the new generation of landplane airliners that would shortly be available.

Thus, when BOAC reopened flying-boat services to Singapore on 31 January 1946 it was with Hythes, on a three-times-weekly basis. Between 17 February and 2 April 1946 G-AGJM 'Hythe' made a 35,313-mile route-survey trip from Poole to Australia, New Zealand, Hong Kong, Shanghai and Tokyo. Captain R.C. Parker was in command, and the BOAC chairman, Lord Knollys, was on board. During the course of the journey the Hythe became the first British civil airliner to alight on the Wang-poo River at Shanghai, and on the Bay of Tokyo. This trip led to the inauguration on 12 May 1946 of the first British post-war UK–Australia flying-boat service, operated twice weekly from Poole to Sydney in conjunction with Qantas .The eastbound service took five-and-a-quarter days to reach Sydney, and called at Marseilles, Augusta (Sicily), Cairo, Basra, Bahrain, Karachi, Calcutta, Rangoon, Penang, Singapore, Sourabaya, Darwin and Bowen. The first eastbound schedule was operated by G-AGJN 'Hudson' as far as Singapore, and by G-AGJL 'Hobart' for the remainder of the journey.

The older 'C' class flying-boats were still in use, and on 29 May 1946 they began a weekly service from Poole to Cairo via Augusta. This was taken over on 30 September by 'G' class flying-boat G-AFCI 'Golden Hind'. This machine had been rebuilt by Shorts at Belfast in late 1945 as a luxurious 24-seater with Bristol Hercules XIV engines. Captain Dudley Travers was in command for the aircraft's first peacetime commercial passenger operation, but the service was to be withdrawn on 21 September 1947, after which 'Golden Hind' was retired from BOAC service. On 13 January 1947 the 'C' class boats ceased operations on the withdrawal of the last surviving leg of the 'Horseshoe' route, from Durban to Cairo. On 12 March 1947 'C' class G-ADHM 'Caledonia' left Durban for Southampton. This was the last 'C' class flight out of Africa, and probably the last BOAC service by the type.

Meanwhile, on 24 August 1946 a weekly 'Dragon' service from the UK to Hong Kong had been opened by Hythes. G-AGIA 'Haslemere' operated the first eastbound service as far as Karachi, with stops at Marseilles, Augusta, Cairo, Basra and Bahrain. From Karachi, G-AGLA 'Hunter' took the service onwards to

Short Solent 2 G-AHIU 'Solway' being demonstrated at the 1949 Farnborough Air Show. (Air-Britain)

Hythe class Short Sunderland G-AGJJ. (The A.J. Jackson Collection)

Calcutta, Rangoon, Bangkok and Hong Kong. Hong Kong was also served by a weekly service from Singapore via Bangkok, which had been inaugurated by G-AGKZ 'Harwich' on 26 August.

Early in 1946 BOAC had been given the opportunity to evaluate the second production Short Seaford 1, G-AGWU, which was a larger, upgraded version of the Sunderland. BOAC was sufficiently impressed to place an order for twelve examples of a development of the Seaford, known initially as the Short Solent 1. BOAC's first Solent, G-AHIL 'Salisbury', was launched at Rochester on the River Medway on 11 November 1946, by which time the production models of the Solent had been re-designated as Solent 2s, and made its first flight on 1 December. The BOAC Solent 2s were powered by Bristol Hercules 637 engines and were fitted out to carry thirty passengers on two decks and a crew of seven. They were actually purchased by the Ministry of Civil Aviation, who leased them to BOAC. The February 1947 BOAC Newsletter carried an announcement that BOAC was to introduce Solents onto the 'Springbok' service to South Africa in place of Avro Yorks. BOAC chairman Sir Harold Hartley professed himself convinced that the flying-boat route to South Africa is the most fascinating in the world, and that it offers great tourist possibilities, with its combination of historical and scenic interest.

Another new flying-boat type joined the BOAC fleet in 1947. Frustrated by delivery delays to the new landplane types on order, BOAC was forced to change its mind and lease nine Pratt and Whitney Twin Wasp-powered Short Sandringham 5s from the Ministry of Civil Aviation. These were to be known as the 'Plymouth' class in BOAC service, and were intended to take over from the Hythes on the routes to the Far East and Australia. In 1948 BOAC were also to order three examples of an improved model, the Sandringham 7. These were furnished to accommodate thirty passengers, and were known as the 'Bermuda' class. On 2 May 1947 the 'Plymouth' class Sandringham 5s entered service with BOAC on weekly flights from Poole to Bahrain and Karachi, with night stops at Augusta and Cairo en route. They also opened a weekly service from Poole to Hong Kong on 23 June 1947, flying via Augusta, Cairo, Bahrain, Karachi, Calcutta, Rangoon and Bangkok and supplementing the existing Hythe services.

On 22 August 1947 Solent G-AHZB was lost at Bahrain Marine Air Base, with ten casualties among the twenty-six occupants. The 'G' class-operated Poole–Cairo service was withdrawn on 21 September, and on 11 December 1947 Hythe G-AHER 'Helmsdale' alighted on the Zambezi River above Victoria Falls during a proving flight for the forthcoming Solent services to Johannesburg. The Hythe was believed to be the first aircraft to land on the river at Victoria Falls. On the same day the Hythe service between the UK and Singapore was withdrawn.

On 19 March 1948 the Plymouth service to Hong Kong was extended eastwards to Iwakuni in Japan. The first flight through to Japan was operated by G-AJMZ 'Perth', under the command of Captain R.C.S. Reid, and the 10,625-mile trip was scheduled to take seven days. From 20 November the service was again extended, to Tokyo.

During early 1948 it became clear that BOAC would have to make major cost-savings. Flying-boat operations from Poole had always been extremely expensive, and it was decided that the fleet could be operated more economically from Southampton, where the aircraft could be moored to floating pontoons, from which the passengers and freight could be loaded directly, without a boat transfer. Moreover, the greater and deeper expanse of water at Southampton meant that the flying-boats could be operated with greater safety margins.

Short Sandringham Mk 7 G-AKCO. (The A.J. Jackson Collection)

BOAC's UK flying-boat base was transferred from Poole to Southampton Water on 31 March 1948. The first departure from there took place on the following day when Hythe G-AGEW 'Hanwell' departed for Sydney, but it was not until 14 April that the terminal at Berth 50 was officially opened by Lord Nathan, the Minister for Civil Aviation. The new terminal featured four waiting rooms, two floating docks, a restaurant and a lounge bar. At the opening ceremony BOAC Solent G-AHIN was named 'Southampton' by the Mayoress of the city. On 8 April Solent G-AHIY 'Southsea' had been launched at Rochester, achieving the sad distinction of being the last aircraft to be built at the famous seaplane works.

On 4 May 1948 the Solents were introduced onto weekly Southampton-Johannesburg services. The first scheduled service was operated by G-AHIT 'Severn', but a 'pre-inaugural' flight for journalists had been made in April by G-AHIN 'Southampton'. The Solent services routed via Augusta, Cairo, Luxor, Khartoum, Port Bell and Victoria Falls, and terminated at Vaaldam, on the Vaal River about fifty-eight miles from Johannesburg. In July the Solents had to be temporarily withdrawn for wing-tip float modifications, and did not return to service until October. From the spring of 1949 the Solent 2s were joined by thirty-four seat Solent 3s. These too were a development of the Seaford, six of which had been loaned free of charge to Short Bros at Belfast by the RAF. After conversion the Solent 3s were sold to the Ministry of Supply, which then leased four of them to BOAC.

On the Solent 3 the thirty-four passengers were accommodated on two decks which were connected by a short spiral staircase. The passenger entrance was on the port side and led directly to a promenade deck. There were two forward-facing seats in this area, and twenty others in three cabins forward of this entrance. 'D' and 'E' cabins, accommodating twelve passengers in total, were on the upper deck, which was reached by the spiral staircase from the forward end of the promenade area. Midships on the upper deck were the cocktail bar, steward's compartment and a fully equipped galley with electric cooker and refrigerator. Forward of these was the flight deck. The crew comprised the Captain, First Officer, Navigating Officer, Radio Officer and Flight Engineer. Among the other on-board facilities provided for the passengers were a library and a dressing-room.

The weekly service to Johannesburg was eventually upgraded to three times weekly. The 5,600-mile journey took four and a half days and included four night stops. The fare of £295.20 return included a visit to the Valley of the Kings during the stopover at Luxor. At all the ports of call along the route there were extensive facilities provided for both the aircraft and their occupants. At Augusta there was attractive passenger night-stop accommodation and staff quarters, featuring 126 rooms. At Alexandria (for Cairo), on land leased from the Egyptian government, BOAC constructed workshops, offices, an aircraft catering kitchen and a lounge. The alighting area on the Zambezi at Victoria Falls was linked to the Falls Hotel by a specially-constructed four-mile stretch of road, and at Vaaldam a new power house, slipway, workshops, stores, offices and living accommodation were built, all for the handful of flying-boat services each week.

On 16 February 1949 BOAC's last Hythe service arrived at Southampton from Sydney, with Captain D.W. Pallett commanding G-AGJO 'Honduras' on the last sector. In BOAC service the Sunderlands and Hythes had flown 25,117,246 miles and carried 79,793 passengers.

On 5 May 1949, Solent 3 G-AKNO alighted on the Thames and taxied to the Tower of London, to be moored there as part of the celebrations marking the thirtieth anniversary of British civil aviation. While it was there, the Solent was named 'City of London' on 10 May by Sir George Aylwen, the Lord Mayor of London.

By mid-1949 the new generation of landplane airliners had begun to displace BOAC's flying-boats from the air lanes. On 26–28 August the Plymouth class were withdrawn from the Far East routes, as Canadair Argonauts were now in service, and on 7 November 1950 the Solent service to Johannesburg was replaced by Handley Page Hermes landplane services. All the Solents were then withdrawn. They had been the last flying-boats in service with BOAC, and their retirement brought to an end the flying-boat operations which BOAC and its predecessor Imperial Airways had maintained continuously since 1924.

7

BOAC Rejects

Three major new British airliners were designed and built with BOAC in mind during the early post-war years, only to be rejected by the Corporation or to fail to secure the necessary government backing to reach production status.

The Avro Tudor

The Tudor design originated in 1943 as a post-war transport derived from the Avro Lincoln bomber. However, as the design was refined it developed into a different aircraft, retaining only the general configuration of the Lincoln. It had longer wings, a single tail fin, and a pressurised fuselage, and was powered by four Rolls Royce Merlin 621 V-12 liquid-cooled piston engines. The first prototype, G-AGPF, made its maiden flight on 14 June 1945 from Ringway, Manchester. Trials with the three prototypes revealed a number of problems, and a new tail unit was substituted. On 10 March 1946 the developed Tudor 2 G-AGSU made its first flight from Woodford. However, on a later flight it was to crash, killing its designer Roy Chadwick.

Throughout the design development of the Tudor BOAC kept revising its specifications for the type, and at the final development meeting on 12 March 1946 insisted on no fewer than 343 further alterations. The Tudor 1 was granted its Certificate of Airworthiness in September 1946, and on 21 January 1947 HRH Princess Elizabeth named the intended BOAC Tudor 1 G-AGRE 'Elizabeth of England' in a ceremony at London Airport. Despite this, BOAC eventually abandoned the Tudor altogether, cancelling its order for twenty-two Tudor 1s on 11 April 1947. Although the type never saw service with BOAC it was used by British South American Airways, and later by British charter airlines.

G-AGPW, the sole Bristol Brabazon to be completed, in flight. (Air-Britain)

The Bristol Brabazon

While the Second World War was still in progress a committee was set up under the chairmanship of Lord Brabazon of Tara to consider the post-war airliner needs of Britain's airlines. Its 1943 report listed five basic types, one of which was a 'London–New York express airliner'. This project, known as Brabazon Type 1, was to have priority in design and production, even though it was expected to take at least five years to have it ready for service. A contract was awarded to the Bristol Aeroplane Company for a design which was based on the company's '100-ton bomber' project. There was some debate over the number of passengers to be carried. BOAC stated its opinion that passengers could not tolerate flights lasting longer than eighteen hours, and recommended the allocation of 200 cu. ft of space per passenger for ordinary services, and 270 cu. ft per passenger for luxury services. The design eventually evolved into a 50-seater, even though BOAC would have preferred a smaller twenty-five-passenger version. By November 1944 the main features of what was then called the Bristol Type 167 had been decided, including propulsion by four pairs of coupled Bristol Centaurus turbo-props. The first prototype was rolled out at Filton in December 1948, and the first flight of the Bristol Brabazon, as it was named, took place on 4 September 1949. In 1950 the Brabazon visited London Airport for demonstration flights, and also appeared at the Farnborough Air Show. For the demonstration flights the rear fuselage was partially furnished with thirty BOAC reclining seats and a bar. The demonstrations to official passengers proved how quietness and freedom from fatigue and claustrophobia could be achieved in a really large aeroplane, and the Brabazon impressed observers with its handling qualities, but the lack of political will to back such a massive project meant that it never saw BOAC service. After less than 400 hours flying time the first prototype and the partially completed second machine were broken up in 1953. However, the experience gained was to aid Bristol in due course with another airliner for BOAC, the smaller, less ambitious Britannia.

The Saunders-Roe S.R. 45 Princess

The Saunders-Roe Princess was an attempt to repeat the pre-war success of the Empire flying-boats utilising the latest technology of the early post-war years. In 1946 the Ministry of Supply authorised Saunders-Roe to proceed with the construction of three Princess flying-boats, registered G-ALUN, G-ALUO and G-ALUP for use by BOAC. They were to be the largest flying-boats ever built. Ten Bristol Proteus turbo-prop engines were to give the Princesses a still-air range of 5,500 miles at a cruising speed of 360mph. The gigantic pressurised hull was to be divided into two decks, on which BOAC planned to carry 105 passengers in First-Class and Tourist-Class cabins. Also to be provided for the passengers were bunks, powder rooms and a spiral staircase.

Technical problems with the pressurisation of the hull, the largest yet built, delayed the maiden flight of the Princess until 22 August 1952, when Geoffrey Tyson took G-ALUN aloft for the first time. The Princess was displayed at the 1952 Farnborough Air Show, but by then BOAC had ceased flying-boat operations. They did carry out a survey of their maintenance base at Hythe to determine what alterations would be necessary to the Princess, but shortly afterwards announced that they were no longer interested in the aircraft.

8

British South American Airways

In February 1944 British Latin-American Air Lines was first registered as a company by a consortium of five British shipping companies operating sea routes to South America, but did not commence operations at that time. On 13 March 1945 a white paper on British air transport revealed the government's intention of setting up a new airline company. This was to be controlled by the shipping company owners of British Latin-American Air Lines, but under the overall control of the government, who would appoint its directors. In June 1945 Air Vice Marshall D.C.T. Bennett was appointed Managing Director, but a month later Britain's new Labour government announced its intention to nationalise air transport. In September 1945 the airline was renamed British South American Airways Ltd, and it commenced operations on 1 January 1946, when Avro Lancastrian G-AGWG 'Starlight', under the command of AVM Bennett, departed London Airport on the first of six proving flights to South America. This was routed London–Lisbon–Bathurst–Natal–Montevideo–Buenos Aires, and on 15 March 1946 BSAA commenced regular London–Buenos Aires Lancastrian services, flying via Lisbon, Bathurst, Natal, Rio and Montevideo. This was the first British commercial air service to South America, and on 5 April the scheduled timing from London to Buenos Aires was cut from seventy-seven hours to fifty-six hours. During the period 22 April 1946–5 May 1946 Lancastrian G-AGWI 'Star Land', again under the command of AVM Bennett, carried out a survey flight over the route London–Buenos–Aires–Santiago (Chile)–Lima–Bogota–Caracas–Trinidad–Natal–Bathurst–London. On 11 June BSAA's first Avro York, G-AHEW 'Star Leader' operated a Shell charter flight to Venezuela. The aircraft returned via Bermuda and Gander, flying Gander–London direct with a full load of twenty-one passengers and seven crew in 10hrs 35mins. A new weekly Lancastrian service from London to Santiago via Bathurst, Natal, Rio and Buenos Aires was inaugurated on 27 June.

On 1 August 1946 the airline was nationalised under the Civil Aviation Act 1946, and became the British South American Airways Corporation. The chairman was J.W. Booth, and the Chief Executive was Air Vice Marshall D.C.T. Bennett. At that time the fleet consisted of six Lancastrians and four Yorks. A unique feature of the airline's fleet was that throughout its entire life it consisted entirely of Avro designs. During the period May–October 1946 twelve new Yorks were acquired, as well as a number of ex-BOAC examples. Six Avro Lancasters were also used for freight services from 1946 onwards. Four of these were modified by the addition of a cargo hold in the forward section of the fuselage. These were used for almost a year, carrying perishable goods on routes to South America. The other two examples were returned to the RAF after a short period of uneconomical service. During the following year, Lancasters were to be used for a series of trial flight-refuelled non-stop services between London and Bermuda. These commenced on 28 May 1947, with Lancaster G-AHJV being refuelled by another Lancaster based in the Azores. On the first trial flight the 4,000 miles was covered in twenty hours.

Meanwhile, on 2 September 1946 Lancastrian G-AGWL 'Star Guide', under the command of Captain Gordon Store, had inaugurated a fortnightly service from London to Caracas via the Azores, Bermuda and Jamaica. On 23 September Dakar was substituted for Bathurst as a stop on the London–Buenos Aires services. On 18 January 1947 the route from London to Venezuela via the Caribbean was extended along the west coast of South America to Lima and Santiago. BSAA called its air hostesses 'Star Hostesses', and one of these was a certain Eve Branson, later to have a son, Richard, who was to make quite a name for himself in the airline industry!

On 5 June 1947 BSAAC commenced a weekly London–Azores–Bermuda–Nassau–Jamaica service, and in August 1947 the Corporation purchased a substantial shareholding in British West Indian Airways, but on 2 August 1947 disaster struck. Lancastrian 3 G-AGWH 'Star Dust', with six passengers and five crew aboard, went missing over the Andes mountains during a heavy storm while en route from Buenos Aires to Santiago. Thirty minutes after take-off a radio message was received reporting turbulence and heavy snow. The final part of the message was 'STENDEC', sent in Morse code. Nobody on the ground knew what that meant. It was not until January 2000 that climbers discovered wreckage and preserved bodies near the peak of Argentina's Tupungato mountain, close to the border with Chile.

On 29 September 1947 BSAAC took delivery of its first Avro Tudor 4 G-AHNK 'Star Lion'. On the following day AVM Bennett commanded this aircraft on a proving flight from London to South America, and the same aircraft was used to inaugurate Tudor 4 services between London and Havana via Lisbon, the Azores, Bermuda and Nassau on 31 October 1947.

The Tudor did not have a happy history. Twelve production Tudor 1s were laid down in response to an order from BOAC which was eventually cancelled. Two were then completed for the Ministry of Supply as Tudor 3 VIP transports. The remainder were sold to BSAAC as Tudor 4s for only £30,000 each. Of these, only six were delivered and used in twenty-eight-seat configuration. During 1946/7 BSAAC envisaged a requirement for six Comet 1 jets to replace the Tudors, but the eventual merger with BOAC was to render this unnecessary.

On the night of 29–30 January 1948 Tudor 4 G-AHNP 'Star Tiger' disappeared between Santa Maria in the Azores and Bermuda. On the first day of February 1948 BSAAC became the first British airline to carry subsidiary mail on scheduled services when it began carrying mail to South America, and on the same date it introduced a three-times-weekly Avro York service between Nassau and Miami. However, during that month AVM Bennett was dismissed from BSAAC, for several reasons but primarily because of his defiance of a Ministry instruction to ground the Tudor fleet. Since 1 January 1946 the airline had suffered seven accidents to passenger aircraft, in four of which a total of forty-six casualties had been incurred. AVM Bennett was eventually replaced on 1 April 1948 by Air Commodore H.G. Brackley.

On 21 August 1948 BSAAC began a weekly Nassau-Havana York service, later upgraded to three times weekly, and that month the airline acquired Bahamas Airways Ltd. During that year BSAAC also played a part in the Berlin Airlift, flying 2,562 sorties with Tudor 5s converted to carry fuel. On 3 December 1948 a weekly Tudor 4 service to Buenos Aires replaced the former Lancastrian operation. The westbound services routed via Keflavik, Gander, Bermuda, Jamaica, Barranquilla, Lima and Santiago, while the eastbound flights routed via the Azores. Three days later a weekly London–Lisbon–Azores–Gander–Bermuda–Nassau–Havana service was inaugurated, but on 17 January 1949 Tudor 4 G-AGRE 'Star Ariel' disappeared in unexplained circumstances between Bermuda and Jamaica with thirteen passengers aboard. This was the second Tudor to disappear in mysterious circumstances, and the Tudors were then withdrawn from passenger service, with the remaining examples being relegated to cargo operations. The subsequent aircraft shortage was one of the factors leading to the merger into BOAC on 30 July 1949, under the Airways Corporations Act 1949. BOAC chairman Sir Miles Thomas DFC then also became chairman of BSAAC.

9

BOAC's Organisation, Staffing and UK Bases

In 1940 BOAC's headquarters and terminal for landplanes was at Whitchurch near Bristol, while the flying-boats operated from Poole Harbour in Dorset. Hythe, near Southampton, became the maintenance base for the flying-boats, and Bramcote, near Nottingham handled landplane maintenance. In addition to the servicing of its own aircraft BOAC undertook the assembly and modification of fighters at Colerne in Wiltshire. In May 1940 the Ministry of Aircraft Production requested BOAC's co-operation in undertaking the repair and modification of military aircraft engines and propellers. Repair shops at Croydon and Hythe were available, but did not have sufficient capacity, so on June 18 1940 an advance party of engineers went to view the Treforest Trading Estate near Cardiff, which had been set up pre-war to help solve local unemployment. By early July a new factory was in full production, and by 26 July engine test-beds had been constructed in a nearby field and the first reconditioned engine was delivered. BOAC engineers also assembled American-built aircraft for the RAF and Royal Navy at Speke, Liverpool, and at Colerne until the work was taken over by RAF and American engineers, and then opened two workshops in Bath for the repair of damaged propellers. On 1 November 1944 the Whitchurch terminal was transferred to Hurn Airport at Bournemouth, and the engineering work at Bramcote was switched to Croydon.

By 1946 BOAC aircraft began wearing the airline's first civilian colour scheme. This consisted of a natural metal finish, with a Union Flag on the tail fin(s) and the 'Speedbird' logo and BOAC titles on the fuselage near the nose.

With the end of the war and the commencement of peacetime commercial operations BOAC faced many problems, the most major of which were caused by obsolete aircraft and overstaffing. In 1947 the combined staff of BOAC and British South American Airways numbered 24,100. By March 1951 this figure had been reduced to about 16,500. In the financial year ending 31 March 1952 BOAC made a profit of £1.25 million before interest of £1 million had been deducted, the first profit in its history, and operating revenue per employee had been raised to the point where the airline could also look forward to making a profit in the years to come. This situation was also due to the introduction of more commercially viable aircraft.

A review of BOAC's re-equipment options in 1947 had decided that the Boeing Stratocruiser was the best available aircraft for the Corporation's North Atlantic operations. It was a proven aircraft, already in service with Pan-American Airways, and although its seat-mile costs were no lower than its rival the L-749 Constellation, it could offer 50 per cent more carrying capacity. It also offered sleeping berths for those passengers willing to pay a supplement, and a downstairs cocktail bar to while away the long overnight journeys. BOAC would normally have had to wait a long time for their order to be fulfilled, but Scandinavian Airlines System and Aer Lingus had recently cancelled options they held, and these were transferred to BOAC as firm orders. For the Empire routes to Australia, the Far East and Africa the government authorised the purchase of Lockheed L-049 and L-749 Constellations, although not in sufficient quantities to handle all the projected traffic. To supplement the Constellations, permission was given to buy Canadair Argonauts with Canadian Dollars, provided the aircraft were powered by Rolls Royce Merlin engines paid for in Sterling. As soon as was practicable these foreign types were to be replaced by British-built Comets and Britannias. The Avro Yorks and the Solent flying boats were to be withdrawn during 1950 as more modern types were phased in.

During 1949 the transfer of staff from various office locations in London to Airways House at Brentford began. This building was situated on the Great West

An engine change being carried out by the night shift on L-049 Constellation G-AHEK 'Berwick' inside No.3 Hangar at London Airport Engineering Base. (Eric Loseby)

Opposite page:

Top: Qantas L-749 Constellation VH-EAN at No.3 Hangar at London Airport for turn-round checks by
BOAC engineers. (Eric Loseby)

Middle: A Skyways L-749 Constellation is prepared for moving sideways into a hangar at the BOAC base
at London Airport by means of tramlines and flat bogies attached to the main undercarriage. (Eric Loseby)

Bottom: Comet 4 aircraft inside Technical Block B at London Airport. (Eric Loseby)

Road, midway between central London and London Airport. An innovation
there was a staff restaurant, where all staff could enjoy a three-course lunch,
served at their table, for only 2s 6d. More than 300 staff enjoyed these lunches
each day. The move was largely completed by June 1950, when the chairman and
deputy chairman transferred their offices from Stratton House, Piccadilly.
However, the location of Airways House proved not to be convenient, and the
transfer of staff to London Airport began in the summer of 1954. On 11 July
1955 the headquarters of BOAC was officially transferred to London Airport,
and the building was sold that year.

In 1949 BOAC's London passenger terminal and reservations office was at
Airways Terminal at Victoria, which had originally opened in June 1938 as the
London terminal of Imperial Airways. In December 1949 a transatlantic reservation system known as 'North America Bookings' was in use. This utilised a large
visual indicator board to control its 'sell and record' bookings. On the board the
booking status of all transatlantic services for the next six months was shown. A
green disc against the flight showed that seats were available for immediate sale,
and a yellow disc meant that prior confirmation from New York was required.
This could be obtained almost instantaneously on an IMCO circuit giving a
direct connection to New York. A red disc meant that the flight was full. Facing
the indicator board were Space Clerks, dealing with incoming telephone calls.
BOAC's first steps with mechanised reservations systems involved the use of a
system called ERS (Electronic Reservations System), which was located in a huge
equipment room in Airways Terminal, and was very successful for its time. The
system was first introduced at Airways Terminal in February 1962. In February
1963 it went online in Canada, followed by New York in September 1963.

Since as long ago as 1957, the airlines had been experiencing problems
with 'no-shows' for flights, and had adopted a policy of controlled overbooking
on flights which had a history of no-shows and late cancellations. In the four
weeks ending 14 September 1957, i.e. during its peak transatlantic season,
BOAC lost £17,000 of westbound transatlantic revenue as a result of late cancellations and passengers not turning up for booked flights, despite operating a
policy of controlled overbooking. Deliberate overbooking was not practiced
however, on those types of accommodation which offered less than thirty seats
on each flight, for example the First-Class compartments on mixed-class
Britannia services.

Throughout the early 1960s Airways Terminal was expanded and modernised in a £3m scheme. Two new wings were added at each side of the original central tower, and at the same time the entire passenger area was redesigned and expanded. The first new wing was opened in 1960, and the addition of the northern wing enabled BOAC to house at Airways Terminal those departments which had hitherto been scattered around the West End of London. In March 1965 a further extension in the form of a six-storey wing incorporating a new arrivals hall was opened, followed in August 1965 by a new ticket office.

During the week ending 21 August 1965, BOAC sold 21,862 seats both into and out of the UK, at a 70 per cent load factor. This compared with 18,111 seats during the same week the previous year, although the load factor was exactly the same.

In the autumn of 1968 all passenger reservations were transferred onto BOAC's new BOADICEA computer, which was based on the use of the new and powerful IBM 360 range machines, and held details of all BOAC flights for a year ahead. All BOAC sales offices and reservations centres throughout the world were then linked to BOADICEA by teletype. The total cost of the BOADICEA system was £43 million.

Prior to the introduction of BOADICEA, Air-Britain member Peter White was involved in a joint BOAC/Standard Telephones and Cables communications study to assess the likely peak-hour traffic for BOADICEA. From this study the new network design was to be finalised in terms of number, capacity and routing of communications links. A survey form was designed, and after a pilot run was distributed to all BOAC reservations offices worldwide. The survey was scheduled for a busy week in mid-July 1966, and involved the reservations clerks filling in a survey form for every single reservations transaction handled during that week. After the forms were distributed BOAC learned of an impending strike by Pan-American Airways, one of their two main transatlantic competitors, set for the very week of the survey. The strike duly took place, BOAC's bookings shot up, and the survey team were swamped with the resulting forms, which took months to process, adjustments having to be made to offset the distortion to the figures brought about by the strike. In November 1968 new small television-type screens were installed in New York and at Airways Terminal, and were rapidly extended to all other stations, putting BOAC ahead of all other airlines in the extent and sophistication of its reservations systems. However, BOADICEA was totally incompatible with BEA's reservation computer BEACON, which was based on the UNIVAC system, and located in BEA's West London Air Terminal in Cromwell Road, London. BOADICEA was operated successfully for many years, and the system was sold to many other airlines, before being eventually succeeded by the British Airways reservations system BABS.

On 1 November 1949 BOAC Chairman Sir Miles Thomas announced that the current year's results were not showing sufficient economies. Currency devaluation meant that the cost of buying fuel and maintaining BOAC stations in 'hard currency' areas would cost about £1 million more, hopefully to be offset by a rise of about £400,000 in dollar revenue brought in by an increased volume of traffic. There was to be a reorganisation of the airline, in which there would be two distinct sections; the operational side, under Deputy Chairman Whitney Straight, would direct all its energies to producing the maximum number of CTMs from the new fleets of aircraft as economically as possible. The commercial side would go all-out to sell the passenger and freight capacity thus created to the best advantage. This new pattern would give practical effect to the benefits accrued from merging BOAC and BSAAC, and was being put into operation consequent upon the delivery of the new Argonaut and Stratocruiser fleets, the impending introduction of the Hermes, and the concentration of activities at London Airport. The new organisation would be implemented progressively, with a view to it being fully operative by the beginning of January 1950. In 1950 BOAC's new 'white-top' colour scheme was introduced. As a result, by 31 March 1951 BOAC's fleet consisted of twenty-two Argonauts, ten Stratocruisers, ten Constellations, sixteen Hermes and ten Yorks (for cargo only).

During 1950–51 London Airport was the maintenance base for all BOAC aircraft types except the Constellations and Stratocruisers, whose major maintenance was still carried out at Filton while work continued on the London Airport engineering facilities. As this progressed, Constellation maintenance was transferred over in 1953 and the Stratocruiser work in October 1954. The first stage of the new engineering base was opened in 1955. It covered 8.5 acres, and comprised four large hangar blocks, with office accommodation at the sides and workshops in the transepts between the hangars. Work commenced immediately on the second stage, which became known as the 'Britannia hangar', and also housed the Britannia simulator. This became operational in 1957. An interesting structural feature for that period was the use of two very long cantilevers to give uninterrupted door openings of 300ft in width. Another new building was erected nearby to house the accounts staff, catering and provisioning departments, and the cabin-crew training department. On the third floor of the office accommodation, room B314 was converted into a 'writing room', for the use of Captains passing through London Airport. Newly decorated, with comfortable furnishings and carpets, this room was the only room in the headquarters building at the time to have papered walls!

A major expense in the mid-1950s was the cost of 'slipping' crews, i.e. overnighting them at en route points along the network to join another service once they had had their mandatory rest period. In 1956 the cost of hotel accommodation and meals averaged £3 15s per person on the Eastern routes, and slightly more than £5 per person on the transatlantic routes. Taking into account the crew's daily overseas allowance and the proportion of their flying pay which was unproductive, the real costs per crew totalled £219,000 per annum, broken down by fleet as follows: Argonaut £32,000, Constellation £40,000, Britannia £45,000, DC-7C £45,000, Stratocruiser £57,000.

Efforts were made at this time to develop the airline's air cargo business, and to cater for lucrative niche cargo consignments. During 1955 BOAC's revenue from the carriage of tropical fish amounted to £75,000. All BOAC staff were also encouraged to find new passenger business for the airline by means of the Staff Sales Incentive Scheme. Every time a BOAC staff member introduced new passenger business, 3*d* out of every £1 of the fare paid was credited to that employee's staff rebate fare. £500 of introduced business would pay for a staff travel return ticket to somewhere such as Tripoli, and spouses were allowed to travel on the same basis. There was also a 'Sale of the Year' award, with a prize of free air transportation for two people to any point on the BOAC route network outside the Dollar area, and one week's free hotel accommodation. The award for 1956 went to DC-7C Flight Captain Bernard Frost, for introducing business worth £12,503.

By the mid–1960s around 5,000 people worked at the Heathrow base, about 25 per cent of BOAC's worldwide total. In early 1970 the first Boeing 747 hangar, '01 Hangar', was completed in time for the arrival of the first wide-bodied member of the BOAC fleet.

Since 1940 BOAC's engine overhauls had been carried out 'in-house' at the factory at Treforest in South Wales. By 1956 it had a throughput of some 2,000 piston engines each year. However, the imminent introduction of turbo-prop and jet engines, with their better utilisation between overhauls, looked set to reduce this figure by two-thirds from 1957 onwards until the early 1960s, when fleet expansion would restore the workload again. In order to keep Treforest busy during the intervening years a large volume of third-party work was secured from other airlines and the RAF.

At the end of March 1951 the staff of BOAC totalled approximately 16,000, of whom around 3,000 were employed at London Airport, and the remainder at stations around the globe. In August 1951 new salary scales were introduced for BOAC and BEA pilots. A Senior Captain First Class had his salary increased from £1,500 to £2,150 per annum, and a First Officer's was increased from £750 to £1,035 per annum, with annual increments of £30, up to a maximum of £1,305 per annum. By 1952, in order to cope with the expansion in services, BOAC was advertising for more Air Stewardesses. A remuneration of £5 17*s* per week when flying, and £2 per week when not was offered, and the advertisements attracted 800 applicants, 3 per cent of whom were eventually selected.

By 1964 BOAC had 734 Stewardesses on its strength, and this figure had risen to 1038 by 1970.

In October 1969 a new range of stewardess uniforms was unveiled, to be introduced in May 1970, to coincide with the projected entry into service of the

The nose of Boeing 747 G-AWNF in the London Airport Engineering Base, along with two Boeing 707s and a Comet 4 G-APDT, used for apprentice training. (Eric Loseby)

wide-bodied Boeing 747. For the first time in twenty-five years radical new designs, new colours and new accessories were to be introduced. The basic uniform colour was still navy blue, but there were also tropical dresses in coral pink and turquoise blue. There were also trousers, which the stewardesses were free to wear at any time except when they were actually serving passengers on board the aircraft.

During the financial year 1952/53, 13.5 per cent of BOAC's passengers travelled in the newly introduced Tourist Class. By the end of the financial year 1954/55 this proportion had increased to 45.2 per cent. In 1954 BOAC's average fare was £80, compared with BEA's £16. BOAC used the brand names 'Monarch' and 'Majestic' for their De Luxe and First-Class services, and 'Coronet' for their Tourist-Class services, except on the North Atlantic routes, where 'Mayflower' was used for flights to the USA, and 'Beaver' for flights to Canada.

By the end of 1955 BOAC's staff totalled 18,411. In October 1956 the average journey length for each BOAC passenger was around 3,500 miles, and each round-trip passenger was worth around £160 in revenue to the airline.

Until 2 August 1956 BOAC's capital requirements had been met by the issue to the public of BOAC stock, as laid down in the Air Corporations Act. However, that arrangement was then discontinued, and to raise capital BOAC had thenceforth to apply to the Ministry of Transport and Civil Aviation for 'exchequer advances'. This left the airline vulnerable to cuts in its capital for non aviation-related reasons, for instance to meet any requirements for cuts in government annual budgets.

In June 1960 the Civil Aviation (Licensing) Act became law. This brought to an end BOAC's statutory right to be the chosen instrument (i.e. sole British operator) on long-haul routes. Henceforth, the independent airlines could apply for, and be granted, scheduled service licences for any route. The applications were to be heard by the Air Transport Licensing Board.

On 16 November 1961 BOAC finally transferred its passenger handling services at London Airport from the temporary buildings on the North Side apron to the new No.3 Building 'Oceanic' (now known as Terminal 3) in the Central Area. At first the new terminal could only be used for departures, and it was not until March 1962 that arrivals could also be handled there. Initially BOAC had the new building all to itself, as foreign airlines were not allowed to transfer across from the North Side until 29 March 1962.

The year 1964 was BOAC's best to date. The total number of passengers carried (scheduled and charter) was 1,212,100, a 16 per cent increase over 1963, and in November the airline announced its highest operating profit to date, £8.7 million.

In July 1969 the Airways Flying Club, jointly owned by BOAC and BEA, staged an airshow at Wycombe Air Park to commemorate its twenty-first birthday. The show was opened by a low pass by BOAC Boeing 707-436 G-APFK, and closed by a flypast by a BEA Trident.

Also in 1969, the new joint BEA/BOAC cargo terminal on Heathrow's South Side became operational at the end of the year, although it was not officially opened until May 1970, when HRH Prince Philip performed the ceremony. The terminal took two years to build, at a total cost of £11 million, of which BOACs contribution was £5 million.

In April 1971 British Overseas Air Charter Ltd was formed as a subsidiary of BOAC for the purpose of operating charter flights worldwide. A large number of these were on the North Atlantic routes, to combat competition from the many charter companies operating 'affinity group charters' to the USA and Canada, but during one week in July 1972 British Overseas Air Charter operated more than eighty charter flights, mainly with Boeing 707 equipment. These ranged from Far East trips to short European legs. Boeing 747s were also used during that summer on a series of weekly charters to Palma. It was during 1972 that BOAC signed its biggest charter contract to date. This was with Kuoni Travel, for Boeing 707 flights during the winter of 1972–73. Weekly flights were operated to Ceylon and Bangkok, and a fortnightly operation from London to Mexico City.

BOAC Chairmen

Sir John Reith	21 January 1939–5 March 1940
The Hon. Clive Pearson	6 March 1940–24 March 1943
Sir Harold Howitt	25 March 1943–25 May 1943
Viscount Knollys	26 May 1943–30 June 1947
Sir Harold Hartley	1 July 1947–30 June 1949
Sir Miles Thomas	1 July 1949–30 April 1956
Gerard (later Sir Gerard) d'Erlanger	1 May 1956–28 July 1960
Sir Matthew Slattery	29 July 1960–31 December 1963
Sir Giles Guthrie	1 January 1964–31 December 1968
Charles(later Sir Charles) Hardie	1 January 1969–31 December 1970
Keith(later Sir Keith) Granville	1 January 1971–31 August 1972
Ross(later Sir Ross) Stainton	1 September 1972–31 March 1974

BOAC Associated Companies

Throughout its post-war history BOAC maintained a large network of subsidiaries throughout the world. These airlines operated regional services which were usually timed to connect with BOAC mainline services, and the companies were grouped together under the collective title of BOAC Associated Companies. In October 1949 BOAC purchased the shares of British Caribbean Airways Ltd. Its services were thereafter operated by chartered Vickers Vikings of British West Indian Airways Ltd. British Caribbean Airways Ltd ceased trading on 31 March 1950. During 1950 the member airlines of BOAC Associated Companies included Aer Lingus Teoranta, British Commonwealth Pacific Airlines Ltd, Cyprus Airways Ltd, East African Airways Corporation, Iraqi Airways Ltd, Malayan Airways Ltd, and Tasman Empire Airways Ltd, plus Egyptian Aircraft Engineering Co SAE. Other subsidiaries, although not part of BOAC Associated Companies, were Aden Airways Ltd, Bahamas Airways Ltd, and British West Indian Airways Ltd. The latter two airlines were originally subsidiaries of British South American Airways Corporation, and were inherited when BOAC took over that company. On 1 October 1951 BOAC acquired a majority shareholding in Gulf Aviation, based in Bahrain, and in 1954 purchased a controlling interest in Middle East Airlines. On 30 November 1957 BOAC Associated Companies Ltd, which had been formed in September of that year, took over responsibility for BOAC's assets and liabilities connected with the Associated Companies and other subsidiaries. On 1 January 1960 BOAC became joint owner, with Qantas and Tasman Empire Airways Ltd, of Fiji Airways, and on 26 April 1960 BOAC Associated Companies Ltd signed a contract for three Avro 748 series 2 turbo-prop aircraft, to be operated by Aden Airways.

10

BOAC Operations after 1950

The North Atlantic Routes

During the late 1940s and the first half of the 1950s BOAC's transatlantic services were maintained by two modern American types, the Lockheed Constellation and the Boeing Stratocruiser.

On 24 January 1946 the Parliamentary Secretary to the Ministry of Civil Aviation announced to the House of Commons that BOAC had ordered five Lockheed L-049-46-25 Constellations for transatlantic services. At the time this order cause some controversy as many people thought that a British design should have been ordered, but in reality there was no suitable home-grown type available. The Avro Tudor 1 was too small to be competitive, and would have been able to accommodate twelve passengers on North Atlantic routes. The Constellation first flew on 9 January 1943 as the C-69 transport, intended for the US military. It was powered by four 2,200hp Wright Cyclone 18-cylinder radial piston engines, and first went into airline service with Pan American Airways on the New York–Bermuda route in February 1946. During 1947 the Bristol Aeroplane Co. proposed meeting a British requirement for a medium-range airliner for the Empire routes by building L-049 Constellations (and later the developed L-749 Constellation) in the UK and fitting them with Bristol Centaurus 662 engines. Lockheed were willing to grant a licence, but in the end the British government refused to sanction the dollar expenditure for these projects, and Bristol then went ahead with its own new Type 175 design, which became the Britannia.

On 16 June 1946 L-049 Constellation G-AHEM 'Balmoral', under the command of Captain W.S. May, operated the first of ten BOAC Constellation transatlantic proving flights, and set a record of 11hrs 24mins for the New York–London journey. These flights paved the way for the inauguration of twice-weekly scheduled services between London and La Guardia Airport, New York on 1 July 1946, with G-AHEJ 'Bristol II' operating the first service under the

Stratocruiser G-ALSC operated BOACs first Manchester-New York service on 7 May 1954. (Air-Britain)

command of Captain O.P. Jones. The Constellation fleet was initially based at Filton as part of BOAC's No.3 Line, but the temporary grounding of all Constellations after an accident to a TWA example meant that BOAC's services were suspended between 10 July and 30 August 1946. The BOAC Constellations were returned to service after modifications to their electrical systems. With the resumption of services the eastbound frequency was upgraded to twice weekly from 31 August, and the westbound from 2 September. The Constellations were fitted out in a one-class forty-three-seat configuration, and the services were initially flown via Shannon and Gander in a scheduled time of 19hrs 45mins. On 11 September BOAC began routing one of its services via Prestwick instead of Shannon, the first Constellation to call at Prestwick being G-AHEM 'Balmoral' which arrived from New York on 12 September. The first non-stop flight from New York to Prestwick was also operated by G-AHEM on 6 December 1946 in 11hrs 2mins. During 27–28 February 1947 BOAC completed its first million miles of Constellation operations, during the course of a New York–Shannon–London service by G-AHEM, commanded by Captain K. Buxton.

On 15 April 1947 BOAC operated its first commercial passenger service to Canada, when it inaugurated a weekly Constellation schedule from London to Montreal. The first three services operated via Shannon and Gander, but from 6 May Prestwick was substituted for Shannon.

Constellations replaced Boeing 314 flying-boats on the route between Baltimore and Bermuda on 17 January 1948, with G-AHEN 'Baltimore' operating the inaugural service that day and also inaugurating Bermuda–New York Constellation services on the following day. On 5 April 1948 BOAC notched up its thousandth Constellation-operated North Atlantic crossing, and

Passengers board BOAC Stratocruiser G-ALSD Cassiopeia at Prestwick, in around 1956. (BOAC photograph 7010 via Peter Berry, copyright British Airways)

Stratocruiser G-AKGH Caledonia in flight. (BOAC photograph, copyright British Airways)

once again the aircraft in question was G-AHEN. The Baltimore–Bermuda Constellation service was suspended on 17 January 1949, but on 15 March the New York–Bermuda service was upgraded to daily in each direction. The service was to be withdrawn on 31 March 1950, but was later reinstated as a Tourist-Class flight. On 21 April 1949 L-049 Constellation G-AKCE made a notable crossing of the Atlantic, from Sydney in Nova Scotia to Prestwick in 6hrs 48mins.

The February–March 1952 edition of *Bradshaw's International Air Guide* shows the 'Bermudian' Tourist-Class service between Bermuda and New York as still being Constellation-operated. Flight BA653 departed Bermuda on Mondays, Wednesdays and Sundays at 1000hrs and arrived at New York (Idlewild) Airport at 1230hrs. The return leg flight BA654 departed Idlewild at 1530hrs on Fridays, Saturdays and Sundays, and arrived Bermuda at 1945hrs. The free baggage allowance was 30kg. In the March 1953 edition of the BOAC timetable the service frequency was reduced to Saturdays and Sundays in each direction. The round-trip fare was US$95. There was also an unnamed weekly Tourist-Class Constellation service between New York and Kingston. Flight BA649 departed New York on Mondays at 1030hrs and called at Nassau and Montego Bay before arriving Kingston at 1940hrs. After an overnight stop the return leg BA650 left Kingston at 0700hrs on Tuesdays and arrived New York at 1545hrs after transiting the same points. The New York–Kingston round trip fare was US$199.

On 1 May 1952 BOAC introduced Tourist-Class services to the USA and Canada, using Constellation equipment. These services operated from London to New York and Boston via Shannon or Prestwick, and from London to Montreal via Prestwick. The Tourist-Class services to the USA were advertised as 'Mayflower' services, and the Canadian services as 'Beaver' services.

The Tourist-Class fares represented savings of over 40 per cent on the First-Class fares. The Constellations were fitted with reclining seats, complimentary light refreshments were provided, and full meals could be purchased. The free baggage allowance was 20kgs. Typical Tourist-Class fares in 1952 were London–New York for £148 19s return during the winter, Prestwick–Montreal for £158 5s return during the peak summer months, and Shannon–Boston for £127 11s return in the winter. Tourist-Class passengers from North America who were travelling onwards with BOAC to the Middle East, Africa, Asia etc, where Tourist-Class services had not yet been introduced, could avail themselves of a through fare to their final destination and still travel in First Class from London onwards, enjoying all the First-Class amenities on the onward legs, such as free meals and free accommodation at compulsory night stops. In the March 1953 BOAC timetable the Tourist-Class 'Mayflower' services to the USA operated twice weekly. Flight BA523 departed London on Wednesdays at 1630hrs and called at Prestwick and Gander, arriving New York at 0900hrs on the following morning. On Fridays flight BA521 left London at the same time but also called at Boston en route, arriving New York at 1015hrs. The 'Beaver' Tourist-Class service to

L-049 Constellation G-AHEL in an early colour scheme, at London Airport in company with a BOAC Lancastrian, an RAF York, and a DC-4. (Michael H. Starritt)

L-049 Constellation G-AHEN Baltimore operated the thousandth North Atlantic crossing by the type in BOAC service on 5 April 1948. (BOAC photograph, copyright British Airways)

L-049 Constellation G-AKCE 'Bedford'. (The A.J. Jackson Collection)

Montreal departed London on Tuesdays and Thursdays at 1630hrs and arrived Montreal (Dorval) at 0825hrs on the next morning, having called at Prestwick and Gander en route. Constellation equipment was still used for these services.

To cover a temporary aircraft shortage in 1955 and 1956 three Seaboard and Western Airlines Lockheed L-1049D Super Constellations were leased by BOAC from the start of the 1955 summer season until April 1956. These were operated in an eighty-six-seat Tourist-Class configuration on three times weekly 'Coronet' services from London to New York via Prestwick and Boston, and daily between New York and Bermuda. Seaboard and Western supplied the flight crews, but BOAC cabin crews looked after the passengers. The New York–Bermuda route was then taken over by British West Indian Airways, using Viscounts.

Powered by four 3,500hp Pratt and Whitney Wasp Major 28-cylinder piston engines, the Boeing Stratocruiser was a transport derivative of the wartime B-29 bomber, with the military XC-97 version flying before VE-Day. BOAC took delivery of its first Stratocruiser G-ALSA 'Cathay' on 15 October 1949, and during November 1949 the airline's first two examples, G-ALSA and G-ALSB, were used for crew training and development flying from Filton, where they were initially based as part of the No.3 Line. BOAC pilots found the Stratocruiser cockpit very roomy. It was three times the size of the Constellation cockpit, each pilot had his own blind flying panel, and the engine instrumentation was kept to the minimum as there was a complete set on the Engineer Officer's panel. About thirty-five Captains and First Officers initially converted onto Stratocruisers from Constellations, with a proportionate number of Navigating, Radio and Engineer Officers. The actual flying training time was reduced to almost 25 per cent of the normal period by a preliminary course on the Dehmel flight simulator at the Pan-American school at La Guardia Airport, New York. BOAC ordered an example of the similar Curtiss-Wright simulator at a cost of more than £100,000, and although this was not ready in time for the initial Stratocruiser conversion programme it was to be used for routine 90hr and 180hr pilot checks, eliminating the need to remove aircraft from service for this purpose.

On 6 December 1949 Stratocruisers were introduced on London–New York services, routing via Prestwick on a 19hrs 45mins schedule. The inaugural service was operated by G-ALSA 'Cathay', but it was not until the beginning of 1950 that the flagship of the fleet G-AKGH 'Caledonia' was named in a ceremony at Prestwick. Despite resurfacing of the runways in 1949 Stratocruiser operations through Prestwick were to prove problematic throughout the type's service, as the direction of the main runway was not suited to the prevailing winds, and the subsidiary runway was not long enough for Stratocruiser operations. Consequently, BOAC Stratocruiser services had to overfly Prestwick on many occasions. On 23 April 1950 Stratocruisers were introduced on the London–Montreal route, and early that year the New York services began to use Idlewild Airport as their terminal instead of La Guardia. At that time the BOAC

Stratocruiser G-AKGL suffered a nose-wheel collapse at Prestwick during its transatlantic career. (The A.J. Jackson Collection)

London–New York return fare was $630 (peak season) and $466 (off-peak). Mr R.W. Findlay worked on Stratocruiser overhauls for BOAC at London Airport, and recalls a period when the type was plagued with engine troubles. It began one evening when the shift foreman went out to do a routine engine run-up, and returned shortly afterwards to report that two of the engines had seized up. During the subsequent three weeks BOAC had a total of twenty-eight Stratocruiser engines suffer the same fate, and had aircraft standing idle awaiting replacement engines. The problem disappeared after that, but a satisfactory explanation was never really found. From 8 November 1950 a twice-weekly Stratocruiser service between New York and Nassau was introduced. On 24 April 1951 a mishap befell G-AKGL, when its nose-wheel leg gave way on landing at Prestwick. Fortunately, no one was injured and the Stratocruiser was repaired on site and returned to service. On 1 March 1951 the De Luxe 'Monarch' service from London to New York was inaugurated, initially on a three-times-weekly frequency, but upgraded to daily from 1 May. The first westbound service was commanded by Captain J.T. Percy, and the first eastbound schedule by Captain O.P. Jones, flying G-ALSB 'Champion'. Captain Jones was almost a legendary figure on the transatlantic services of this period, commanding most of the inaugural services, as befitting his great experience. The Stratocruiser had the widest passenger cabin of any piston-engined airliner, and on payment of a premium surcharge to the fare the passengers could enjoy the standards of comfort and service normally only found on the ocean liners of the period. A short spiral staircase led to a downstairs cocktail lounge, and after complimentary cocktails the passengers could enjoy a dinner of caviar, turtle soup, cold Inverness salmon, strawberries with fresh double cream, cheese and fresh fruit, complimented by free champagne and liqueurs. The gentlemen passengers were presented with exclusive 'Monarch' ties, and for a further small supplement to the fare the passengers could reserve sleeper berths which folded down from the cabin walls and came complete with mattresses, blankets, pillows and linen sheets. The flights to New York entailed a stop at Gander, and sometimes at Shannon as well. They departed London at around 2000hrs and took roughly twelve hours to reach Gander, arriving there at about 0400hrs local time. After a one-hour refuelling stop the Stratocruiser took off with a fresh crew for New York, arriving there at about 0800hrs local time. The Stratocruiser pilots that regularly flew on the North Atlantic routes were nicknamed by their colleagues the 'Atlantic Barons'. This was because of a myth created by them that the North Atlantic was the most demanding of all routes, and required pilots of exceptional skill and experience to cope with the additional risks of flying over vast expanses of ocean. When the Comet 1 was introduced, these pilots tried to resist the awarding of pay increases to jet pilots.

During 1952 BOAC's transatlantic load factors were 65 per cent in First Class and 67 per cent in Tourist Class.

The February–March 1952 edition of *Bradshaw's International Air Guide* showed daily London–New York services. The De Luxe 'Monarch' flight BA509 left London at 2000hrs on Tuesdays, Fridays and Saturdays, and arrived at 0800hrs on the following day. The return leg, flight BA510, left New York at 1700hrs on Wednesdays, Fridays and Sundays and arrived London at 0930hrs the following morning. Both services were scheduled as non-stop, and the free baggage allowance was 30kg. On the other days of the week, BOAC's normal services left London at the same time, but did not arrive New York until 0930hrs or 1000hrs, as they involved stops at Prestwick or Shannon, and sometimes Boston as well. The return legs departed New York at 1700hrs, and also stopped either at Prestwick or at Boston and Shannon. Sometimes it was also necessary to make an additional stop at Gander. In the March 1953 BOAC timetable the 'Monarch' De Luxe service had been upgraded to a daily frequency. There was also an additional First-Class Stratocruiser service on Thursdays from London. Flight BA513 departed at 1900hrs and called at Prestwick and Boston en route to New York (Idlewild). Passengers joining at New York could check in for their flight at the Waldorf-Astoria Hotel two hours before departure. Stratocruisers also operated the 'Canadian Monarch' De Luxe service from London to Montreal (Dorval). This non-stop service operated as flight BA607 on Fridays only, returning on Saturdays as flight BA608. There was also a Monday First-Class Stratocruiser flight BA601 to Montreal via Prestwick, returning on Tuesdays. Montreal-originating passengers could check in at the Laurentian Hotel ninety minutes before flight departure. On Stratocruiser First-Class services to both New York and

Montreal, sleeper berths were available at a supplement of US$35 or CA$35 each way.

By March 1953 the De Luxe 'Bahamian' Stratocruiser service between New York and Nassau was operating on a five-times-weekly basis. There was also a once-weekly First-Class Stratocruiser service which continued onwards to Montego Bay. At Nassau and Montego Bay, British West Indian Airways provided onward flights to Kingston, using Vickers Vikings operating under BOAC flight numbers. These were also used on flights between Kingston and Montego Bay and on services from Nassau to Havana, as well as on daily services between Miami and Nassau. Bahamas Airways provided seaplane services from Nassau to many destinations throughout the Bahamas, using Grumman Goose and Consolidated Catalina equipment.

From 23 January 1954 a weekly non-stop New York–Montego Bay Stratocruiser service called 'The Jamaican' was introduced. On 7 May 1954 BOAC commenced its first services from Manchester to New York, as a stop on the Stratocruiser flights which now routed London–Manchester-Prestwick-New York. The first service from Manchester was operated by G-ALSC, and initially the services were First Class only, until Tourist Class was introduced on the route on 24 May 1955.

On the night of 29–30 June 1954 Captain James Howard was in command of BOAC flight 510-196 from New York to London via Goose Bay, operated by Stratocruiser G-ALSC. The flight left New York at 2103hrs GMT. About thirty minutes later, nearing the boundary of New York Air Traffic Control, Captain Howard was instructed by Boston ATC to hold somewhere near the east coast of Rhode Island. No reason was given. After some ten to twelve minutes he was cleared to proceed, provided he accepted a detour via Cape Cod, rejoining his original track well north of Boston. About three hours later, crossing the St Lawrence estuary near Seven Islands, Quebec, and flying at 19,000ft above broken cloud at about 14,000ft, he saw 'strange flying objects, moving at about the same speed as us (approximately 230kt) on a parallel course, maybe three to four miles north-west of us'. Initially the objects appeared to be below the cloud base at about 8,000ft, but soon after crossing the coast into Labrador the cloud layer was left behind, and the objects became clearly visible, seemingly having climbed much nearer to the altitude of the Stratocruiser. At the time, the sun was reported to be low to the north-west, with clear skies and unlimited visibility. The Captain and flight-deck crew had time to study and sketch the objects as they accompanied G-ALSC for some twenty minutes. Some passengers also reported seeing the objects out of the port side windows. According to Captain Howard there was one large object and six smaller globular ones. The small ones were strung out in line, sometimes three ahead of and three behind the large one, sometimes two ahead and four behind, but always at the same level. The large object appeared to be continually changing shape, rather like a swarm of bees.

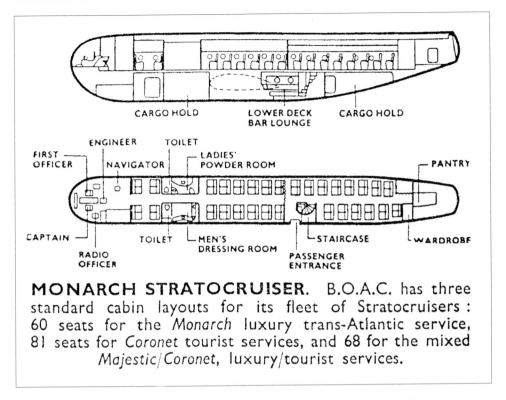

CARGO HOLD — LOWER DECK BAR LOUNGE — CARGO HOLD

ENGINEER — TOILET
FIRST OFFICER — NAVIGATOR — LADIES' POWDER ROOM — PANTRY

CAPTAIN — TOILET — MEN'S DRESSING ROOM — STAIRCASE — WARDROBE
RADIO OFFICER — PASSENGER ENTRANCE

MONARCH STRATOCRUISER. B.O.A.C. has three standard cabin layouts for its fleet of Stratocruisers : 60 seats for the *Monarch* luxury trans-Atlantic service, 81 seats for *Coronet* tourist services, and 68 for the mixed *Majestic/Coronet*, luxury/tourist services.

Seating layout of Stratocruiser in 'Monarch' De Luxe transatlantic configuration. (via Author)

After watching the objects for ten minutes or so the Captain judged he was within VHF range of Goose Bay, so he asked the co-pilot to request information on the objects from air traffic control there. Goose Bay asked them to describe what they were seeing, and said that they had a radar-equipped F-94 2-seater interceptor on patrol. A little later they were asked to change frequency and talk direct to the F-94 pilot. On doing so they were told that the interceptor had their Stratocruiser on radar, but there was no mention of any objects being plotted. The Captain gave the F-94 a bearing to the objects, and as he did so he noticed that the small objects had disappeared (the navigator said that they had appeared to converge on, and enter, the large object). As the F-94 approached the Stratocruiser's position the large object appeared to dwindle in size, while still flying parallel with the Stratocruiser, and after a few more seconds it disappeared. Captain Howard then commenced his descent into Goose Bay for refuelling, and landed there at 0145hrs GMT on 30 June. At Goose Bay the crew were questioned at length by USAF intelligence officers, who told them that there had been several other sightings in the Labrador area.

In the twelve months ending 5 December 1954 BOAC's Stratocruisers flew more than 22,000 hours and made a total of 1,264 Atlantic crossings. However, on 25 December 1954 disaster struck. G–ALSA 'Cathay' was approaching

Prestwick en route from London to New York, with twenty-five passengers and eleven crew. The aircraft was too high during the final stages of a Ground Controlled Approach, and was put into a steep descent, but was then flared out too late. The Stratocruiser struck the ground short of runway 31, became briefly airborne again, and then crashed onto the runway at 0325hrs, finishing up inverted. The aircraft's commander, Captain L. Stewart, survived the crash along with six other crew members and a solitary passenger. The Stratocruiser was also carrying around £1 million pounds worth of industrial diamonds, of which about 90 per cent were recovered.

By early 1955 BOAC's Stratocruiser fleet had increased to sixteen machines, with the acquisition of six second-hand examples from United Airlines. Along with two more machines from the original BOAC batch, these were converted to an 81-seater Tourist-Class layout for use on the North Atlantic routes. The work was carried out by Lockheed Aircraft Service International Inc at Idlewild Airport, New York, with a BOAC acceptance inspection team on hand. Among the modifications necessary to the ex-United aircraft were a revision of the flight deck layout from three-crew to six-crew operation, and the installation of crew bunks. The first completed conversion, G-ANUB, was delivered to BOAC on 6 April 1955.

In 1955 BOAC's transatlantic load factors were 64.1 per cent in First Class and 63.4 per cent in Tourist Class.

During the summer of 1955 BOAC operated nine First-Class and seven Tourist-Class services each week between London and New York, and three First-Class and three Tourist-Class services each week between London and Montreal. The Stratocruisers carried fifty passengers on First-Class services, and eighty-one on Tourist-Class flights. During 1955 Stratocruiser utilisation rose by 4 per cent. 35,670 operational hours were flown, giving a daily average utilisation of 6.68 hours per aircraft, the highest annual average to be achieved by BOAC's Stratocruisers.

On 4 October 1955 BOAC's Stratocruiser-operated transatlantic night operations into Manchester began using the longer runway at RAF Burtonwood on a temporary basis while the runway at Ringway was lengthened. During that month three services in each direction called in at Burtonwood each week, decreasing to once weekly from the commencement of the winter timetable in November. As there were no civilian passenger terminal facilities at Burtonwood the passengers were transported by car from Manchester to the Patten Arms Hotel at Warrington, near Burtonwood, where the necessary documentation and formalities were carried out in a private lounge. There were only about eight BOAC staff based at Burtonwood. They were issued with a radio receiver so that they could ferry the passengers to Burtonwood just before the Stratocruiser landed, and the best turnaround time recorded there was just 9mins 30secs from chocks on to chocks off. There was once a story circulating, which may or may not have been true, that a Stratocruiser once landed in error at the nearby former

Fleet Air Arm airfield at Stretton, mistaking it for Burtonwood. Realising his error, the pilot promptly took off again and flew the short distance to Burtonwood.

During this period BOAC was making strenuous efforts to attract US-originating passengers, and these were offered a range of inclusive tours from New York to Europe and the Holy Land. A 1956 BOAC Tours brochure offered a twenty-nine-day tour taking in London and Shakespeare country, the Swiss Alps, Rome, Beirut, Jerusalem, Cairo and Paris for only US$1,834 flying First Class off-peak, or US$1,350 flying Tourist Class. During the peak season a supplement of US$50 applied. For those with less time (or cash) to spare, a fifteen-day tour taking in London, Paris, Rome and Madrid cost US$1,217 off-peak flying First Class, or US$840 flying Tourist Class. To help American tourists afford these tours, BOAC offered a 'Fly Now-Pay Later' budget plan. Under this scheme, travellers paid a 10 per cent deposit and could take up to twenty months to pay the balance in monthly instalments. The airline also offered a Family Plan for travel during the period 1 November–31 March, whereby the head of the family paid the full rate, and the spouse and any sons or daughters between the ages of twelve and twenty-five received discounts of US$200 or US$300, depending on the class of travel.

On 1 May 1956 Stratocruisers were used to inaugurate BOAC's new London –Detroit service, but by the time the November 1957 BOAC timetable came into effect Stratocruiser North Atlantic operations were restricted to a daily 'Monarch' De Luxe flight in all 'sleeper-seat' configuration between London and New York. The westbound flight BA509 departed London at 2000hrs and flew non-stop to New York, arriving at 0845hrs the following morning. The return leg flight BA510 left New York at 1700hrs and arrived London at 1000hrs the next day.

BOAC planned to introduce the turbo-prop Bristol Britannia onto the North Atlantic routes in the mid-1950s, but lengthy delays in putting this aircraft into service meant that stop-gap measures needed to be taken in order to protect the airline's competitive position. Consequently, in March, BOAC were given permission to order ten Douglas DC-7C aircraft for delivery between October 1956 and April 1957. The total price was £5 million, and the airline was allowed to pay for the fleet in US dollars and import the aircraft free of import duty, on the condition that the DC-7Cs would be resold for US dollars once the Britannias were in service. The DC-7C was a development of the Douglas DC-7B, designed to meet a Pan American Airways requirement for an airliner capable of flying the North Atlantic non-stop in both directions. Called the 'Seven Seas' by many airlines, the DC-7C first flew on 20 December 1955. It was powered by four 3,400hp Wright R-3350 turbo compound engines, and, along with the Lockheed L-1649 Starliner, represented the ultimate development of the piston-engined airliner.

BOAC's first DC-7C, G-AOIA, was handed over in a ceremony at Santa Monica, California, on 15 October 1956. During a proving flight on 11 November a BOAC DC-7C flew non-stop from London to New York in the record time of 10hrs 40mins. The inaugural service, on 6 January 1957, was on the 'Monarch' De Luxe service from London to New York, and was operated by G-AOIA with Captain Gordon Store in command. On 10–11 March the DC-7Cs were placed onto London–San Francisco services, with a night-stop in New York en route. At San Francisco the BOAC flights connected with Qantas services to Sydney. The first service through to San Francisco was operated by G-AOID, with Captain W.M. Reid commanding as far as New York, and Captain B.C. Frost taking the aircraft onwards to San Francisco. On 1 April 1957 DC-7Cs were introduced onto the Manchester-New York route to compete with SABENA flights using the same type, and by June 1957 up to twenty services each week between London and New York were being operated by DC-7Cs.

The BOAC timetable for November 1957 showed DC-7Cs scheduled to operate from London to New York daily except Mondays and Fridays. On Tuesdays and Fridays flight BA557 departed at 2015hrs and called at Manchester and Prestwick, arriving New York at 0720hrs the following morning. On Wednesdays and Saturdays flight BA551 departed London at 2130hrs and flew via Prestwick to Boston and New York, arriving Boston at 0620hrs the following morning, and New York at 0830hrs. There was an additional flight on Tuesdays, operating to the same schedule as the Thursday flight. This was flight BA581, which flew direct from London to New York, night-stopped there, and continued onwards to San Francisco, arriving there at 1630hrs. DC-7Cs also operated flight BA563 on Thursdays and Saturdays from London to Chicago via Prestwick, Montreal and Detroit. On the other days of the week the flight terminated at Montreal. On some of these days the service called at Manchester only, some days at Manchester and Prestwick, and some days at Manchester, Prestwick and Gander. On the inbound legs from Montreal on Tuesdays and Thursdays a 'flag stop' was made at Gander if requested in advance. The DC-7C services were operated in a mixture of De Luxe, First-Class and Tourist-Class configurations. De Luxe services were furnished with forty-two 'Sleeper Seats', and First-Class services featured sixty of these seats. In addition to these seats, thirteen overhead bunks were on offer to De Luxe and First-Class passengers at a supplement of £26.80 each way. The DC-7Cs could also be configured in various mixed-class layouts, such as twenty-four De Luxe seats (plus six overhead bunks) plus twenty-six First-Class seats (with five overhead bunks), or thirty First-Class seats (with six overhead bunks) plus thirty-one Tourist-Class seats, or twenty-four De Luxe seats (with six bunks) plus thirty-one Tourist-Class seats. On 18 December 1957 DC-7Cs were introduced onto a weekly non-stop service between Montreal and Nassau.

In April 1958 the DC-7C services between London and New York via Manchester and Prestwick were selected for a trials involving the playing of recorded music in the passenger cabin. This only took place during passenger embarkation, take-off and landing, and the DC-7C services were selected because of the number of stops involved. A thirty-minute tape of specially recorded light orchestral music was played on a standard battery-driven tape-recorder and relayed through the aircraft's public address system. After the flights the passengers were given a questionnaire to complete. In answer to the questions, 100 per cent said they enjoyed the music, and 95 per cent said they would like to have it available throughout the flight as well as on take-off and landing.

Although Britannia turbo-props entered transatlantic service in mid-December 1957, the February 1961 BOAC timetable still featured DC-7C services to Canada twice weekly, but in Economy-Class only layout. The Thursday flight BA623 departed London at 2330hrs and called at Prestwick en route to Montreal and Toronto. The Saturday flight BA627 departed London at the same time but called at Manchester instead of Prestwick. On the return legs both flights called at Montreal and Prestwick. At one point BOAC was considering having its DC-7Cs re-engined with Rolls Royce Tyne turbo-props. In this form it would have been known as the DC-7D, but the idea was not proceeded with.

The turbo-prop Britannia series 312 made its delayed debut on the North Atlantic on 19 December 1957, the type having entered BOAC service in its smaller series 102 form on the Africa and Far East routes earlier that year. The inaugural transatlantic service was operated from London to New York by G-AOVC, under the command of Captain A. Meagher. It took off from London at 1035hrs and flew overhead Prestwick, the southern tip of Greenland, Gander and Boston, landing at Idlewild Airport, New York at 2310hrs, having encountered severe headwinds en route which necessitated a 350-mile detour from its intended course. The distance of 3,750 miles was covered at an average ground-speed of 305mph. The return leg left Idlewild at 2312hrs on 21 December, and routed via Gander, the south of Ireland and Bristol, landing at London at 0800hrs on 2 December. This was the first transatlantic scheduled service by a turbo-prop airliner, and the first North Atlantic scheduled service to be operated by a British-built aircraft. Initially the Britannias were operated just one round-trip each week, with DC-7Cs making the remainder of the crossings for BOAC. The westbound service was flown wholly in daylight on Fridays, and the eastbound leg overnight on Sundays. On transatlantic flights the Britannias were fitted out in a fifty-two-seat, all First-Class 'Majestic' configuration, with twenty-six 'Slumberette' fully-reclining sleeper seats and twenty-six conventional First-Class reclining seats. At the rear of the cabin were two spacious dressing rooms with specially toned lighting. There was also a ladies powder room with a dressing table and cushioned seating. Yardley toiletries were provided for the gentlemen, and Elizabeth Arden cosmetics for the ladies.

Because of the low number of passengers carried, most of the crossings could be made non-stop, although strong headwinds could still force a refuelling stop at Goose Bay or Gander. The eastbound flight duration was scheduled at twelve hours, although it was frequently operated in less. In 1958 one service took just

DC-7C G-AOIE was later to serve with Caledonian Airways on North Atlantic charters. (Air-Britain)

9hrs 30mins. The westbound service was scheduled to take 11hrs, due to the usually favourable westerly winds. The normal operating crew was two pilots, a flight engineer and a navigator. Two crew bunks were provided, one above the other, just aft of the flight deck. Navigation over the ocean depended primarily on the LORAN system, whereby 'master' and 'slave' systems on land transmitted pulses that the navigator translated from his cathode ray tube. He then referred to a chart overprinted with the LORAN chain lines. There was also a periscopic sextant for astro-navigation, and assistance could also be obtained from radar-equipped weather ships, whose position was marked on the aircraft's charts. The air conditioning and heating systems kept the passenger cabin at a comfortable temperature in winter, but not so the flight deck, and crews would often wear their uniform overcoats over their jackets when the outside air temperature was exceptionally low.

By 31 December 1957 six series 312s had been delivered to BOAC. However, the delayed entry into service of the Britannia meant it entered service just ten months before the first jet services (by Comet 4 and Boeing 707) across the Atlantic, where BOAC had once anticipated a three-year lead. On 17 April 1958 G-AOVL inaugurated Britannia 312 services from London to Chicago, with en route stops at Prestwick, either Shannon or Gander, Montreal and Detroit. On 6 May, Britannia 312s replaced DC-7Cs on the London–New York–San Francisco services. At the end of the first year of transatlantic Britannia operations, figures were published which showed that 645 transatlantic crossings had been made, of which 522 (81 per cent) had been non-stop. Only 50 per cent of the services had arrived within one hour of the scheduled time. A loss of £500,000 had been incurred on Britannia 312 operations, but this was mainly attributed to the still-developing San Francisco and mid-west services, as the New York services had made a profit.

In November 1957 agreement was reached between the competing airlines on the North Atlantic for the introduction on 1 April 1958 of Economy Class on transatlantic flights. Economy-Class fares were about 20 per cent lower than Tourist Class. Seat pitch, i.e. the distance from the front of one seat to the front of the seat in the row ahead, was reduced to 34ins. The minimum number of seats that could be fitted across the cabin width was also governed by regulations. In order to attract this type of passenger to its services BOAC introduced a new design of Economy-Class seat, giving 14ins foot-room clearance under the seat in front. When aircraft were operated in an all-Tourist layout, a minimum number of seats had to be fitted to comply with the regulations. In the DC-7C this was seventy-seven seats, in the Britannia 312 it was eighty-seven seats, and in the Stratocruiser it was eighty-one. Where Tourist-Class seating was provided in a mixed-class configuration, the degree of comfort provided was not to exceed that provided in an all-Tourist-Class layout. Rules also governed the meal service in the respective classes. In Tourist Class, hot meals could be provided, but in Economy only sandwiches with coffee or tea, milk or mineral water could be served. Alcoholic and non-alcoholic drinks could be sold in Tourist Class, but neither was to be made available in Economy. The new lower fares proved so popular that by March 1959 around half of BOAC's North Atlantic capacity was allotted to Economy Class. However, not all of this was new traffic, as there was a substantial switch from Tourist Class. Nevertheless, during 1958–59 BOAC experienced a 30 per cent increase in total transatlantic business, compared to the 5 per cent of other airlines.

On 24 December 1958 one of the Britannia 312 fleet was lost during a test flight in connection with the renewal of its Certificate of Airworthiness. G-AOVD took off from London, and after carrying out tests it began an approach to Hurn in thick fog, but struck the ground near Winkton. Out of the twelve people on board, nine lost their lives.

DC-7C G-AOIC in flight. (BOAC photograph, copyright British Airways)

Planning to fly
this year?

Wherever your destination, fly by B.O.A.C. . . . world leader in air travel. B.O.A.C.'s convenient world-wide route network enables you to enjoy the finest value in air travel to 51 countries on all 6 continents. B.O.A.C. takes pride in offering you the world's finest passenger service . . . that particular blend of comfort, good food and personal attention which makes experienced air travellers unhesitatingly choose B.O.A.C.

For full details of de Luxe, First Class and Tourist services world-wide, consult your local B.O.A.C. Appointed Travel Agent or any B.O.A.C. office.

World leader in air travel

B·O·A·C

takes good care of you

Remember—it costs no more to fly by B.O.A.C.

BRITISH OVERSEAS AIRWAYS CORPORATION WITH S.A.A., C.A.A., QANTAS AND TEAL

January 1958 BOAC magazine advertisement featuring a DC-7C model. (via Author)

On 16 April 1959 Britannia 312s replaced DC-7Cs on services between Manchester and Montreal, and during the financial year ending in March 1960 Britannias contributed 58 per cent of BOAC's total capacity. On 1 May 1960, after much argument between member airlines, the International Air Transport Association introduced a 7 per cent propellor-driven fare differential on the North Atlantic routes, theoretically helping operators of types such as the Britannia to remain competitive by charging lower fares than all-jet operators. However, in practice this resulted in a fare reduction on Britannia flights of only £7 or so each way, a small incentive to switch away from the much faster Boeing 707 and DC-8 jets being introduced by BOAC's competitors.

The year 1961 was the last complete year of Britannia operations by the full fleet. The February 1961 BOAC timetable still listed Britannia scheduled services across the Atlantic. On Mondays, Thursdays, Fridays and Saturdays they operated non-stop from London to New York, departing at 0001hrs and arriving at 0650hrs. On Mondays, Wednesdays and Thursdays there was also a stopping service to New York via Manchester and Prestwick (the Wednesday service also stopped at Boston). Britannias were also still in use on overnight services to Canada. On Sundays, Thursdays and Fridays they flew from London to Montreal and Toronto, with en route stops at Manchester, Prestwick and Shannon. On Wednesdays the service flew via Manchester, Prestwick and Gander and terminated at Montreal. First and Economy Classes were offered on flights to the USA and Canada. By November 1961 Britannia transatlantic operations had been reduced to a daily London–New York overnight service which called at Prestwick and Shannon and on Tuesdays and Fridays continued onwards to Detroit and Chicago, and a daily except Tuesday all-Economy service to Canada.

During 28 and 29 June 1961 and the period from 9 July 1961–21 July 1961 a BOAC engineers' strike at Heathrow saw Prestwick become the temporary main operating base for the BOAC Britannia 102, Britannia 312 and DC-7C fleets. A much modified schedule was operated, with these aircraft types, along with Britannias of Ghana Airways and El Al, being turned round at Prestwick, and their passengers being ferried to and from London in an assorted of chartered aircraft which included Dan-Air Airspeed Ambassadors, Derby Aviation Dakotas, and Capitol Airways Super Constellations.

The final official transatlantic scheduled service by BOAC Britannia was operated by G-AOVH on 1 March 1964. However, they continued to be utilised for a while afterwards on charter flights from Manchester and Prestwick, and it was not until 26 April 1965 that G-AOVL operated BOAC's final Britannia 312 service, from Bermuda to New York. BOAC's total investment in the Britannia (including the earlier series 102s used on Far East and African routes) was £42 million including spares, and the airline was believed to have lost some £12 million as a result of the type's late introduction and truncated service life once jets had appeared on the scene. However, despite several mishaps, the Britannia

L-1049D Super Constellation N6503C was leased from Seaboard and Western Airlines in 1955–56 for Tourist-Class transatlantic services. (The A.J. Jackson Collection)

fleets had achieved an unblemished safety record, flying over 5,000 million passenger-miles without injuring a single passenger.

BOAC had originally planned to initiate jet services across the North Atlantic with the De Havilland Comet 3, which was a development of the Comet 1 and Comet 2, neither of which had true transatlantic range. It was expected that the Comet 3 would be ready for service in 1956, and that it would be able to fly from London to New York in under seven hours. To prepare for Comet 3 operations the 'Comet Flight', which had been suspended in 1954 was re-formed in 1957. Two Comet 2Es were fitted with Rolls Royce Avon 524 engines in the outer engine positions and flown extensively on trials over BOAC routes, including the North Atlantic. They were also flown intensively between London and Beirut, flying nine round trips each week between 16 September and 9 November 1957, and eleven round trips weekly after that.

By 4 January 1958 these aircraft had amassed 1421 hours on the proving flights, and by 5 March 1958 this figure had increased to 2350 flying hours. Sharing the flying were two Captains, eight Engineer Officers and one Radio Officer. Each aircraft was crewed by three pilots, with one of them acting as the navigator, plus an engineer. The Comet 3 differed from the Comet 2 in being 3ft longer, having more powerful Avon engines, more fuel capacity and significantly greater range. The design held great promise, and BOAC ordered five, for operation on the North Atlantic in fifty-eight-seat, all-First-Class configuration. However, De Havilland eventually decided not to put the Comet 3 into production. Instead, a radical redesign was rapidly completed, and the result was the Comet 4. This was to be powered by four 105,000lb thrust Rolls Royce Avon 525 single-shaft turbojets, and a fleet of nineteen was ordered by BOAC.

In 1958 BOAC announced tentative plans to introduce the Comet 4 on to routes to Australia from February 1959. It was about that time, however, that rumours began to circulate that Pan-American Airways was planning to put the new Boeing 707-120 into service across the North Atlantic. The projected date was uncertain, but BOAC immediately began feasibility studies to see how best to counter this threat with its own jet services. The first Comet 4 intended for BOAC, G-APDA, made its first flight from Hatfield on 27 April 1958, piloted by John Cunningham, and began a series of route-proving flights in September. On 30 September 1958 BOAC took delivery at London Airport of G-APDB and G-APDC, the first two of the nineteen Comet 4s ordered. At that time BOAC was still negotiating with the Port of New York Authority for permission to operate jets on scheduled services into Idlewild Airport. However, on 2 October G-APDB carried BOAC Chairman Basil Smallpeice and a party of journalists on 'Pre-Inaugural Proving Flight' CPF 001 from London to New York via Gander, thus ensuring that the aircraft was in position for the start of scheduled services as soon as permission was granted. It had been decided to operate simultaneous inaugural flights in both directions. Shortly after 1700hrs New York time on 3 October Basil Smallpeice stood on a chair at BOAC's Speedbird Club in New York and announced that permission had finally been received, and that Comet 4 services would start the next morning. Thus, on 4 October 1958, BOAC operated the first commercial jet services across the North Atlantic, beating Pan American's Boeing 707s into service by just under three weeks. The westbound flight, captained by R.E. Milllichap, flew from London to New York in a total time of 10hrs 22min, including a technical stop at Gander. The actual flying time was 8hrs 53mins at an average groundspeed of 404mph. The eastbound service, under the command of Captain T.B. Stoney, the BOAC Comet Flight Manager, made a spectacular take-off from Idlewild, reaching a height of 1,850ft while still inside the airport perimeter and then throttling back to satisfy the noise abatement requirements. Thanks to a 92mph tailwind and priority handling from the UK air traffic controllers the eastbound crossing was achieved in the record time of 6hrs 11mins. At 1335hrs GMT and at position 47 degrees West the two

DC-7CF G-AOIJ, one of two converted in November 1960. (Air-Britain)

BOAC Britannia 312 G-AOVP on final approach. (Air-Britain)

Comets passed each other about 300 miles apart, and the chairman of BOAC, Sir Gerard D'Erlanger, and its Managing Director exchanged congratulatory radio messages.

The Comet services were intended to be once weekly in each direction, but after only a few flights had been completed BOAC's North Atlantic services were disrupted by a strike. When the Comet flights resumed on 13 November 1958 they were on a daily basis. The Comets operated in various configurations, either forty-seat 'Monarch' De Luxe service, or fifty-six-seat First-Class service, or in mixed-class layouts, including 16 De Luxe seats plus forty-three Tourist-Class seats. In November 1958 BOAC announced that Comet 4s would be operating to Canada from December, and on 19 December a weekly Comet service from London to Montreal was inaugurated by G-APDC under the command of Captain Hengle. By this time bookings for the New York–London flights had increased by 50 per cent. There was a particularly high demand for De Luxe seats, so the mixed-class cabin layout was modified to accommodate twenty of these instead of sixteen. During1958, 3913 passengers were carried, with load factors bettering 80 per cent. The Comets were officially approved for a service life of 2,900hrs between overhauls. The first non-stop Comet service from London to

Britannia 312 G-AOVJ was delivered to BOAC in April 1958. (Air-Britain)

Britannia 312 G-AOVG later made many more Atlantic crossings in the hands of British Eagle. (Air-Britain)

Comet 2 G-AMXK was leased to BOAC for route-proving flights for the forthcoming Comet 4. (W. McGill)

New York was accomplished in 7hrs 45mins on 24 March 1959, by G-APDH under the command of Captain R.C. Alabaster.

On 21 June 1959 Comet G-APDB was making a daylight approach to Idlewild Airport, New York, when it struck a blast fence 65ft short of the runway threshold. The landing was completed safely and there were no injuries, but damage was caused to the main undercarriage and the flaps. The suspected cause was a sudden downdraught of unexpected severity.

At the end of the Comet's first year in service, BOAC's Managing Director, Basil Smallpeice, said that 'the Comet was largely responsible for the fact that between 1 April 1959 and 19 September 1959 traffic was up by 40 per cent on the North Atlantic compared to the summer period of 1958'. On 1 March 1960 BOAC began operating Comets to Toronto, and on that day a revenue-pooling agreement between BOAC and Trans-Canada Airlines came into effect. From that date BOAC operated two Comet and two Britannia 312 services each week between London and Toronto. Another new Comet route, from London to Boston, was inaugurated on 13 June 1960, but a few months later, after almost exactly two years of transatlantic operations, the Comets were withdrawn from the routes as they simply did not have the range for regular non-stop flights in the westbound direction. Boeing 707s were by then in service, and the last scheduled transatlantic Comet service was operated from New York to London on 16 October 1960. During the period 4 October 1958–16 October 1960 a total of 2,304 North Atlantic crossings had been made by the Comet fleet, an average of just over three per day. In addition to the New York services, 94,000 passengers had been carried on routes from London to Montreal, Toronto and Boston, at a load factor of 74 per cent.

The Comet 4s continued in service with BOAC on Far Eastern routes, and in August and September 1964 they made a temporary comeback on the North

Atlantic, as back-up aircraft to meet an unexpectedly high demand for seats from Scotland. BOAC-Cunard, who were operating the routes at the time, laid on three extra services each week from Prestwick, with the Comets making a stop at Gander on the westbound leg and returning non-stop.

On 24 October 1956 the British Government announced approval of the purchase of fifteen Boeing 707 jets by BOAC for use on transatlantic routes. It was recognised that such a purchase was going to be necessary if BOAC was to remain competitive on the North Atlantic, but funding was only granted on condition that the 707s would be powered by Rolls Royce Conway turbojets, and on the understanding that no further dollars would be made available for aircraft purchases for other routes. A contract was signed with the Boeing Aircraft Company on 8 November 1956 for the purchase of the aircraft, which would be designated as Boeing 707-436s.

The Boeing 707 had already been granted a US Certificate of Airworthiness, but in order to serve with BOAC it would require a British one as well. From their experience of the initial 707 models, the Boeing test pilots thought that the handling could be improved by some design modifications, and after discussions with BOAC Chief Engineer Charles Abell it was agreed to modify the BOAC machines in four respects: 1). The tail fin was to be extended by some 3ft. 2). Full rudder boost was to be provided. 3). The yaw damper was to be improved. 4). A shallow ventral fin was to be fitted below the tail. Boeing agreed to carry out these modifications free of charge, but only at the end of the first year of service with BOAC. However, when the Air Registration Board test pilot D.P. Davies came to flight test the 707 he expressed concern about the effect on handling that the heavier and more powerful Rolls Royce engines would have, and he refused to grant a British Certificate of Airworthiness until the modifications had actually been incorporated. The delay involved in complying with this requirement meant deferring the delivery of the aircraft from the intended December 1959

Comet 4 G-APDA at the 1958 Farnborough Air Show, before entering regular service with BOAC. (Maurice Marsh)

Passengers boarding Comet 4 G-APDE for the 'Monarch' service to New York on 14 November 1958. (British Aerospace PLC)

until several months later, with BOAC losing the use of the 707s for at least part of the 1960 summer season. However, when the modified aircraft was flight tested, it was indeed found to be so much better to handle that Pan-American Airways retrospectively introduced the modifications onto their 707s already in service, and their senior pilots expressed their great appreciation of the contribution to flight safety made by BOAC and the British ARB.

BOAC's first Boeing 707, G-APFD, arrived at London on its delivery flight from Seattle on 29 April 1960. Under the command of Captain T.B. Stoney, BOAC's Manager, 707 Flight, the aircraft made the 4,900-mile journey non stop in 9hrs 44mins. Crew training was carried out at RAF St Mawgan, Newquay, and on from 3 May 1960 a series of proving flights was operated between New York and London via Prestwick. The first such flight was operated by G-APFD under the call-sign Jet Speedbird 001. Proving flights were also operated from London to Toronto via Prestwick, the first such flight, by G-APFD as Jet Speedbird 010 on 17 May 1960 inaugurating the new extension to runway 13/31 at Prestwick. On 27 May 1960 Captain Stoney commanded G-APFD on the inaugural BOAC Boeing 707 scheduled service, from London to New York. The next day, Captain Nisbett was in charge of the same aircraft on the inaugural eastbound service. On 1 June 1960 the inaugural 707 scheduled service from

Comet 4 G-APDB operated the worlds first jet schedule from New York to London on 4 October 1958. (The A.J. Jackson Collection)

A night-time shot of Britannia 312 G-AOVD at Idlewild Airport, New York in February 1958. (Bristol via Michael Harrison)

Within weeks of BOAC's inaugural transatlantic Comet services, Pan-American were operating Boeing 707-121s such as N707PA in competition. (Air-Britain)

G-AOVC operated BOACs inaugural Britannia transatlantic service on 19 December 1957. (Bristol via Roger Jackson)

London to Toronto via Prestwick and Montreal was operated by G-APFB as flight BA615A. The initial cabin layout for these flights comprised thirty-four First-Class and ninety-seven Economy-Class seats. The 707 was the first BOAC aircraft type to dispense with curtains on the passenger cabin windows, being fitted with sliding opaque and smoke-tinted blinds instead. By August 1960 BOAC were operating nine transatlantic services each day, using a mixed fleet of Boeing 707s, Comet 4s and Britannia 312s. Once all fifteen 707s had been delivered, BOACs worldwide network would be operated 51 per cent by jets, 42 per cent by turbo-props, and only 7 per cent by piston-engined types. The overall break-even load factor would be reduced to 55 per cent, and BOAC would have attained second place in the league table of the world's international airlines, second only to Pan-American.

Since 1959 BOAC had been able to make greater use of the traffic rights in the UK/US bilateral agreements, and could combine two or more US destinations on the same service, instead of only operating to New York. This facility was used to greatly increase the earning power of the new 707s at little extra cost, and on 20 September 1960 they were introduced onto a twice-weekly London–Prestwick–Montreal–Detroit–Chicago service. From 24 September a weekly New York–Nassau-Montego Bay-Kingston 707 service was inaugurated by G-APFB, and on 20 October 1960 the London–New York service was extended twice weekly to San Francisco. Also during October, the 707s replaced Britannia turbo-props on the Manchester-New York route.

In the February 1961 timetable BOAC 707s were scheduled to operate the daily 'Monarch' flight BA509 from London to New York in a mixed First and Economy-Class configuration. This service flew non-stop, departing London at 1500hrs

Britannia 312 G-AOVP later flew transatlantic charters for Lloyd International Airways. (The A.J. Jackson Collection)

Boeing 707-436 G-APFD in the original colour scheme worn by the type. (Air-Britain)

Boeing 707-436 G-APFF was later transferred to BEA Airtours. (Air-Britain)

G-APFI, a Boeing 707-436 in the later colour scheme worn by the type. (Air-Britain)

and arriving at 1740hrs. The return leg BA510 departed New York at 2100hrs and arrived London at 0830hrs the next day. The 707s were also utilised on flight BA539, which flew from London to New York via Manchester, Prestwick and Boston four times each week, and on a twice-weekly non stop London–Los Angeles service. From 2 June 1961 flight BA563 operated London–Prestwick–Detroit–Chicago three times each week. In the summer of 1961 the fare from Prestwick to New York by jet service was £309 5s return in First Class or £164.0.0 return in Economy Class. The winter 1961 BOAC timetable included three-times-weekly Boeing 707 service BA537 to New York and continuing onwards to Washington/Baltimore (Friendship) Airport.

In April 1964 Boeing 707s replaced Britannias on Manchester-Montreal services, and on 20 September 1964, at the height of 'Beatlemania' the Beatles pop group returned from New York to London aboard a BOAC 707 at the conclusion of their US tour.

From 1965 onwards BOAC began to receive examples of the improved Boeing 707-336 model, in both the convertible cargo/passenger 336C and the all-passenger 336B variants. These were the first BOAC aircraft to be fitted with in-flight entertainment systems for use on long daylight sectors, the first usage being on the London–Miami route. As wide-bodied Boeing 747s came into service some of the earlier Boeing 707-436s were withdrawn, renovated and sold to BEA Airtours for use on inclusive-tour flights. Others were converted to all-Economy configuration for service with BOAC subsidiary British Overseas Air Charter on North Atlantic charter flights.

If events had turned out differently, BOAC could well have been operating a British-built jet on the North Atlantic well before the Boeing 707 or Comet 4 entered service. Since around 1952, Vickers had been working on the Vickers 1000, a military transport project for the RAF, based on the Vickers Valiant design philosophy. The Vickers 1000 resembled the Valiant, but had four Rolls Royce Conway turbojets buried in the roots of its low wing. A proposed civil version, the Vickers VC7, was also conceived in very close co-operation with BOAC. This had a large diameter fuselage for those days, and would have been the first airliner with what was to become the standard configuration for the first generation of big jet airliners; six-abreast seating with a centre aisle. The VC-7 would have been capable of crossing the Atlantic non-stop, which the early versions of the 707 could not. However, in September 1955, when the first prototype Vickers 1000 was within six months of completion, the RAF pulled out of the project, ostensibly because it needed transport aircraft in a quicker timescale than Vickers could manage, and because Britannias were more readily available. At this point BOAC decided not to proceed with an order for the civil VC7. A statement made in the House of Commons at the time said that BOAC was quite content to manage with turbo-props on the North Atlantic throughout the 1960s.

Following the cancellation of the VC-7 project, Vickers put its own money into studies for a jet version of its Vanguard turbo-prop (the 'Vanjet'). One of these studies was designated the VC-10, and on 22 May 1957 BOAC announced that this design best met its needs for the 'Empire' routes to Africa and the Far East. To meet the stringent operating requirements of the airfields along these routes at the time, the VC-10 was fitted with four rear-mounted Rolls Royce Conway engines and a very aerodynamically clean wing, with many

MENU
and Wine List

Rolls-Royce 707
Inaugural Flight

LONDON — LOS ANGELES
March, 1961

*

BRITISH   OVERSEAS   AIRWAYS   CORPORATION

Cover of menu for the inaugural BOAC Boeing
707 service London–Los Angeles, March 1961.

A landing shot of Boeing 707-436 G-APFD, which operated BOAC's first service by the type on 27 May 1960. (The A.J. Jackson Collection)

lift-generating devices. Early in the development programme, studies were insti-gated into the development of a higher capacity version for North Atlantic routes, providing extra seating capacity at the expense of the standard VC-10s exceptional 'hot and high' performance. This version was to emerge as the Type 1150 Super VC-10, propelled by four of the more powerful 22,500 lb thrust Conway 550 engines. These were fitted with thrust reversers on all four units, and until the advent of the Boeing 747 they were the most powerful in airline service. An additional fuel tank in the fin would permit an extra 1,350 imp gallons to be carried, and a fuselage stretch of 13ft over the standard VC-10 would boost the maximum passenger capacity to 174.

Soon after his appointment at the end of 1959 the Minister of Aviation, Duncan Sandys, had set about the task of rationalising the British aircraft industry. There were to be two major firms only. De Havilland was to be merged into Hawker Siddeley Aviation, and Vickers-Armstrong, the Bristol Aeroplane Company and the airframe interests of English Electric were to be merged to form the British Aircraft Corporation. The latter consortium had few outstanding orders, so BOAC were asked by the Minister if they would order ten examples of the Super VC-10, for delivery from 1965. The airline found it economically impossible to justify such a purchase on top of their existing order for thirty-five standard VC-10s for the 'Empire' routes for delivery from 1964, and suggested converting the last ten machines of this order into Super VC-10s, but under pressure from the government they gave in and signed on 23 June 1960 a £25 million contract for ten Super VC-10s. It soon became apparent that the improved economics of the Super VC-10 would reduce the need for so many standard VC-10s, and in early 1961 the combined order was changed to 15 VC-10s and 30 Super VC-10s. The recession in 1961 reduced the need for standard models still further, and the order was cut back to 12 VC-10s and 30 Super VC-10s. Subsequently, the Super VC-10 order was also cut back to seventeen examples with delivery spread over a number of years. At one stage there were people in high places in BOAC who put forward a case for disposing of the Boeing 707s and standardising on the Super VC-10, but the airline eventually compromised on a mixed 707/VC-10 fleet.

During the early 1960s various developments of the VC-10/Super VC-10 were considered. In 1962 BOAC asked Vickers to meet a requirement for non-stop London–Los Angeles flights, a distance of 4,730 nautical miles, with a third version of the VC-10. If a suitable design has been produced, BOAC would have considered ordering six or more, and reducing its Super VC-10 order by a like amount. In 1963 it was proposed that eight of the thirty Super VC-10s on order should be developed as mixed passenger/cargo aircraft, commencing with the thirteenth example towards the end of 1965. This variant would have had a moveable bulkhead, and would have carried either all passengers, or all cargo, or various combinations of passengers and palletised cargo. A large freight door, similar to that on the RAF's VC-10s, was to have been installed on the port side, forward of the wing. BOAC also evaluated a Vickers proposal for a 265-seat double-decker development of the VC-10, powered by three Rolls Royce RB178 engines and retaining the VC-10 'T-tail' configuration. This was

Boeing 707-436 G-ARRA, seen here in the original livery, was delivered in February 1962. (The A.J. Jackson Collection)

Boeing 707-436 G-ARRA at Manchester Airport, with an Adria Airways DC-6B in the background. (Barry Abraham)

designated by Vickers the Super 265, and BOAC gave it the project name 'Superb'. In the end, BOAC decided that its requirement for a high-capacity long-range airliner would be better met by the Boeing 747, and without a firm order from them the project was dropped.

The first flight of the Super VC-10 was made from Weybridge by G-ASGA on 7 May 1964. By February 1965 the Super VC-10 flight test programme was sufficiently advanced for Vickers to loan G-ASGC and G-ASGD to BOAC for initial crew training at Shannon. Because of the similarities between the standard and Super VC-10, BOAC was able to train pilots to fly either version, and by the time the complete fleet was in service, which was not until 1969, no less than 900 flight deck crew and 500 cabin attendants were deployed on the two versions. The inaugural service of the Super VC-10 took place on 1 April 1965 when G-ASGD, operating a BOAC-Cunard service, flew from London to John F. Kennedy Airport, New York. The type initially operated on the 'Monarch' service to New York and Bermuda, with one service each week going onwards to San Francisco instead of Bermuda. The Super VC-10s were configured to carry sixteen First-Class and 123 Economy-Class passengers, and had an interior designed by British designer Robin Day. This featured cherry red carpeting, charcoal grey seat covers, and a striking black and white print of seventeenth-century London on each bulkhead wall. BOAC's attitude towards the VC-10 was strangely ambivalent. The airline publicly criticised the economics of the type, and demanded a government subsidy for operating it. However, it realised the undoubted passenger appeal of the VC-10's smooth ride and quiet passenger cabin, and its advertising described it as 'triumphantly swift, silent and serene'. A publicity brochure for BOAC's First-Class service on the type promised 'sumptuous seven-course meals served on crested china from a buffet trolley'. On 28 February 1966 Super VC-10s replaced Boeing 707s on London–Montreal–Chicago services, and in the spring they were introduced onto the Manchester–Prestwick–New York run.

The January–March 1968 BOAC timetable showed the 'Monarch' service from London to New York as being operated by a mixture of Super VC-10 and Boeing 707 equipment. On most days there were three flights to New York by Super VC-10, and on some days these were supplemented by an additional 707 service. There was also the 'Scottish Monarch' service, operated daily from Manchester and Prestwick to New York by Super VC-10 as flight BA537. The First-Class return fare was £291 8s from Manchester or £281 18s from Prestwick. 707s maintained the three-times-weekly BA671 service from London to Miami, and also operated to Toronto via Manchester and Prestwick, while the Super VC-10s flew direct from London to Montreal.

A short-lived Super VC-10 service from Belfast to New York was introduced in May 1968, and on 29 April 1969 G-ASGD operated to New York on BOAC's first scheduled non-stop transatlantic service from Manchester.

In order to cope with the contingency of a VC-10 being stranded 'down the line' with engine failure, a pod was developed which could be installed under the starboard wing of another VC-10 and used to ship out a spare Rolls Royce Conway out and bring the damaged one back for repair. As the Conway was also used to power BOAC's early Boeing 707s, the VC-10 pod installation could also be used to rescue its rival!

During 1972 a new 1800hrs Super VC-10 service from London to New York was introduced. The Super VC-10 fleet was absorbed into British Airways in the 1974 merger, and the type was finally withdrawn from British Airways service in 1981.

In 1961, faced with a decline in liner travel across the North Atlantic, and with substantial numbers of passengers being lost to the airlines, the Cunard Steamship Company applied to the Air Transport Licensing Board for a licence to operate scheduled air services between Britain and the USA, in competition with BOAC. In order to be able to operate such flights, Cunard acquired the UK independent airline Eagle Airways, and set up a subsidiary called Cunard-Eagle Airways. Two Boeing 707s were ordered to operate the proposed transatlantic routes, and at an initial hearing in May 1961 Cunard-Eagle was granted licences for transatlantic services. However, BOAC then appealed, and on 21 November 1961 the licences were revoked. BOAC then approached Cunard with the idea of setting up a joint company to operate transatlantic services. The joint company would operate the two 707s on order and would take advantage of Cunard's prestigious reputation and network of sales offices in the USA. An agreement establishing BOAC-Cunard Ltd was signed on 6 June 1962, with BOAC taking a 70 per cent shareholding and Cunard holding the balance.

BOAC-Cunard's inaugural service departed Heathrow for Manchester, Prestwick, New York and Bermuda on 24 June 1962. By the autumn of 1963 the joint venture had started to yield profits, and these built up during 1964 and 1965. The flights were operated initially by the Boeing 707s, but on 1 April 1965 the Super VC-10 entered BOAC-Cunard service, G-ASGD operating the type's inaugural service to New York. During the summer of 1965 the Super VC-10s also inaugurated a five-times-weekly service to Boston and Detroit and, from 24 October 1965, a three-times-weekly service to Lima. The BOAC-Cunard aircraft wore the standard BOAC colours, but with BOAC-Cunard titling on the forward lower fuselage instead. In May and June 1966 the UK shipping industry was hit by a national seamen's strike which cost the Cunard Group at least £3.75 million. In the middle of that year BOAC warned Cunard that orders would have to be placed for more and bigger aircraft for the North Atlantic, and asked Cunard for 30 per cent of the additional capital investment required. This was beyond Cunard's means at that time, as they were committed to purchasing the new 'Q4' liner (later to be christened the 'Queen Elizabeth 2') and so, in September 1966, BOAC bought out Cunard's 30 per cent shareholding for £11.5 million and the BOAC-Cunard services reverted to BOAC.

By 1966 it was apparent that if BOAC was to remain competitive on the North Atlantic it would have to join Pan American and TWA in ordering the Boeing 747 wide-bodied jet, and so on 2 September 1966 the Corporation signed a contract for six Boeing 747-136s, powered by four Pratt & Whitney JT9D-3A turbofans, at a total price of around $160 million. This order was later increased to eleven machines, and then in 1968 to twelve. The total cost of the revised order was £165,473,000, including associated equipment.

The Boeing 747 first flew on 9 September 1969, and first entered service with Pan American on 22 January 1970, on the New York–London route. On 22 April 1970 BOAC took formal delivery of its first example, G-AWNA, at the Boeing factory in Seattle, and this was delivered to Heathrow on 23 May 1970. In September 1970 the airline decided that it wanted to take up its option on four more 747s, for delivery in March and April 1973, to bring the total fleet to sixteen. The purchase of these was approved, but a pilots' dispute delayed the inauguration of Boeing 747 services for nearly a year, and the option was not formally taken up with Boeing at that time. During the dispute the first three BOAC 747s, G-AWNA, G-AWNB and G-AWNC, stood idle at Heathrow. Eventually the inaugural BOAC Boeing 747 service took place on 14 April 1971, from London to New York, with G-AWNF taking off from Heathrow at 1203hrs

A BOAC-Cunard Boeing 707-436 at Heathrow, with a Middle East Airlines Comet 4C in the background. (Maurice Marsh)

under the command of BOAC's 747 Flight Manager, Captain D. Redrup. Initially the frequency was twice weekly, but this was increased to daily from May 1971. The introduction of the 747 brought about a quantum leap in airliner size, offering as it did roughly two and a half times the passenger capacity of the 707, and airports worldwide had to adapt to handle the wide-bodied jets. Terminal buildings were extended, and telescopic weatherproof boarding 'fingers' were built on to permit embarkation without the use of steps. BOAC's 747s were configured to carry twenty-seven First-Class and 335 Economy-Class passengers on the North Atlantic routes during the summer. In winter this was altered to thirty-six First Class and 315 Economy Class. The First-Class seats were of 42in pitch, and First-Class passengers also had access to the Monarch Lounge on the upper deck. This was reached by a spiral staircase from the First-Class cabin, and featured four 'club-style' swivel chairs plus settee seating for sixteen

Two BOAC-Cunard Boeing 707-436s at Heathrow. (Maurice Marsh)

people. The Economy-Class cabin was divided up into three sections, each with its own decor, in order to provide a more intimate feel. The basic seat pitch was 34in, although some rows were at 33in pitch. Six galleys and two microwave ovens were fitted. In First Class a special catering unit enabled special dishes to be cooked to order, and in Economy Class 288 meals could be heated simultaneously. The 747s featured an in-flight entertainment system, first introduced by BOAC on its Boeing 707-336 flights to Miami. Films and audio entertainment were available to all passengers on payment of an IATA-specified charge of $2.50. In addition to the usual range of perfumes and souvenirs sold on board, specially designed 747 cuff-links, tie tacks, ties and scarves were available from the cabin crew. Because of their higher cruising speed, the 747s were able to trim fifteen minutes off the London–New York flight time by 707 or Super VC-10. In May 1972, 747 services from London to Miami and Chicago were introduced. The 747s operated daily to Chicago, replacing Super VC-10s, and

BOAC-Cunard Super VC-10 G-ASGC, now preserved at Duxford. (Air-Britain)

Super VC-10 G-ASGI was delivered to BOAC in February 1966. (Air-Britain)

BOAC's first Boeing 747, srs 136 G-AWNA. (Maurice Marsh)

flew to Miami three times each week, with 707s operating on the remaining four days. By July 1971 the 747s were also in service on routes to Bermuda, Montreal and Toronto. During 1972 wide-bodied transatlantic services were extended to include Boston and Detroit. A Manchester–Prestwick–New York 747 service was also introduced for the summer 1972 timetable. The explosion in transatlantic travel brought about partly by the introduction of the 747s enabled fares to be slashed, and in 1972 BOAC was offering excursion fares from London to Detroit of £102.10 return, To Philadelphia the excursion fare was only £89.80 return. In order to fill the vastly increased number of seats on offer, BOAC was arranging inclusive-tours to Europe for American tourists, and one such package on sale during the winter of 1972–73 offered US residents an eight-day theatre tour to London, inclusive of air fare and theatre tickets, at prices starting at US$270.

The 747s were also operating daily between Bermuda and New York as flight BA491, and in August 1973 a record number of passengers was carried on this route. The total of 8,640 passengers averaged 278 passengers on each northbound flight, a load factor of 77.85 per cent.

The last Boeing 747 to be delivered in the BOAC colour scheme was the thirteenth example G-AWNM in May 1973. The next two machines were delivered in British Airways livery in anticipation of the forthcoming merger, and by the time of the completion of the amalgamation with BEA in 1974 fifteen 747s were in service.

By 1960 the volume of cargo being carried on transatlantic flights had reached the level where dedicated freighter aircraft could be profitably utilised, and during November of that year two examples of the DC-7C fleet, G-AOII and G-AOIJ, were converted to DC-7F freighters. The conversion entailed fitting the aircraft with two double freight doors, the forward one being 91in wide by 67in wide and the rear one 124in wide by 78in high. As freighters the DC-7Fs could carry 14 tons of cargo, and the inaugural cargo service was operated by G-AOIJ under the command of Captain Froom from New York to London via Prestwick on 3 December 1960. The first westbound service departed London on 7 December, but had to return with engine trouble. The first successful westbound flight left London on 10 December and operated to New York via Manchester, Gander and Montreal. The flight was severely delayed, mainly by bad weather, and was 35hrs 17mins behind schedule by the time it even arrived at Montreal . The November 1961 BOAC timetable included twice-weekly DC-7F all-cargo flights between London and New York. On Wednesdays flight BA573 departed London at 2200hrs and flew via Manchester, Prestwick and Montreal, arriving New York at 0930hrs the following day. If required, a 'flag stop' at Boston could also be incorporated. The Thursday service BA577 departed at 2200hrs and operated via Prestwick to New York, arriving at 0830hrs on Friday. Again, subject to demand, 'flag stops' at Montreal and Boston could also be inserted. The DC-7F services were supplemented by flights using leased L-1049D Super Constellation freighters of Seaboard and Western Airways. Six overnight services each week were operated from London to New York. One flight was non-stop (though with a 'flag stop' at Prestwick if requested), and the others flew via Shannon, with one of these stopping at Prestwick as well. Including the flights operated for them by Seaboard and Western, and passenger flights offering cargo capacity, BOAC offered thirty-three scheduled cargo-carrying services each week between the UK and North America.

From the end of September 1963 the DC-7Fs were replaced by a Canadair CL-44 turbo-prop freighter leased from Seaboard World Airlines, the new name for Seaboard and Western. Although still US-registered as N228SW this aircraft wore full BOAC Cargo Service markings. On 30 September 1963 it carried out its first revenue operation for BOAC, transporting to New York fifteen out of the nineteen British racing cars entered for the Watkins Glen Grand Prix race at Buffalo. This was claimed to be the largest single airlift of cars recorded at that time. The CL-44 commenced regular transatlantic services on the following day. By 1965 the CL-44 was operating six overnight transatlantic services each week, equipped with ten pallets giving it a 25-30 tons capacity. The Seaboard World lease was terminated on 31 October 1965, but after that date further CL-44s were chartered from the Flying Tiger Line until the entry into service of four convertible cargo/passenger Boeing 707-336Cs, purchased by BOAC in 1965. These were fitted with a side cargo door, and carried BOAC Cargo titles. Transatlantic all-cargo services with the 707s commenced on the London–Manchester–Prestwick–New York route on 13 January 1966. By the spring of 1968 they were operating five-times-weekly to New York via Manchester and Prestwick, with additional stops at Montreal twice a week and Philadelphia once weekly.

The Seaboard World CL-44 was not the last propeller-driven airliner to wear the BOAC colour scheme. From 1972 two elderly Viscount 701 turbo-props were hired from Cambrian Airways to provide feeder flights from Prestwick to Belfast, and from Prestwick to Edinburgh and Aberdeen. These flights were timed to connect with BOAC transatlantic services passing through Prestwick. The two Viscounts, G-AMOG and G-AMON, were named 'Scottish Prince' and 'Scottish Princess' respectively, and wore the full BOAC dark blue and gold livery of the time. They entered service on the feeder flights in April 1972 and June 1973, by which time they were over twenty years old. They were still in service on the feeder routes at the time of the BOAC merger with BEA, and were then repainted in British Airways colours.

11

South American and Caribbean Services

Until July 1949, British air services to the Caribbean area and South America were the domain of the British South American Airways Corporation, but the merger of that airline into BOAC meant that the latter company then took on the responsibility, although for a while afterwards the two airlines still retained their own identities and flight numbers. The November 1949 joint BSAA/BOAC timetable showed BSAA flight BA103 leaving London each Friday at 1005hrs and flying via Lisbon, Dakar and Natal to Rio, arriving there at 1525hrs on the following day. After a night stop the journey resumed at 0800hrs on Sunday to Sao Paulo, Montevideo and Buenos Aires, arriving there at 1835hrs. On Wednesdays and Sundays BOAC flight BO501 flew from London to New York via Shannon and Gander. From New York the service continued onwards to Bermuda as BOAC flight BO654. At Bermuda, BSAA flight BA511 offered connections to Nassau and Kingston. Connecting flights from Nassau to Miami and Havana were provided by BSAA, and Bahamas Airways services connected Nassau with West Palm Beach and points throughout the Bahamas. Once BSAA was fully absorbed, BOAC took over that airline's BA flight prefix for its own services.

On 16 March 1950 Canadair Argonauts began operating BOAC services to South America, slashing eighteen hours off the timing for the London–Buenos Aires–Santiago route. On 3 October 1950 Lockheed L-049 Constellations were introduced onto the route to Chile via the west coast of South America, replacing Avro Yorks. The first Constellation service was operated by G-AHEJ 'Bristol II'. The February–March 1952 edition of *Bradshaw's International Air Guide* shows BOAC services to South America as being Argonaut-operated, while Constellations maintained the routes to the Caribbean area. Argonauts flew to South America on three days each week, but the Thursday flight BA351 was the longest routing. Departure from London was at 0900hrs, and stops were made at Madrid, Lisbon, Dakar, Recife, Rio de Janeiro and Montevideo before arrival at Buenos Aires at 2130hrs on Friday. A night stop was made there, and on Saturday

Britannia 312 G-AOVR was delivered to BOAC in October 1958. (Air-Britain)

morning the flight continued onwards to Santiago, finally arriving there at 1430hrs on the Saturday. The aircraft rested at Santiago until 1630hrs on Sunday, before beginning the long journey back to London as flight BA352.Constellation flight BA455 departed London at 1630hrs on Mondays, and flew to Kingston via Lisbon, Santa Maria (Azores), Bermuda and Nassau, arriving Kingston at 1615hrs on Tuesday. At Nassau a connecting flight was available to Havana.

During 1953 Constellations were also used to operate Tourist-Class services to Trinidad via Bermuda and Barbados. BOAC had originally planned to have Comet 2 jets in service on the South Atlantic for the summer of 1953, but a series of crashes with the Comet 1 and its subsequent grounding brought an end to these plans. The resultant shortage of aircraft also led to the suspension in April 1954 of all BOAC services to South America until replacement propeller aircraft had been found to return the fleet to full strength.

In the March 1953 BOAC timetable a weekly First-Class Stratocruiser service was offered between London and Montego Bay. Flight BA457 departed London at 1900hrs on Mondays and flew via Gander (optional stop), Bermuda and Nassau, arriving at Montego Bay at 1700hrs on the following day. The return leg flight BA458 set off from Montego Bay at 0815hrs on Wednesdays, and arrived London at 1045hrs on Thursdays. Sleeper berths were available at a supplement of US$35 each way. On 7 October 1953 a London–Trinidad Constellation schedule was inaugurated, flying via Prestwick, Gander, Bermuda and Barbados.

At the end of June 1955 BOAC introduced its first mixed–class services on the London–Trinidad route, using Boeing Stratocruisers. At the rear of the cabin were twenty-two First-Class seats. The occupants of these seats had the use of a lower-deck lounge, and there were also five sleeping-berths available on payment of a supplement. In the forward part of the cabin were fifty Tourist-Class seats. The service operated once-weekly via Gander, Bermuda and Barbados. That summer the Stratocruisers were also utilised on a weekly First-Class service from London to Montego Bay, carrying sixty passengers. By November 1957 the

Stratocruisers were still in use on Caribbean services. On Saturdays and Tuesdays flights BA681 and BA683 respectively operated from London to Kingston via Bermuda, Nassau and Montego Bay, departing at 1900hrs and arriving at Kingston at 1915hrs on the following day, with BWIA Dakotas flying the final leg from Montego Bay to Kingston. On Thursdays flight BA691 from London to Port of Spain was operated by Stratocruiser throughout, departing London at 1900hrs and arriving at 1840hrs on the Friday after an en route stop at Bermuda. All of these services offered both De Luxe and First-Class seats, with sleeper berths also available at extra cost, and two of the services also offered Tourist-Class accommodation.

On 28 October 1958 BOAC resumed services to South America, after a four-year gap. This time it was with turbo-prop Bristol Britannia 312s, with G-AOVL inaugurating twice-weekly services from London to Port of Spain and from London to Caracas, both via Bermuda and both with an optional stop at Barbados. These were the first ever turbo-prop scheduled services between Europe and South America. The journey time was scheduled at 21hrs 25mins, if the stop at Barbados was omitted. The Britannia 312s were also used to inaugurate a new service from London to Bogota via Port of Spain, Bermuda and Caracas on 7 January 1960. The service took thirty-two hours, and the Britannias were furnished with thirty-four First-Class and thirty-nine Tourist-Class seats. Shortly afterwards, on 25–26 January 1960, BOAC re-opened services to Brazil, Uruguay, Argentina and Chile, using Comet 4s. These were the first services across the South Atlantic to be operated by a British jet. The inaugural service was operated by G-APDO and flew London–Madrid–Dakar–Sao Paulo–Montevideo–Buenos Aires–Santiago. Captain Andrew was in command as far as Dakar, where Captain Perry took over. The return leg called at Lisbon instead of Madrid, and the service operated twice-weekly. The scheduled timing for the

Britannia 312 G-AOVL wearing British West Indian Airways titles whilst on lease. (Air-Britain)

In January 1960 Britannia 312s inaugurated a new 32-hour schedule to Caracas via the Caribbean. G-AOVK was later to serve with British Eagle. (The A.J. Jackson Collection)

On 28th October 1958 Britannia 312 G-AOVL inaugurated the first turbo-prop services between Europe and South America. (Bristol via Roger Jackson)

Comet 4 G-APDT later survived at Heathrow as an apprentice training airframe. (Air-Britain)

In January 1960 BOAC Comet 4s inaugurated the first British jet services across the South Atlantic. G-APDG illustrated. (Derek King)

twice-weekly journey from London to Santiago was around twenty-six hours, and the flying time for the round trip of 14,073 statute miles was 40hrs 2mins. On 30 January 1960 the Comet 4 route to New York was extended onwards to Nassau and Montego Bay. Comet 4s were also used on services to Rio, being able to cover the 5844-mile journey in just under fourteen hours, with just one stop en route.

On 10 October 1960 BOAC and Cunard-Eagle Airways began operating in conjunction low-fare, low-frequency 'Skycoach' services over the London–Bermuda–Nassau route. Both airlines used Britannias, taking it in turns to operate alternate flights. The fare of £130 was only available to British residents, and the revenue was split between the two airlines on a pro-rata basis. Five days later a monthly 'Skycoach' Britannia service from London to Montego Bay and Kingston was inaugurated, and on the same day BOAC and Cunard Eagle began a fortnightly London–Bermuda–Nassau–Miami service offering both First-Class and Economy-Class seats. A week after that a 'Skycoach' service from London to Port of Spain via Barbados was introduced, with one flight every four weeks.

On 2 June 1961 Boeing 707-436 G-APFI was en route Antigua–Barbados on a charter flight when it encountered severe turbulence at 23,500ft, and one fatality was sustained.

The Super VC-10 was introduced onto the South Atlantic routes from 21 July 1964, However, in the spring of 1965, continuing losses on the South American

In 1960 BOAC and Cunard-Eagle Airways commenced low-fare, low-frequency 'Skycoach' services to the Caribbean. BOAC used Britannia 312s such as G-AOVG. (Bristol via Roger Jackson)

routes resulted in the handing over of BOAC's South Atlantic routes to British United Airways, who also operated them with VC-10 equipment.

On 3 April 1965 Super VC-10s were placed onto the flights to Nassau, Montego Bay and Kingston, and they were also used on a three-times-weekly service to Lima from 24 October 1965. In the spring of 1968 the Super VC-10s were offering daily services from New York to Nassau or Freeport and Kingston as an extension of the 'Scottish Monarch' transatlantic service, and on three days a week this service continued onwards to Lima. Boeing 707s flew the majority of services from London to the Caribbean and South America, serving Mexico City via Bermuda and Kingston, Bogota via Bermuda, Barbados, Port of Spain and Caracas, and Georgetown via Bermuda, Antigua, Barbados and Port of Spain. A Super VC-10 service to St. Lucia was inaugurated on 20 July 1971, with flight BA699 calling at Barbados en route. The return leg, flight BA698, incorporated a stop at Antigua instead.

12

The Comet 1:
The Magnificent False Start

As early as 1944 De Havilland had started development work on a jet airliner design. This followed the lines suggested by the Brabazon Committee's type IV requirement, although the company were confident they could improve on the specified performance. A contract was signed on 21 January 1947, whereby the Ministry of Supply ordered two prototypes to meet Specification 22/46, and the project was given the name Comet in December 1947. Avro Lancastrian VM703 was modified as a test-bed for the De Havilland Ghost 50 engines proposed for the Comet, and two of these engines were fitted onto its outer engine positions. The Comet was also originally intended to use rocket boosters on take-off, and the Lancastrian test-bed was also fitted with two captured German Walter 109-500 rocket engines under its fuselage for test purposes. Meanwhile, a second Lancastrian, VM729, was also fitted with Ghost engines. This machine was to handle the final development and certification flying of the Ghost 50, so that when the Comet made its first flight it would be powered by reliable and mature engines. At the time that the design team was authorised to proceed with the final design back in February 1945 it was still thought that the type would be suitable for North Atlantic services, but the flight trials were to show that this was impractical.

By the time the Comet made its first flight, BOAC had revised its jet fleet requirements a number of times. In 1946–47 the Corporation had wanted eight, with a further six for its subsidiary BSAAC. When that airline was merged into BOAC the total order remained at fourteen, but when the specification for the Comet was finalised as a 36-seater the order was reduced to ten. The prototype Comet G-ALVG made its maiden flight from Hatfield in the hands of John Cunningham on 27 July 1949. On 17 November 1949 BOAC Chairman Sir Miles Thomas had his first flight in the still-unpressurised prototype. Despite having to wear an oxygen mask he found the experience exhilarating, and was convinced that the Comet would give BOAC a strong commercial advantage. At around this time Flight Refuelling Ltd was investigating the possibilities of extending the range of the Comet by the use of in-flight refuelling. During late 1950 and early 1951 a series of test flights took place involving the Comet prototype and Flight Refuelling's Avro Lincoln tanker RA657. However, the poor longitudinal control of the Comet at the low speeds necessary for the refuelling process caused concern, and instead a 'reverse refuelling' scheme was proposed, with the Comet trailing a hose and drogue and the tanker aircraft approaching from the rear to engage the drogue with its probe and then pump fuel into the Comet. Some trials of this method did take place, using Avro Tudor G-AGRI as the 'tanker', although without a probe and using ballast to simulate the fuel load. BOAC observers were aboard the Comet during these trials and commented unfavourably on the oscillation of the Comet during the trials and the adverse effect this would have on passenger comfort. The scheme was finally abandoned, however, when it was realised that the weight of the receiving equipment at the rear of the Comet would only worsen its already poor low-speed handling qualities.

On 23 March 1951 the second prototype Comet G-ALZK was delivered on loan to the BOAC Comet Unit at Hurn for route proving and crew training until 24 October 1951. The Comet Unit had been set up in September 1950 by Captain M.R.J. Alderson. BOAC was soon to set up its own crew training course based at the Comet Development Unit at London Airport, but initial crew training was carried out at Hatfield. Comet crews were recruited from many sources, including former flying-boat Captains and ten former BSAAC pilots. Initially the courses had a high 30 per cent failure rate, but this was found probably to be due to the newly-devised training techniques. When these were modified the failure rate was much reduced. Once qualified, the Comet crews succeeded in negotiating pay rises on the grounds that the jet was more demanding to fly, particularly with regard to fuel flow calculations and the estimation of fuel reserves for the 'thirsty' Ghost engines. The Comet Development Unit had many new problems to solve initially, including how to calculate the aircraft's True Air Speed. The Unit's Captain Majendie devised a method for converting Indicated Mach Number and temperature into True Air Speed, and also developed new methods of navigating the Comet using DME and the reliable MF beacon. Before fare-paying passengers were carried a series of 'freight' flights to Johannesburg were undertaken, each one complying with the strict operating procedures which had been drawn up for passenger services. On 22 January 1952 a Certificate of Airworthiness was granted to Comet G-ALYS, the first one ever issued to a turbojet airliner.

The world's first regular passenger services by a jet airliner commenced on 2 May 1952, when Comet G-ALYP inaugurated services from London to Johannesburg via Rome, Beirut, Khartoum, Entebbe and Livingstone. The aircraft was under the command of Captain A.M. Majendie as far as Beirut, Captain J.T.A. Marsden to Khartoum, and then Captain R.C. Alabaster for the

BOAC coaches deliver passengers to G-ALYP for the inaugural Comet 1 service to Johannesburg on 2 May 1952. (British Aerospace PLC)

final leg. With thirty-six passengers on board, it covered the 6,724 miles in an elapsed time of 23hrs 34mins. The same aircraft left Palmietfontein Airport, Johannesburg, on 5 May for the inaugural northbound service, and reached London in 23hrs 51mins. On 15 May 1952 BOAC began a series of eighteen Comet proving flights over the London–Singapore route, and these were followed on 3 July by the first proving flight from London to Tokyo. The remainder of the Comets on order were delivered at regular intervals during the summer of 1952, with the last one, G-ALYZ arriving in September. Meanwhile, in June, a special Comet flight was laid on so that Members of Parliament could experience the revolutionary new mode of transport. On 11 August BOAC commenced a weekly Comet service from London to Colombo via Rome, Beirut, Bahrain, Kuwait, and Bombay. The 5,925-mile journey was scheduled to be covered in 21hrs 35mins, cutting 12hrs 10mins off the previous Canadair Argonaut schedule. The inaugural service by G-ALYU arrived Colombo as planned on 12 August, but the first westbound service on 13 August had to be diverted to Prestwick on arrival because of fog, and eventually landed at London 3hrs 42mins behind schedule. On 14 October 1952 BOAC inaugurated another new Comet routing, again using G-ALYU. This flew London–Rome–Cairo–Bahrain–Karachi–Calcutta–Rangoon–Bangkok–Singapore in a scheduled time of 25hrs, compared to two and a half days by Argonaut.

The first accident to a BOAC Comet occurred on 26 October 1952. G-ALYZ, on a scheduled service from London to Johannesburg with thirty-five passengers and eight crew aboard, had made an intermediate stop at Rome and during its take-off from there the speed failed to build up normally. After becoming airborne for a few seconds the aircraft's captain decided that there was a lack of engine thrust, throttled back the engines and aborted the take-off. The Comet came to rest close to the airport boundary. Two passengers were slightly injured and the aircraft sustained considerable damage. The subsequent accident enquiry found that all the engines were delivering maximum power and that all fuel flows, temperatures and pressures were normal. The pilot was blamed for 'not appreciating the excessive nose-up attitude of the aircraft during take-off' and was transferred to Avro York freighters. However, on 3 March 1953 a new Comet 1A of Canadian Pacific Air Lines, on its delivery flight to Sydney where it was to be based, failed to become airborne during take-off from Karachi, killing the eleven people on board. Again, pilot error was implied as the cause, but, following this enquiry, the British Airline Pilots Association campaigned for the investigation into the BOAC crash to be re-opened, as it believed the BOAC operating manuals were misleading. BALPA believed that during take-offs at high weights in high temperatures and humidities the Comets stalling speed would be some 9 knots higher than quoted. It had also been found that increasing the fuselage incidence to 9 degrees resulted in the wing, which had a symmetrical aerofoil section, becoming partially stalled. After these accidents, BOAC twice

Passengers boarding Comet 1 G-ALYP at London on 2nd May 1952 for the worlds first scheduled jet passenger service. (British Aerospace PLC)

altered the recommended take-off technique, increasing the unstick speed by 6 knots, and thenceforth placed more emphasis on this in crew training.

On 3 April 1953 BOAC Comets began operating to Tokyo, on the fastest air service to the other side of the world, 10,000 miles in under thirty-six hours, with no night stops en route. The full routing was London–Rome–Beirut–Bahrain–Karachi–Delhi–Calcutta–Rangoon–Bangkok–Manila–Okinawa–Tokyo, and the actual scheduled journey time was 33hrs 15mins, including 28hrs 30mins flying time. This compared with the previous journey time of 86hrs by Canadair Argonaut. The inaugural service was operated by G-ALYX, and the first westbound flight left Tokyo on 6 April, to complete the round trip in a record time of 74hrs 45mins, with 55hrs 59mins actual flying time. The service was later upgraded to twice weekly, with one service calling at Cairo instead of Beirut. By that time BOAC was operating Comets on almost half of its total route network, and during the type's first year of scheduled operations the Comet fleet flew 9,443 revenue-hours and carried around 28,000 passengers. However, on 2 May 1953, the first anniversary of Comet passenger operations, disaster struck. G-ALYV, commanded by Captain Maurice Haddon, one of BOAC's original Comet Captains and a very experienced pilot, took off from Calcutta at 1059hrs on a flight to Delhi with thirty-seven passengers and six crew aboard. Six minutes later the aircraft crashed in flames while flying through a thunder squall, and all passengers and crew were killed. The accident enquiry found that structural failure had been sustained as a result of 'either severe gusts encountered in the thunder squall, or overcontrolling or loss of control by the pilot when flying through the thunder squall'.

Despite this accident Comet operations continued, albeit not without mishaps. On 16 July 1953 a BOAC Comet 1 was landed in error at Juhu Aerodrome, the old airport for Bombay. The runway there was only 1,250 yards long, and there was a tailwind. The Comet did not touch down until it was some 500 yards past the runway threshold, but it still came to a standstill in the remaining distance, sideways on and close to the boundary fence. Nobody was hurt in the incident, and the only damage to the aircraft consisted of burst tyres. On 24 July the lightly loaded Comet was flown out again, taking off in less than 650 yards and attaining a height of 500ft by the airfield boundary. On the following day another Comet was lost when G-ALYR was written off at Calcutta, fortunately without fatalities.

On 27 August 1953 the maiden flight of the developed Comet 2 G-AMXA took place at Hatfield in the hands of John Cunningham, and during the period 13–19 September Comet 2X G-ALYT made a 11,760-mile proving flight over the route London–Lisbon–Dakar–Recife–Rio–Natal–Dakar–Casablanca–Madrid–London, in preparation for BOAC's eventual introduction of Comet 2s on the South Atlantic routes. The total flying time was 31hrs 40mins, with Captains A.P.W. Cain and A. Majendie in command.

Comet 1 G-ALYR failed to get airborne from Calcutta in July 1953. (Derek King)

From 4 October 1953 South African Airways began using BOAC Comet 1s in their markings for their 'Springbok' services between London and Johannesburg.

Disaster struck again on 10 January 1954. Comet 1 G-ALYP, on a service from the Far East to London, departed Rome (Ciampino) at 0931hrs with twenty-nine passengers and six crew aboard for the last leg of the journey. At approximately 0951hrs the Comet was at an estimated 27,000ft, and began a radio conversation with BOAC Argonaut G-ALHJ, also airborne in the vicinity. A transmission from the Comet began 'George How Jig from George Yoke Peter, did you get my...' and was suddenly terminated in mid-sentence. A short time later, witnesses on the ground saw flaming wreckage falling into the sea. The Comet had crashed some 16km south of Elba, Italy, with the loss of all on board. The weather in the area at the time was generally good. A massive search for the wreckage, involving several Royal Navy salvage vessels searching at depths of between 70 and 100 fathoms, and utilising television cameras for the first time for this type of operation, succeeded in recovering about 70 per cent of the airframe, 80 per cent of the engines and 50 per cent of the aircraft's equipment. All BOAC Comet operations were suspended, and modifications were made to the power plants and other parts, including the installation of armour-plated shields between the turbine blades and the fuel tanks. After the accident enquiry found no definite cause for the accident, the Air Safety Board decided that 'everything humanly possible has been done to ensure that the desired standard of safety shall be maintained. This being so, the Board sees no justification for imposing special restrictions on Comet aircraft. The Board thus recommends that the Comet aircraft should return to normal operational use after all current modifications have been incorporated and the aircraft have been flight tested.' On

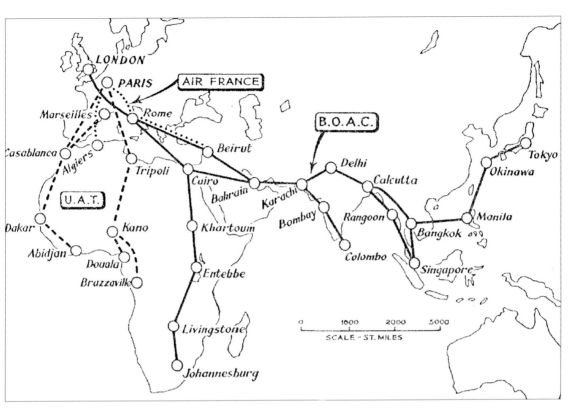

Map showing extent of Comet 1 services by all three operators in 1953. (via Derek King)

Comet 2 G-AMXA, which was destined never to enter BOAC service, and was transferred to RAF Transport Command instead. (Air-Britain)

12 March 1954 G-ALYW made a test flight with the modifications incorporated, and the Comet 1s returned to service on 23 March 1954, when G-ALYX operated a London–Johannesburg flight.

Meanwhile, BOAC had demonstrated its confidence in the Comet by signing a contract for five examples of the much-developed Comet 3 on 1 February. However, within weeks another Comet 1 crashed. This time it was G-ALYY that was lost, operating a London–Johannesburg service on behalf of South African Airways on 8 April 1954. The aircraft had taken off from Rome for Cairo at 1832hrs, and was climbing normally to its cruising altitude of 35,000ft. The last radio transmission from it was a routine report to Cairo at 1905hrs, giving its estimated time of arrival. Once again, there were no survivors among the fourteen passengers and seven crew. Once again, no definite cause for the accident was found by the initial enquiry. BOAC suspended Comet 1 operations again on 12 April 1954, and the fleet's Certificates of Airworthiness were withdrawn. This time the grounding was permanent. The Comet 1s had flown almost 25,000hrs, representing a total flown mileage of 10 million miles. All the surviving Comet 1s were used in an extensive programme of tests to determine the cause of the accidents. At first, an in-flight explosion of fuel vapours was thought to be a possible cause. However, after repeated pressure testing of the fuselage of G-ALYU in a water tank, to simulate the pressurisation cycles of a series of flights, the cause of the crashes was traced to a fatigue failure of the pressure cabin, starting at a corner of one of the small windows on the flight deck. This led to a catastrophic break-up of the aircraft in mid-air.

At the time of the final Comet 1 grounding, production of the developed Comet 2 was well under way. This was a slightly longer aircraft, powered by Rolls Royce Avon 503s, and with an additional 1,000-gallon fuel capacity. It had accommodation for forty-four passengers, and the first deliveries to BOAC were expected in July 1953. Having insufficient range for transatlantic services with a full load without a refuelling stop, the Comet 2 was scheduled to enter service on routes to South America in the summer of 1953. Once these services were established, the Comet 2s were to begin exploratory flights to North America, to prepare the way for scheduled transatlantic services by the further developed Comet 3, probably in 1956. The Comet 2s were also to be used for scheduled services along the 'Empire' routes to the Far East and Africa. After the grounding of the Comet 1s, all but four of the twelve Comet 2s on order were delivered to RAF Transport Command instead. Two examples of these were completed in 1957 as civil development aircraft, with Rolls Royce Avon 524 engines in the outer positions, and were flown extensively on BOAC routes, including the North Atlantic.

13

Middle East and African Services

In April 1947 the Ministry of Supply ordered a fleet of Handley Page Hermes airliners, powered by four 2,100hp Bristol Hercules 763 14-cylinder radial sleeve-valve engines, for use by BOAC on African routes, with deliveries commencing in June 1948. However, deliveries of the developed Hermes 4 did not in fact begin until 1950, by which time the aircraft which was to replace the Hermes, the Canadair Argonaut, was already in service. On 11 June 1950 the Minister of Civil Aviation, Lord Pakenham, christened G-ALDI, the flagship of the Hermes 4 fleet, 'Hannibal', in a ceremony at London Airport. BOAC Hermes operations commenced on 6 August 1950, when the type replaced Avro Yorks on the London–Tripoli–Kano–Lagos–Accra route, with G-ALDJ 'Hengist' operating the inaugural service. The Hermes fleet was based at London Airport as part of BOAC's No.2 Line, and the aircraft carried forty passengers and a crew of five. From 24 September 1950 the Solent flying-boat services from Southampton to Lake Naivasha were replaced by four-times-weekly London–Rome–Cairo–Khartoum–Nairobi Hermes services, with two of these flights also calling at Entebbe. The scheduled timing for the service was 27hrs, or 28hrs 15mins when the stop at Entebbe was made. The Solents were also displaced by Hermes land-planes on the route to Johannesburg from 7 November 1950. The Hermes services operated three times weekly from London, calling at Tripoli, Kano, Brazzaville and Livingstone (for Victoria Falls). Flight BA111 departed London Airport on Tuesdays, Fridays and Sundays at 1100hrs and arrived at Johannesburg at 2125hrs on the following day. The return leg flight BA112 departed Johannesburg at 0001hrs on Mondays, Wednesdays and Fridays and arrived London at 0640hrs on the following day. The inaugural London–Johannesburg service was operated by G-ALDR 'Herodotus'. During the period 26 January–10 February 1952 the Hermes services to East Africa were re-routed via Tripoli and Khartoum because of rioting in Cairo. The February–March 1952 edition of *Bradshaw's International Air Guide* lists BOAC flight BA251 as departing London at 1415hrs daily except Mondays, and arriving at Accra at 1125hrs on the

Avro York G-AGSL 'Morley' served with BOAC from 1945 to 1951. (The A.J. Jackson Collection)

following day. Dinner was served while in the vicinity of the Massif Central, and refuelling stops were made at Castel Benito (Tripoli) at 2200hrs, at Kano at 0600hrs, and at Lagos at 0955hrs. A full English breakfast was served at Kano. The return leg, flight BA252, departed Accra daily except Wednesdays at 1015hrs and arrived London at 0805hrs on the following day. The free baggage allowance was 30kg. The Hermes fleet was also deployed on daily London–Nairobi services. Flight BA159 departed London Airport at 1045hrs and flew via Rome, Cairo and Khartoum, arriving Nairobi at 1355hrs on the following day. On Wednesdays and Sundays, however, an additional stop at Entebbe was included, and the Hermes landed at Nairobi at 1610hrs.

On the night of 25–26 May 1952 BOAC Hermes G-ALDN 'Horus', commanded by Captain Robert Langley, departed Tripoli for Kano with ten passengers and eight crew aboard. Acting as navigator on the flight, although he was actually a pilot and not a fully qualified navigator, was Trevor De Nett. At the start of the flight he misinterpreted the figures on the variation-setting control of the CL2 Gyrosyn compass master unit, not realising that each digit on the control should be multiplied by ten to give the true value. He thus set an initial variation of 30 degrees West on the compass instead of the intended 3 degrees West, and later increased this to 60 degrees West instead of 6 degrees. The Captain did not cross-check this compass against the aircraft's P12 magnetic compass because he had earlier decided that it was unserviceable and had continued the flight without further reference to it. In doing so, he was going against BOAC Fleet Standing Instructions, and in fact the magnetic compass was later discovered to have been serviceable all along. De Nett also took astro fixes from the periscopic sextant, but these too were inaccurate, and the error was not discovered until 0400hrs, when the sun came up in the 'wrong place', behind the aircraft instead of on its port side. By this time the aircraft was 54 degrees off course to the west, and was some 900 nautical miles from Kano. The Hermes did not have enough fuel to make Kano, and so Captain Langley decided to head for Port Etienne, on the west coast of Africa. His SOS calls provoked no response until 0612hrs, when both Accra and Lagos acknowledged his messages, and Accra accepted control of the flight. However, neither station pointed out to him that there was a closer alternative airfield at Atar in Mauretania. At 0812hrs Captain Langley radioed that he would be unable to make Port Etienne as his fuel was

Hermes G-ALDD in the 'white-tail' BOAC livery. (The A.J. Jackson Collection)

Handley Page Hermes G-ALDS was later sold to Skyways Ltd. (Air-Britain)

almost exhausted, and he made the decision to put the Hermes down on the desert sand. After one circuit of a small nomad encampment a wheels-up forced landing was made at 0900hrs on the Adrar plateau, ninety miles southwest of Atar. During the landing the port wing was torn off in a collision with a sand dune, but all the passengers and crew escaped from the aircraft with what appeared to be relatively minor injuries, although First Officer Edward Haslam had a nasty gash on his head. Within ten minutes the two stewards had prepared a meal of baked beans, biscuits and salad, and then served tea while the group sat under a nearby tree and waited for help to arrive. A group of nomads appeared on the scene, and at 1800hrs a French Air Force Ju 52 from the garrison at Atar circled the spot. Half an hour later another one parachuted in a doctor, two medical orderlies, a radio team and supplies. Back in London, BOAC arranged for Canadair Argonaut G-ALHS, under the command of Captain Frank Taylor and with BOAC's Deputy Director of Operations, Jackie Harrington on board, to fly down to Atar with to help co-ordinate the rescue operation. The occupants of the Hermes spent the nights of 26 and 27 May, and the intervening day, at the crash site, while a convoy of half-tracks sent to rescue them got bogged down in the sand about fifteen miles away.

1 Not all of BOAC's fleet had wings. A double-decker bus of 1960s vintage poses alongside preserved Britannia 312 G-AOVF. (Philip Lamb, Presbus Publishing Services)

2 Cover of ticket issued to the author for a BOAC-Cunard Boeing 707 flight Heathrow-Manchester-Prestwick in July 1965. (via Author)

3 BOAC's last Super VC-10 G-ASGR on take-off. (British Aerospace PLC)

4   BOAC Super VC-10 G-ASGP at Prestwick in May 1970. (Peter Berry)

5   BOAC-Cunard Super VC-10. (J. &C. McCutcheon Collection)

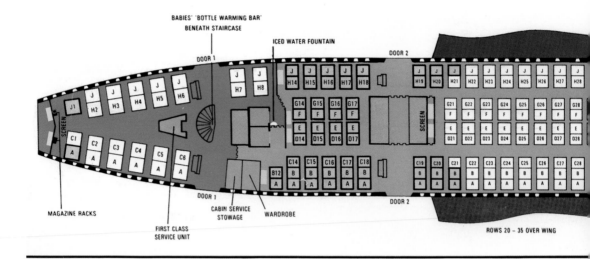

BABIES' 'BOTTLE WARMING BAR'
BENEATH STAIRCASE

ICED WATER FOUNTAIN

DOOR 1

DOOR 2

DOOR 2

SCREEN

SCREEN

MAGAZINE RACKS

DOOR 1

DOOR 2

CABIN SERVICE
STOWAGE

WARDROBE

FIRST CLASS
SERVICE UNIT

ROWS 20 – 35 OVER WING

747 CONFIGURATION PLA

6 *Above:* Boeing 747 configuration plan (initial North Atlantic services). (via Author)

7 *Left:* A side view of a row in the First-Class cabin of the 747.

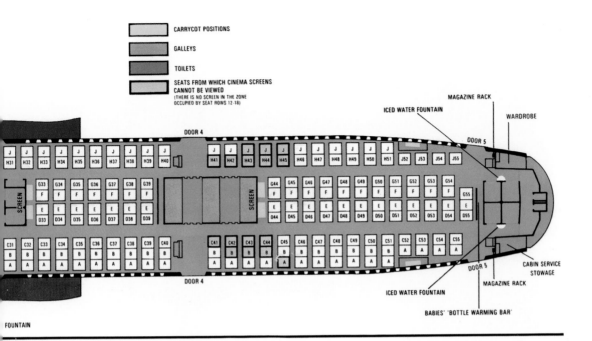

CARRYCOT POSITIONS

GALLEYS

TOILETS

SEATS FROM WHICH CINEMA SCREENS
CANNOT BE VIEWED
(THERE IS NO SCREEN IN THE ZONE
OCCUPIED BY SEAT ROWS 12-18)

MAGAZINE RACK

ICED WATER FOUNTAIN

WARDROBE

DOOR 4

DOOR 5

SCREEN

SCREEN

DOOR 4

DOOR 5

CABIN SERVICE
STOWAGE

ICED WATER FOUNTAIN

MAGAZINE RACK

BABIES' 'BOTTLE WARMING BAR'

FOUNTAIN

he configuration shown, with 27 First Class and 335 Economy seats is used on

orth Atlantic Summer operations. This is altered to 36 First Class and 315 Economy on Winter services,

d may be further modified on other routes to meet market requirements

8 A side view of the 747's Economy
Class.

9   Menu from BOAC New York-Prestwick-Manchester service in November 1972. (via Mrs Mary Smith)

10   A BOAC BOEING 707-436 from a period BOAC postcard, given away to passengers. (J. & C. McCutcheon Collection)

11   The 747 offered passengers luxury in every aspect of their journey, down to iced drinking water and cosmetics available in the toilets.

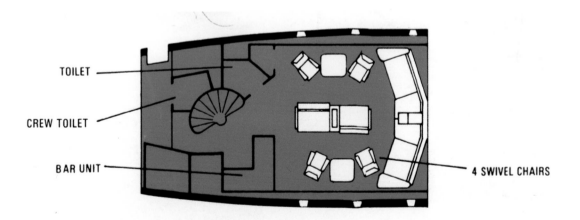

TOILET

CREW TOILET

BAR UNIT

4 SWIVEL CHAIRS

12   Artist's impression of Monarch Lounge on Boeing 747 (initial North Atlantic services). (via Author)

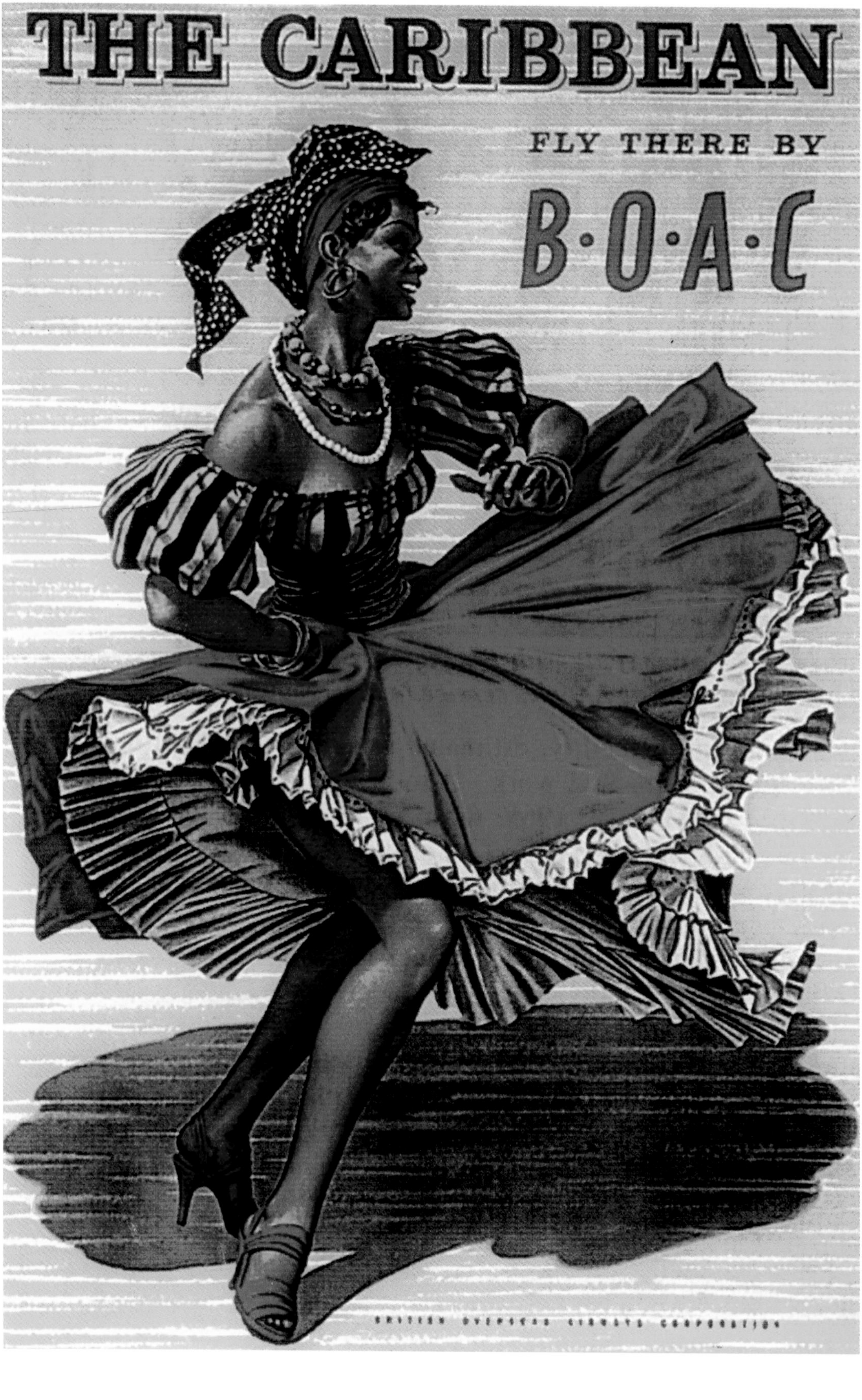
THE CARIBBEAN
FLY THERE BY
B·O·A·C

13   *Opposite:* BOAC poster for its Caribbean services. (via Derek King)

14   *Above:* During 1965 BOAC-Cunard introduced Super VC-10s onto services from London to Lima. (British Aerospace PLC)

You'll love *The Whispering Giant*

...it's the fastest most spacious airliner in the world

15   *Above:* Pre-service advertisement for the BOAC Britannia 102. (Bristol Aero Collection)

16   *Left:* Certificate presented to Mary Scarlett on the inaugural Britannia 102 service to Lagos, 13 April 1959. (Mary Dixon)

17, 18 *Opposite:* Illustrations from BOAC brochure on the VC-10. (via Derek King)

It's the personal touch

Unseen chefs blend their culinary skills for this fabulous restaurant in the sky

Only the best is good enough for the Very Important Passengers of BOAC. The finest foods are prepared by BOAC chefs in London and around the world; superlative service aboard transforms your VC10 jetliner into a truly memorable restaurant. And if you'd care for a cocktail or an after-dinner cognac, the VC10 bar is stocked with the finest wines, spirits and liqueurs. Life is *good* aboard the BOAC VC10. There is no finer way to fly.

19, 20, 21   *Above and opposite:* Illustrations from BOAC brochure on the VC-10. (via Derek King)

22   *Above:* VC-10 G-ARVC in flight. (British AerospacePLC)

23   *Opposite above:* Super VC-10 G-ASGR was the last VC-10 to be built. (British Aerospace PLC)

24   *Opposite below:* BOAC advertisement for its forthcoming Concorde operations. (via Derek King)

25 *Above:* BOAC postcard of a DC-7C in flight. (J. & C. McCuttcheon Collection)

26 *Below:* Matchbox covers from a BOAC flight. (via Drew Craigie)

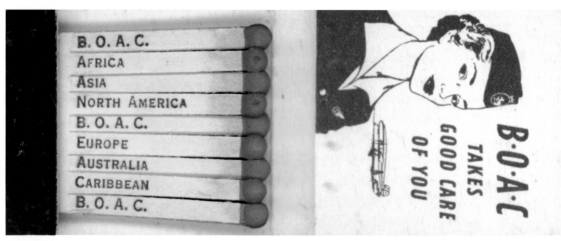

On 27 May the Argonaut arrived at the crash scene and made several passes at 500ft before heading down to Dakar, where its occupants liaised with the French. Eventually, some nomads brought camels to the wreck, and the party set off on camels and on foot on a night-time trek to the oasis at Aioun Lebgar, twenty-three miles away. This was reached after a sixteen-hour journey, but sadly First Officer Haslam, who had given up his place on one of the camels to an eight-year old boy, perished of heat exhaustion on the morning of 31 May. In 2002 an expedition was mounted to the crash site, to try to excavate the fuselage of the Hermes, which was believed to be buried more or less intact under a sand dune. Although engine and wing components were found on the surface, the fuselage was not located, and is believed to have been cut up and sold for scrap metal by the local inhabitants.

On 17 November 1952 the Hermes fleet was used to introduce Tourist-Class services to Africa, at savings of up to 28 per cent. The initial destinations were the Sudan, Uganda and Kenya, and these were followed by Tourist-Class services to Dar Es Salaam from 21 November. On 1 March 1953 Lusaka also received the benefits of Tourist-Class travel, with a once-weekly service from London via Rome, Cairo, Khartoum, Entebbe and Nairobi. The Hermes was configured to seat fifty-six passengers, and the journey took 51hrs 15mins, with a night stop en route. In the meantime, on 4 February 1953, a London–Rome–Cairo–Aden Hermes service had been introduced, with the Cairo–Aden sector being worked under a charter arrangement with Aden Airways.

The Hermes had a tendency to fly in a tail-down attitude, which reduced its speed and increased the fuel consumption. It was consequently uneconomical, and once the Comet 1 was in service alongside Stratocruisers, Constellations and Argonauts BOAC had no work for the aircraft. Argonauts took over on the East African routes on 1 October 1953, and the Hermes fleet was withdrawn after only three years in service. However, the aircraft shortage brought about by the Comet 1 crashes and their subsequent grounding in April 1954 led to a temporary return to service of the Hermes on the East African routes from 18 July 1954 until the final withdrawal of the type from scheduled services on 4 December 1954. Even then, the Hermes could still have been found useful work with BOAC if only the Corporation had been permitted to operate trooping flights to places such as Hong Kong and Singapore. By 1953 almost 50 per cent of the troop movements between the UK and the garrisons in the Middle East and Far East were by air. Government policy decreed that these flights were all allocated to the independent charter operators, and despite efforts to get this policy reversed BOAC was forced to sell off the Hermes fleet to the independent operators at knockdown prices, incurring a capital loss of £3 million. Fears of redundancy among BOAC engineering staff led to a union ban on the work needed prior to sale, and the fleet was to remain cocooned at London Airport for six months until the dispute was settled.

Hermes G-ALDH was later to see service with Airwork Ltd. (Air-Britain)

The successor to the Hermes on the African routes was the Canadair Argonaut. Canadair had been formed in 1944 to take over and develop the Canadian Vickers factory at Cartierville near Montreal, and the Canadair C-4 was the company's first venture. The design was basically a development of the Douglas C-54 airframe, but utilising some components of the later DC-6, and powered by four 1760hp Rolls Royce Merlin 626 engines instead of Pratt and Whitney Twin Wasps. This was because the British engines could be imported without duty being charged. The Canadair C-4 first flew in July 1946, and the first examples to be delivered, to the Royal Canadian Air Force, were unpressurised. However, the DC-4M-2 models delivered to Trans-Canada Air Lines as 'North Stars', and subsequent examples were fully pressurised. BOAC ordered twenty-two machines for use on the Empire routes as the 'Argonaut' class. They differed from the Trans-Canada models in having a separate crew entrance door, and in making the maximum use of British equipment in order to reduce payments in non-sterling currency to around $200,000 per aircraft.

On 29 March 1949 BOAC's first Argonaut, G-ALHC, was delivered to London Airport. The last example, G-ALHY 'Arion', arrived at London on

11 November 1949, delivery of the whole fleet having been accomplished eight months ahead of schedule! On board the last aircraft were food parcels donated by the United Emergency Fund for Britain, including 3,500lbs of provisions from the people of Windsor, Ontario for the needy of Windsor, England. These were accompanied by a message of good wishes from their Mayor. The Argonauts were assigned to BOAC's No.1 Line at London Airport, and were fitted with a periscopic sextant for astro-navigation. BOAC were the first regular users of this device, which eliminated the need for an astrodome on the aircraft. After initially entering service on the long runs to the Far East, the Argonauts replaced Avro Yorks on the London–Rome–Cairo route on 2 November 1949, reducing the journey time to 11hrs 30mins. Three days later a weekly Argonaut service to Kuwait was inaugurated, and on 7 November Argonauts replaced chartered Skyways DC-4s on a weekly London–Rome–Damascus–Abadan service. More routes soon received Argonaut services, with weekly schedules

BOAC Hermes G-ALDM in flight off the Needles, Isle of Wight. (BOAC photograph, copyright British Airways)

London–Rome–Damascus–Kuwait–Bahrain service on 12 November, and London–Rome–Damascus–Baghdad on 16 November. The previous day they had replaced Yorks on the weekly routing to Lydda via Rome. On 3 June 1950 they displaced Yorks from another run, this time a weekly London–Rome–Nicosia or Lydda–Tehran service, with G-ALHS 'Astra' operating the inaugural Argonaut service.

By February 1952 the service to Bahrain had been re-routed to operate via Zurich, Rome, Beirut and Kuwait. Flight BA212 departed London at 1300hrs on Wednesdays and arrived Bahrain at 1305hrs on the following day. The return leg flight BA213 set off from Bahrain at 1530hrs on Thursdays, arriving London at 0935hrs on Fridays. The free baggage allowance on this service was 30kg. On Tuesdays flight BA214 operated from London to Baghdad via Rome and Damascus, and on Sundays BA208 flew to Tehran via Rome and Tel Aviv. Once a week Cairo was also served by BOAC Argonauts. Flight BA318 departed London on Wednesdays at 0845 and flew via Rome, arriving at 2205hrs. At midnight the return leg departed as BA319, arriving in London at 1045hrs on Thursday.

The Argonauts were also utilised on a weekly service to Lisbon only. On 2 June 1950 BEA had withdrawn from the Lisbon route because of capacity limitations imposed by the Portuguese, and BOAC had taken over British operations. Flight BA373 left London on Saturdays at 1015hrs and arrived at 1510hrs. The return leg flight BA374 departed Lisbon at 1030hrs each Sunday, arriving London at 1515hrs.

During late 1952 the introduction of Comet 1s onto the prestige services to the Far East released Argonauts for use on Tourist-Class services to the Middle East and Africa. Following modifications to strengthen the cabin floor, the Argonauts were introduced in a fifty-four-seat configuration on a weekly Tourist-Class schedule to Lod (Israel) from 7 April 1953. The service operated via Frankfurt and Rome, and the journey took thirteen hours. On 1 October 1953 the Argonauts replaced Hermes aircraft on all BOAC's routes to East Africa, with the first service being operated by G-ALHK 'Atalanta'. During the first week of October they opened a Tourist-Class service from London to Lagos and Accra, and also extended Tourist-Class services to include the Persian Gulf, India, Pakistan and Ceylon. Between 14 August and 30 September 1955 a series of Argonaut flights from Nigeria to London was carried out, conveying 500 West African students to Britain. Eleven flights were made from Lagos to London, plus one from Kano, and for these special flights the Argonauts were configured to carry just forty passengers. During the financial year 1954–55 the Argonaut fleet achieved its highest annual utilisation. 74,679 revenue flying hours were logged, representing 98.5 per cent of the total hours flown.

On 21 September 1955 G-ALHL was lost while approaching Idris (Tripoli) from Rome, on a London–Kano service. Visibility was poor at the time, with strong winds. Three aborted landing attempts were made, and on the fourth

Argonaut G-ALHE crashed on take-off from Kano, Nigeria on 24 June 1956. (The A.J. Jackson Collection)

approach the Argonaut descended too low and struck trees some 1,200ft short of the runway. Out of the forty-seven people on board, thirteen passengers and two crew members were lost. On 24 June 1956 another Argonaut was lost. At 1640hrs G-ALHE arrived at Kano on a Lagos–Kano–Tripoli–London service. At 1721hrs the aircraft lifted off again from runway 25 at Kano with forty-five people on board. At that time the reported weather was a 2,500ft cloud base, wind 270 degrees at 20kts, visibility 1,500yds in moderate rain. The undercarriage was raised, and the Argonaut passed over the runway threshold at 100ft at an airspeed of 125kt. As the power was reduced a slight updraft was noticed. Having entered an area of heavy rain, a normal rate of climb was maintained until a height of around 250ft. Suddenly, the airspeed dropped to 103kts, close to the 97kt stalling speed. Full power was applied and the nose was lowered slightly in

Argonaut G-ALHD 'Ajax' in the later 'blue-tail' livery. (Air-Britain)

an attempt to regain speed, but to no avail. The aircraft descended rapidly until only 15–20ft above the ground. A tree dead ahead forced the pilot to bank to the right. The Argonaut impacted a 35ft high tree with its left wing, rupturing the fuel lines. The left outer wing detached as the aircraft crashed into the trees and caught fire. Twenty-nine passengers and three crew were killed. The accident enquiry gave the probable cause as loss of height and airspeed caused by the aircraft encountering at approximately 250ft after take-off an unpredictable thunderstorm cell which gave rise to a sudden reversal of wind direction, heavy rain, and possible downdraft conditions.

During 1955 one of BOAC's busiest out-stations was at Cairo. Aircraft types handled by the staff there included Argonauts, Constellations and Super Constellations, Vikings, Yorks and Dakotas, operated by eight different airlines including BOAC. By 1956 130 hotel rooms were needed each night to cater for transiting passengers and crews, and the cargo section there was handling heavier loads than any other station except New York. Each of the traffic staff could speak at least three languages, most of them four, and some of them six or more.

In 1957 a radio teletype circuit between London and Lagos was opened as the first link in the Overseas Fixed Telecommunications Service, developed by BOAC and the West African Airways Corporation (later to be renamed Nigerian Airways), to eventually connect London with all the BOAC stations in Nigeria and Ghana.

On 8 April 1960 BOAC's final Argonaut service arrived at London from Abadan. The flight was operated by G-ALHG 'Aurora', under the command of

Captain E.N. Wright. In BOAC service the Argonauts had flown nearly 107 million miles, and had carried around 870,000 passengers.

Lockheed Constellations were also used for a short period on the African and Middle East routes. On 23 May 1955 they took over on weekly First-Class services from London to Johannesburg, operating in a thirty-eight-seat configuration. It is interesting to note that during 1955, of the 78,702 people who travelled to South Africa and back, only 11 per cent of them travelled by air, the rest going by ship. For this reason, BOAC at that time considered that its main business was to sell people on the idea of air travel, and after that to convince them that BOAC air travel was the best they could buy. From the summer of 1957 the Constellations began to be replaced on these services by Bristol Britannia turbo-props, and BOAC's last Constellation service was operated on 6 October 1958, from Abadan to London via Kuwait, Beirut and Rome. The aircraft was G-ANTG 'Bournemouth', flown by Captain Smith and Captain A.G. Payne.

Stratocruiser service came to the Middle East on 4 September 1954 when the 'Monarch' De Luxe service from New York to London was extended onwards

G-ANTX inaugurated BOAC Stratocruiser operations to West Africa on 1 March 1958. (Air-Britain)

The tail of Stratocruiser G-ANUC at London Airports North Side terminal, alongside a PIA Super Constellation. (via Author)

to Cairo, with the first westbound service from Cairo departing on 7 September. Following their ousting from front-line transatlantic services the Stratocruisers were also introduced onto BOAC's West African routes from 1 March 1958, flying twice weekly from London to Lagos and once weekly to Accra. Both these routes incorporated a stop at Barcelona, and the inaugural service was flown by G-ANTX 'Cleopatra' under the control of Captain Bellingham. On 16 July 1958 Ghana Airways began operating its own services between London and Accra, although still using chartered BOAC Stratocruisers for the purpose. The first Ghana Airways service was operated by G-ANTZ 'Cordelia'. On 30 and 31 May 1959 BOAC operated its final Stratocruiser services. G-ANTY 'Corolianus', commanded by Captains Carr and Campbell flew London–Barcelona–Kano–Accra, and on the following day the same aircraft flew the return leg, this time with Captains Campbell and Reynolds in charge. Between 1949 and 1959 BOAC had operated a total of seventeen Stratocruisers.

The next aircraft to operate on the routes to Africa and the Middle East was the turbo-prop Britannia 102. The first prototype Britannia had made its maiden flight from Filton as long ago as 16 August 1952, but its development was protracted. The first two BOAC examples, G-ANBC and G-ANBD, were flown from Filton to London Airport and handed over on 30 December 1955, following the issue of the Britannia's Certificate of Airworthiness by the Air

Stratocruiser G-ANUB at the BOAC Engineering Base at London Airport in November 1959. (Clive Dyball)

Britannia 102 G-ANBA was used for tropical trials before delivery to BOAC in August 1957. (Air-Britain)

Britannia 102 G-ANBM was leased to Nigeria Airways during 1959–60. (Air-Britain)

Registration Board a few hours earlier. The aircrafts' log books were ceremoni-ally handed over to Sir Miles Thomas, chairman of BOAC, by Sir Reginald Verdon Smith, chairman of the Bristol Aeroplane Company. G-ANBC was equipped as a ninety-four-seat Tourist-Class aircraft, and G-ANBD was furnished in a fifty-four-seat First-Class layout, complete with horseshoe-shaped lounge bar amidships. Six more examples were delivered during 1956, but before the aircraft began scheduled services they made their first revenue-earning flights carrying British troops from Hurn, where the Britannias were temporarily based for crew training, to Cyprus. In August 1956 Egyptian government claims to ownership of the Suez Canal led to fighting in the Middle East, and it was decided to reinforce the British military bases in Cyprus. The Britannia was ideal for this task, as it could carry up to 116 troops non-stop to Nicosia. The first trooping flight departed Hurn at 0700hrs on 5 August 1956, and a total of sixty-eight such flights were operated by G-ANBE and G-ANBJ. The BOAC Britannias were also used in the evacuation of British civilians after rioting in Lebanon in the autumn of 1956, and the aircraft proved its usefulness as a load carrier by carrying 200 British wives and children from Bahrain to Aden on a single flight. The BOAC Britannias were also utilised to carry refugees from Vienna to London during the Hungarian uprising against Soviet occupation. Twenty-four sorties were carried out during November and December 1956, transporting 2,699 refugees in the course of 1307 flying hours.

The Britannia finally commenced scheduled services on 1 August 1957. G-ANBI, with Captain F.A. Taylor in command for the first leg, operated the inaugural London-Johannesburg Britannia service. Three flights per week were scheduled, flying via Rome, Khartoum and Nairobi, with an optional stop at Salisbury. The Britannias operated in a mixed-class layout, with nineteen First-Class and forty-eight Tourist-Class seats, and the total journey time to Johannesburg was scheduled at 22hrs 50mins. When the Britannia commenced scheduled operations it was the largest airliner in service in the world, exceeding by some 3,000lb the weight of its nearest rival. It was also the fastest and the quietest, its Bristol Proteus turbo-prop engines justifying its advertising slogan 'The Whispering Giant'. For the next five years the Britannia 102s were to serve on BOAC's African and Eastern networks, replacing Argonauts, Constellations and Stratocruisers. On 22 August 1957 Britannias superseded Constellations on the London–Rome–Khartoum–Aden route, reducing the total journey time to 15hrs. During the second half of 1957 the Britannia fleet began to be painted in BOAC's new colour scheme, with the dark blue cheat line being extended to cover most of the nose area, and a dark blue tail fin in place of the previous white one. By December 1957 Britannia's annual utilisation had reached 3,000hrs per

Britannia 102 G-ANBC wears Ghana Airways titles while on lease to them in 1960. (Air-Britain)

Britannia 312s replaced series 102s on the London–Johannesburg route on 27 July 1958. G-AOVB
illustrated. (Bristol via Roger Jackson)

aircraft, but during the first eight months of service there had been no fewer than
forty-nine unplanned engine changes and sixteen engine failures due to icing
problems. These problems had been first encountered in early 1956, during route
familiarisation flights to South Africa. They only occurred during flight in certain
cloud conditions found in tropical zones, and had not been detected during the
Britannia's icing trials, which had been carried out in the completely different
climatic conditions of Canada. The problems were eventually found to be caused
by the design of the Proteus engine's air intake. This curved through 180 degrees,
and in certain weather conditions dry ice crystals could form on the inner walls
of the cowlings. When the crystals reached sufficient thickness they would break
away and enter the compressor in quantities large enough to cause either a 'bump
stall' (caused by the interruption of the airflow through the compressor), or a
'flame-out', where the engine had to be restarted in flight. Modifications were
introduced, and the problems were eventually overcome.

During 1958 one of BOAC's major Middle East stations was at Khartoum, where 195 staff were employed. In addition to handling twenty-four BOAC services each week, the staff also handled the services of SAS (four services), Aden Airways (six services), Central African Airways Corporation (four services), East African Airways Corporation (two services) and South African Airways (six services). Contracts were also held to handle when necessary all RAF and USAF Military Air Transport Service flights, and for the technical handling of KLM and Air France aircraft. Night stop accommodation was provided at the Grand Hotel in Khartoum at the rate of £1 11s plus 5 per cent service charge.

On 27 July 1958 Britannia 312s replaced the earlier series 102s on the London–Johannesburg route, and on 6 October G-AOVJ inaugurated Britannia 312 services to East Africa.

On 6 January 1959 series 102 G-ANBA was used to inaugurate a new Middle East routing, London–Rome–Beirut–Kuwait–Bahrain–Doha. By March 1959 all of the series 102s and the later series 312s ordered by BOAC had been delivered,

Britannia 312 G-AOVE was delivered to BOAC on 21 December 1957. (Bristol via Roger Jackson)

and on 13 April 1959 series 102 G-ANBL inaugurated Britannia services to West Africa, flying from London to Lagos. Three days later G-ANBK introduced Britannia operations to the London–Accra route. On 9 August the London–Lagos route was upgraded to an eight-times-weekly 'express' service, incorporating for the first time a daylight crossing of the Sahara. The 11hrs 30mins schedule included just one stop en route, at Barcelona.

In November 1959 series 312s were used to re-open BOAC services to Tel Aviv, operating alongside the services of sister airline BEA. During the financial year ending March 1960 the Britannia 102 and 312 fleets contributed 58 per cent of BOAC's total capacity. On 13 April 1960 Britannia 102s took over from Argonauts on London–Beirut–Damascus–Abadan services, operating to a 13hrs 25mins schedule, and on 1 December a twice-weekly service to Tripoli and Benghazi was inaugurated. Meanwhile, on 11 November 1960, series 102 G-ANBC was en route to Khartoum with eighteen passengers and nine crew aboard when a problem occurred at 20,500ft. A loss of hydraulic fluid was accompanied by a reduction in airspeed from 210kt to 180kt. During the descent into Khartoum it was discovered that the landing gear could not be lowered and locked down by the use of either the normal or the emergency systems. The Britannia was landed by Captain Alfred S. Powell and his crew on a strip alongside the runway with the nose wheel up and the main landing gear trailing. Thanks to the skill of the crew, nobody on board was injured. The problem was later traced to a failure of the support member for the starboard main-gear uplock. This had permitted the gear to extend under gravity during flight, damaging the hydraulic system lines. Captain Powell was later awarded a BOAC Certificate of Commendation for his 'outstanding qualities of leadership and airmanship'.

The Comet 4 fleet was also used on the Middle East route network, not always without incident. On 9 April 1959 G-APDF was forced to make an emergency landing back at Beirut Airport, some nine minutes after taking off from there. A tyre had burst, causing damage to the wing. Because the aircraft was over its maximum landing weight, four more tyres burst on landing and a fire started in the main-gear assemblies. There were no injuries among the sixty-four passengers and nine crew. The incident was attributed to overheating of the brakes during a previous aborted take-off attempt some eleven minutes earlier.

On 2 December 1959 Comet services to Johannesburg resumed, having been previously operated by Comet 1s until their grounding. The inaugural Comet 4 service was operated by G-APDK, commanded by Captain Bailey for the first leg to Rome, and reached Johannesburg on 3 December. The return northbound leg departed on the same day, but was forced by bad weather at Rome to divert to Naples instead, arriving at London on 5 December. The round-trip journey of 11,169 miles was accomplished in a flying time of 32hrs 29mins.

On 23 December 1959 G-APDL was inadvertently landed 'wheels-up' at Ciampino Airport, Rome after a flight from London. Despite needing the

On 2 December 1959 Comet 4 G-APDK re-instated BOAC Comet services to Johannesburg, previously pioneered by the ill-fated Comet 1s. (The A.J. Jackson Collection)

replacement of the undercarriage doors, engine cowling doors and inner flaps, and the replacement of all four engines as a precautionary measure, the aircraft was repaired by BOAC engineers assisted by De Havilland engineers in the remarkably short time of forty-five days. Delivery of the Comet 4 fleet was completed by G-APDJ on 11 January 1960. Nineteen examples had been delivered in sixteen months, all of them ahead of schedule.

On 1 November 1960 Comet 4s were introduced onto the London–Rome–Beirut–Abadan–Doha–Kuwait route, with G-APDA, under the command of Captains Latus and Hitchins, operating the inaugural service. On the same day Middle East Airlines began jet operations using Comet 4s chartered from BOAC. Their first service was on the routing London–Geneva–Beirut–Dhahran–Bahrain, using G-APDG under the command of Captain Bailey. During 1960, BOAC Comet 4s flew well over 100,000 unduplicated route miles. On 25 January 1961 G-APDM was nearing the end of the first leg of a London–Rome–Khartoum–Nairobi–Salisbury–Johannesburg service. The crew presumed they were on approach to the newly-opened Fiumicino Airport at Rome, but they were actually some sixty miles away from it. The Comet struck treetops at a height of 1,740ft. One flap was sheared in two places, but despite the damage the aircraft was safely landed with no injuries to the forty-four passengers or the crew. An inspection after landing revealed pieces of tree branches in the compressor

VC-10 G-ARVB at Heathrow wearing Nigeria Airways titles during a lease. Iraqi Airways Trident in background. (Maurice Marsh)

stages of the engines. The Italian investigation into the incident found that an incorrect approach chart had been used, and various other navigation procedures had been incorrectly applied. It also discovered that no crew familiarisation flights had been made into the new airport. G-APDM was repaired and put back into service, only to be involved in another landing accident at Stansted on 3 August 1962. Once more it was repaired and returned to service.

To replace the Comets on the Empire routes BOAC originally wanted an anglicised version of the Boeing 707, built under licence in the UK by Vickers-Armstrong, but the airline was told it would have to order a new design from a British manufacturer. Vickers had a project designated the VC-10, and on 22 May 1957 BOAC announced that this design came closest to meeting the airline's requirements. The BOAC specifications were exceptionally severe, and were exclusive to that carrier. The aircraft chosen had to be suitable for operations into the 'hot and high' airport at Nairobi, and of flying non-stop from

Singapore to Karachi against a headwind. At that point in time, with the existing runway lengths, the 707 could not meet these conditions. However, it was only a matter of time before all the world's major airports extended their runways to accommodate the Boeing jet. The final VC-10/type 1100 specification was for an aircraft with the same cabin width as the Douglas DC-8, capable of accommodation 135 passengers in a two-class layout or up to 151 in an all-Economy, six-abreast configuration. It was to be powered by four 20,370lb thrust Rolls Royce Conway 540 two-shaft turbofans, and a rear-engined layout was chosen, to give an aerodynamically clean and very efficient wing. This had continuous lift-generating devices on both the leading and trailing edges. The wing was equipped with leading edge slats, outboard ailerons, upper wing spoilers and massive Fowler flaps. A feature was the use of split control surfaces, each driven by separate power units, managed by two autopilots, each monitoring the other. The result was a very high level of systems reliability which later enabled the VC-10 to become one of the first airliners certified for completely 'hands off' automatic landings in nil visibility. The four engines at the rear of the fuselage were attached to a steel cross-member, which incurred a weight penalty of some 12,000lbs. Also, because of the greater weight at the tail, the wings and fuselage had to be strengthened, adding a further 5,000lb. Because of the weight penalty, the VC-10s direct operating costs were some 17 per cent higher than the 707.

VC-10 G-ARVF at Heathrow in its later BOAC colours. (Maurice Marsh)

Landing shot of VC-10 G-ARVF in its original BOAC livery. (The A.J. Jackson Collection)

However, the rear-engined layout did result in landing and take-off speeds being some 20kt lower than the Boeing, and also produced a smoother and quieter ride for the passengers, a selling point BOAC was to exploit in its advertising.

Before the VC-10 entered service with BOAC the airline was embroiled in a battle to offer lower fares on the African routes. The UK independent airlines had been granted permission by the British government to operate low-frequency 'Colonial Coach' services at special low rates on the 'cabotage' routes to the British colonies in Africa and Asia. Although these flights only operated on a weekly or fortnightly basis, their fares were up to 40 per cent cheaper than BOAC's, and they attracted high load factors. In their first full year of operation they had siphoned off as much as £5.5 million from BOAC. At that time, BOAC were not permitted to offer a third class of fare to compete, only First Class and Tourist Class. At the 1958 IATA Traffic Conference BOAC again pressed for Economy-Class fares on African and Far East routes, as had already been introduced on their transatlantic routes, but they were again turned down. Eventually, after consultation with the Minister over ways of generating work for the additional VC-10s it had been obliged to order for political reasons, BOAC was granted permission on 15 December 1959 to offer fares which matched the Colonial Coach fares of the independents. In late 1959 BOAC signed a revenue-pooling agreement with East African Airways, Central African Airways and

South African Airways, covering all their flights from London to Salisbury, Nairobi and Johannesburg.

On 4 October 1960 new low-fare 'Skycoach' services came into operation on the cabotage routes between the UK and East Africa and Central Africa. The services were operated jointly by BOAC, British United Airways, Central African Airways and East African Airways, using sixty-two-seat Viscount 800s of British United Airways.

The prototype VC-10, G-ARTA, made its maiden flight from Brooklands on 29 June 1962, using less than half of the 4,500ft runway. BOAC accepted its first VC-10, G-ARVI, on 22 April 1964, and the last example, G-ARVB, was delivered on 6 February 1965. The inaugural VC-10 service was operated from London to Lagos on 29 April 1964. G-ARVJ departed London at 1157hrs, with fifty-nine fare-paying passengers and many journalists and BOAC officials aboard. Five hours and fifty minutes later it touched down at Lagos after the 3,100-mile journey. That summer BOAC scheduled five VC-10 services each week from London to West Africa. Flight BA283 operated London–Lagos non-stop, and the other services incorporated stops at Kano or Accra en route. The introduction of the VC-10 also saw the appearance of aircraft in the new BOAC colour scheme, with a dark blue fin emblazoned with a gold 'Speedbird' logo, and gold fuselage titles. VC-10 services to East Africa commenced on 6 June 1964, with G-ARVJ opening a route to Dar Es Salaam via Nairobi, and on 22 June VC-10 services to the Gulf region began. By July 1964 seven VC-10s had been delivered, and before the end of the year the type was in service on routes to Johannesburg and Karachi. On 16 March 1965 VC-10 services to Aden were inaugurated, slashing 90mins off the previous Comet 4 journey time, and from the spring of 1965 VC-10 services were expanded to include routes to Amman, Tel Aviv, and several other Middle East destinations. During its first year of service the VC-10 achieved load factors of 80 per cent on West African routes, and an incredible 98 per cent on Central African and South African services. On 2 April 1966 London–Dubai VC-10 services were inaugurated.

During the 1960s BOAC's marketing people were trying all sorts of ploys to attract customer loyalty to the BOAC brand, and one of these, aimed at junior passengers, was the BOAC Junior Jet Club. On their first flight with BOAC, children were enrolled into the club and presented with a Junior Jet Club lapel badge, made to resemble a set of pilots wings, and a smart log book in the BOAC colours in which to record their flights on BOAC. This could be sent up to the flight deck during their journey for the Captain to fill in and sign, and doubtless encouraged many youngsters to ensure that their parents always booked with BOAC!

By the beginning of 1968 VC-10s were in service to Bombay, Karachi and Delhi, calling en route at Middle East points such as Tel Aviv, Tehran, Baghdad, Beirut, Kuwait, Bahrain and Dubai. There was also a direct London–Tel Aviv

Boeing 747s were introduced onto the London–Johannesburg route from December 1971. (Air-Britain)

service. They also served on the African network, with daily flights to Nairobi, which on various days continued onwards to Ndola, Lusaka, Dar Es Salaam and Mauritius, as well as calling en route at Entebbe on two days each week. West Africa was served by VC-10 services to Lagos on four days each week, and on Tuesdays and Thursdays flight BA241 flew non-stop London–Tripoli. There was a daily VC-10 service to Johannesburg, with extra flights on two days each week, and an excursion fare return ticket could be purchased for £268 7s.

By 1970 Super VC-10s were also in use on routes to the Middle East. On 9 September 1970 Super VC-10 G-ASGN had just taken off from Bahrain for Beirut as flight BA775 when it was hijacked by members of the Popular Front For The Liberation Of Palestine. A landing was made at Beirut before the crew were made to fly the aircraft to Zerqa (also known as Dawsons Field). a military airfield some twenty miles north of Amman. Here the Super VC-10 was joined by a TWA Boeing 707 and a Swissair DC-8, in what was one of the largest mass hijackings in history. Fortunately, the hijackers released all the passengers and crews before they blew up all the aircraft on 12 September 1970.

On 3 July 1971 VC-10s inaugurated BOAC's new London–Seychelles service, flight BA051, and during that summer the VC-10s were still in regular service on the run to Johannesburg, flying via either Frankfurt, Zurich or Rome and Nairobi or Entebbe. They also operated on London–Nicosia–Entebbe–Blantyre and London–Zurich–Entebbe–Lusaka routings, as well as to Dar Es Salaam via Rome, Khartoum and Nairobi. One route that was Boeing 707-operated however, was a Tuesday service direct from London to Tripoli. In the summer

1972 schedules the VC-10s still operated to Dar Es Salaam via Nairobi and Entebbe, and to Blantyre via Nicosia and Nairobi, but the Johannesburg services had been taken over by wide-bodied Boeing 747s, which had been introduced onto the route in December 1971. These services were flown via Frankfurt or Rome and Nairobi. On 5 January 1973 VC-10s inaugurated a new routing, from London to Addis Ababa via Nicosia. By that summer the 747s were flying direct from London to Nairobi en route to Johannesburg on some days. The fare from London to Johannesburg at that time was £708.30 return in First Class or £421.60 return in Economy Class, but excursion fares were also available for only £273 return. The VC-10s were also still in evidence in Africa, flying to Blantyre via Nicosia, Nairobi and Dar Es Salaam, and to Lusaka via Khartoum and Nairobi.

At the time of the amalgamation of BOAC with BEA in 1974 the standard VC-10 fleet had been reduced by aircraft sales to nine examples. These were initially taken over by British Airways, along with the surviving Super VC-10s, but the standard VC-10s were then withdrawn from service.

14

Asian and Australasian Services

During the early 1950s the BOAC routes to India, the Far East and Australia were predominantly operated by two types of airliner, the Lockheed Constellation and the Canadair Argonaut (plus, for a short time, the ill-fated Comet 1).

On 1 December 1948 BOAC began operating L-749 Constellations on the London–Sydney run, with Captain G.R. Buxton taking charge of G-ALAL 'Banbury' on the inaugural service by the type. By 1952 the February-March edition of *Bradshaw's International Air Guide* was showing flight BA704 as departing London at 0800hrs on Tuesdays, Fridays and alternate Sundays. The service operated via Rome, Beirut, Karachi, Calcutta, Singapore, Jakarta and Darwin, with night stops at Beirut and Singapore, arriving Sydney at 0700hrs on Saturdays, Tuesdays and alternate Thursdays. The UK–Australia free baggage allowance was 40kgs for holders of roundtrip tickets and 30kg for one way passengers. One of the fleet was lost on 13 March 1954 at Singapore's Kallang Airport. G-ALAM was inbound with thirty-one passengers and nine crew aboard when it landed short of the runway, striking a sea wall with its undercarriage. The undercarriage collapsed as the aircraft touched down, the right wing broke off as the Constellation slid along the runway, the aircraft rolled to the right and came to rest inverted. There were thirty-three fatalities.

On 19 April 1954 a BOAC Constellation service from Sydney to London was the setting for a bizarre Cold War spy scenario involving Mrs Evdokia Petrov, whose husband Vladimir had until recently been based at the Soviet Embassy in Canberra as a Third Secretary. In fact he was really a Soviet intelligence officer, assigned to establish a network of agents in Australia. On 3 April 1954 he defected to Australia. On 19 April, Mrs Petrov, who had not at that point defected with her husband, was arrested by armed KGB men and taken under escort to Sydney Airport for transportation back to the Soviet Union via the BOAC flight. Alerted by press reports, an angry mob was waiting at the airport, where Mrs Petrov was forced on board the Constellation. The aircraft was due to make a stop at Darwin before finally leaving Australian airspace, and en route a

Russian-speaking BOAC stewardess spoke to Mrs Petrov and ascertained that she did not want to return to Russia and wanted to stay with her husband in Australia. The pilot contacted Darwin, and on landing the flight was met by Australian police and security officers, who disarmed and restrained her Soviet minders, and reunited Mrs Petrov with her husband, who had travelled to Darwin to meet her.

The grounding of the Comet 1s in 1954 involved BOAC in an urgent search for replacement aircraft. By 1955 the airline had acquired some more L-049 Constellations from Qantas, and an L-749A from Howard Hughes, who was then chairman of TWA, but used the aircraft as his personal transport. The seven L-049Es then in service were disposed of in an exchange deal with the American carrier Capital Airlines, which brought BOAC seven L-749A-79-24 models. These had higher gross weights and the improved payload/range capability needed for the Commonwealth routes. The deal enabled BOAC to standardise on the L-749A model, but entailed a cash adjustment of £1,375,000 in Capital's favour. BOAC also had the expense of refurbishing the ex-Capital aircraft to their own standards, including the replacement of the cabin interiors, galleys and associated fittings, and the installation of long-range radios. In 1955 some of the BOAC Constellations were re-configured to accommodate sixty passengers in all-Tourist-Class layout, with five-abreast rows of Vickers reclining seats. On 9 May 1955 they inaugurated weekly Tourist-Class services to Sydney. The type was still used for First-Class services, however, and on 19 May 1955 they commenced a weekly London–Hong Kong 'Majestic' First-Class service, with an onward extension to Singapore from 22 May. On 14 June Constellations took over the weekly First-Class London–Singapore service, and on 25 June they replaced Argonauts on the First-Class service to Karachi. On the First-Class services to Hong Kong and Singapore they carried thiry-eight passengers, with only thirty-four being carried on the Sydney run.

On 11 August 1957 G-ANNT 'Buckingham', under the command of Captain F.K. Bainbridge, and with seventeen people on board, was approaching London from Frankfurt on the last leg of a service from Singapore when it suffered a hydraulics failure which prevented the port main undercarriage from being lowered. For about three hours the Constellation circled London Airport, burning off fuel and making repeated approaches to runway 28 Left, while the crew tried unsuccessfully to get the port gear down. Eventually, as the light was fading, an emergency landing was made on runway 23 Left, so as not to block the active main runway. The Constellation came to rest just before the intersection with runway 28 Left, with no injuries to passengers or crew.

BOAC operated a total of seventeen Constellations. In BOAC service they flew 308 million miles and carried more than 500,000 passengers.

On 14 June 1949 Canadair Argonaut G-ALHD 'Ajax', commanded by Captain A.P.W. Cane, set off from London on a 26,000-mile proving flight over

Argonaut G-ALHD 'Ajax' served with BOAC from May 1949 to May 1959. (Air-Britain)

Argonaut G-ALHX Atalanta in the last of three liveries worn by the type. (Air-Britain)

BOAC's Far East route network. The Argonauts were introduced onto scheduled services to the Far East on 23 August 1949, commencing with a weekly London–Rome–Cairo–Basra–Karachi–Calcutta–Rangoon–Bangkok–Hong Kong schedule. This was BOAC's first all-landplane service to the Far East, and the inaugural flight was operated by G-ALHJ 'Arcturus'. One of the major drawbacks of the Canadair C-4 family was excessive engine noise inside the passenger cabin, caused by the unmuffled exhaust stacks being vented directly against the fuselage. Trans-Canada Air Lines developed a quieter crossover exhaust system for their Canadair North Stars, and BOAC engineers introduced the system onto the Argonauts, but it did not completely cure the problem.

On 26 August BOAC used G-ALHK 'Atalanta' to inaugurate a weekly London–Yokohama (for Tokyo) Argonaut service, the journey taking a total of eighty-six hours, and on the following day a twice-weekly Singapore-Hong Kong Argonaut service was introduced. However, within two weeks of entering service the entire fleet had to be temporarily withdrawn because of problems with the cooler pumps. The trouble was quickly cured, and the Argonauts were soon back in service. On 16 November 1949 they replaced Lancastrians on services to Colombo via Rome, Cairo, Bahrain and Bombay, reducing the journey time to 32hrs. The following day they displaced Yorks on a twice-weekly London–Malta–Cairo–Bahrain–Karachi–Delhi–Calcutta routing. By February

Argonaut G-ALHJ, seen here after retirement, in use as an apprentice-training airframe at the London Airport engineering base. (Author)

Argonaut G-ALHX Atalanta in flight. (BOAC photograph, copyright British Airways)

1952 the Argonaut fleet was operating services through to Tokyo. On three days a week there was a 2200hrs departure from London, calling at Rome (and also Zurich once a week), Cairo or Beirut, Basra, Karachi (plus Bahrain once weekly), Delhi (once weekly), Calcutta and Rangoon, where a night stop was made. The following morning the flight continued onwards to Bangkok, Hong Kong (where another night stop was made), Okinawa (optional technical stop) and finally Tokyo.

During late 1952 the prestige services to the Far East began to be taken over by the new Comet 1 jets, and in 1953 the Argonauts were modified to carry fifty-four Tourist-Class passengers on many routes, including those to the Persian Gulf, India, Pakistan and Ceylon. Following the grounding of the Comets the Argonaut fleet returned briefly to First-Class service on the London–Karachi route from 14 May 1955, but by 25 June they had been replaced by Constellations.

On 2 March 1957 turbo-prop Britannia 102s were introduced onto the London–Sydney route.

The Britannias slashed journey times wherever they were introduced, and they cut the overall journey time to Sydney by nearly 30hrs. Three services were operated each week on the routing London–Zurich–Istanbul–Karachi–Calcutta–Singapore–Jakarta–Darwin–Sydney. One of these was a 'Majestic' First-Class service with only thirty-nine seats, and the other two were mixed-class services, with nineteen First-Class and forty-two Tourist-Class seats.

On 17 September 1957 Britannia 102s replaced Constellations on the route to Colombo via Frankfurt, Beirut and Bombay, reducing the total journey time to 22hrs 30mins. BOAC had begun regular peacetime services to Colombo in 1947, using the RAF Transport Command airfield at Negombo. At first, Haltons were used, then Yorks and then Lancastrians. By 1952 the original airstrip at Ratmalana had been lengthened to 6,000ft and all civil operations moved back there. With the introduction of Argonaut services BOAC became the major carrier operating through Ceylon. During 1957 two London–Singapore-Hong Kong Argonaut Tourist services night-stopped at Colombo each week, and a weekly Constellation service terminated there until the Britannia 102s took over. The staff at Colombo also handled a weekly Qantas Super Constellation service.

On 16 July 1957 BOAC inaugurated Britannia services to Tokyo, and on 8 February 1958 Britannia 102 G-ANBE, under the command of Captain Sanderson, broke the Hong Kong-Tokyo record, covering the route in an airborne time of 4hrs 43mins at an average groundspeed of 419mph. On 3 May 1958 the type began operating London–Melbourne services.

A mishap befell G-ANBC on 8 September 1958 when the aircraft overran the end of the runway at Rangoon while landing in drizzle. None of the forty-two

L-749 Constellation G-ANTF was purchased from Qantas. (The A.J. Jackson Collection)

Britannia 102 G-ANBB wears the later 'blue-tail' colour scheme at the London Airport engineering base. (Air-Britain)

Britannia 102 G-ANBM was leased to Malayan Airways during 1961 and 1962. (Air-Britain)

Blue-tailed Britannia 102 G-ANBO served BOAC from 1957 to 1962. (Air-Britain)

people aboard were injured, but the Britannia was seriously damaged. After temporary repairs on site it was ferried back to the manufacturers at Filton for major rebuilding. It was eventually re-delivered to BOAC on 20 August 1959, after the most extensive repair operation undertaken up to that time on a commercial aircraft by a British company. The aircraft re-entered commercial service two days later, only to be written off in another accident in 1960.

By March 1959 all of BOAC's Britannia 102s and 312s had been delivered. On 23 February series 312 G-AOVC had set off from San Francisco on a trans-Pacific proving flight to Tokyo, and this duly led to BOAC's inaugural Round The World Service on 31 March 1959. On that date Britannia 312 G-AOVT departed London for Japan on a transpacific routing, flying westbound to Tokyo via New York, San Francisco, Honolulu and Hong Kong. Meanwhile, Comet 4 G-APDH departed London for Tokyo on 1 April, travelling in an eastbound direction and arriving there on 3 April. On the following day it returned to London via the same eastbound routing to complete the global circuit begun by the Britannia. However, delays in obtaining full traffic rights meant that the start of regular Round The World Services had to be postponed until 22 August 1959, when they were re-opened by Captain Gibson flying Britannia 312 G-AOVF.

In 1961 BOAC started advertising its Britannia 102 fleet for sale, but Britannias were still used to inaugurate a new through-plane service to Mauritius in January

Britannia 102 G-ANBA was delivered to BOAC in August 1957. (Bristol via Roger Jackson)

1962. The Economy-Class fare was £309.60 return, and the First-Class return fare was £489.60. First-Class passengers travelled in a cabin equipped with five toilets and two dressing rooms, and were served a seven-course dinner. In November 1962 all the series 102s were withdrawn. The final BOAC series 102 service was operated from Hong Kong to London by G-ANBH on 22 November 1962, although a few aircraft continued to fly on lease to Malayan Airways.

On 21 January 1959 BOAC began Comet 4 proving flights on the London–Tokyo route, using G-APDC, as a prelude to placing the type onto scheduled services to the Far East from 1 April 1959. Once in service, the Comets would fly from London to Tokyo with four en route stops in a total time of less than twenty-six hours. Comet 4 schedules to Singapore were inaugurated by G-APDE, which departed London on 1 June 1959 and arrived at Singapore on 3 June. The Comet 4 was ideally suited to BOAC's Asian route network, as its high power-to weight ratio resulted in dramatic take-off and climb-away

Britannia 102 G-ANBH at the London Airport engineering base in November 1959. (Clive Dyball)

Britannia 102 G-ANBM made its first flight on 8 March 1957. (The A.J. Jackson Collection)

Nov 1961

BRITISH OVERSEAS AIRWAYS CORPORATION

INVITE ENQUIRIES FOR

BRISTOL BRITANNIA 102 AIRCRAFT

★ Delivery during 1962

★ Current British Certificates of Airworthiness

★ Choice of seating layouts

★ Supporting components and spares available

Further information available from:
Manager, Aircraft Sales, B.O.A.C. Building 209, London Airport, Hounslow, Middx.   Phone: Skyport 5511, ext. 2404

BOAC attempted to find buyers for the Britannia 102 fleet in anticipation of the types retirement. This advertisement appeared in November 1961. (via Derek King)

Comet 4 G-APDH was written off in an accident at Singapore on 22 March 1964. (Air-Britain)

performances from the hot and sometimes windless runways found in the tropics. However, G-APDA suffered problems while attempting to land at Dum Dum Airport at Calcutta on 8 June 1959, as part of flight BA931 from Tokyo to London. The aircraft was approaching in turbulent conditions when a sudden decrease in airspeed caused it to strike some trees on the approach path before the power could be increased sufficiently. The Comet was climbed away safely and another approach was made to a different runway, but the crew had made insufficient allowance for the aircraft's increased stalling speed in its damaged condition, and once again it came into contact with trees and the landing was aborted. The third landing attempt was successful, and as a result of this incident it was recommended that the Comet 4 approach speed be increased by 5 knots. On 26 July 1959 BOAC inaugurated a high-speed, same-day Comet service between Hong Kong and London, stopping only at Rangoon, Karachi and Beirut. This reduced the journey time to less than 22hrs, a reduction of about seven hours.

During the period 1 April–19 September 1959 the Comet 4s were responsible for a 22 per cent increase in passenger traffic on the Far East route network. Worldwide, their punctuality was better than any other type in the BOAC fleet, with no in-flight engine failures. However, the odd mishap did still occur, and in October 1959 a Comet landed at Rome with the undercarriage still retracted.

Comet 4 G-APDD in Malaysian Airlines colours at the BOAC engineering base at Heathrow. (Air-Britain)

Comet 4 G-APDB with Malaysian Airlines titles. (Derek King)

Comet 4 G-APDF later became XV814. (Derek King)

Following this incident an undercarriage warning horn system was installed, and the pre-landing checklist was amended.

Joint BOAC/Qantas Comet 4 'Kangaroo' services to Sydney commenced on 1 November 1959, with the inaugural flight from London being operated by G-APDL, under the command of Captain Barnett as far as Beirut. The aircraft arrived Sydney on 3 November, and the first Sydney–London service set off on the following day, arriving London on 5 November. The roundtrip journey of 23,384 statute miles was completed in 60hrs 57mins flying time, at an average of 383.66 mph. For the Singapore-Sydney and vice-versa portions of the route the Comets were operated on charter to QANTAS. Comet 4 services to Manila began on 31 October 1961, and in April 1963 a twice-weekly Comet 4 service to Auckland was inaugurated, taking one and a half days.

During 1964 BOAC began to look for buyers for its Comet 4 fleet. One example was advertised for sale at £600,000, and an enquiry was received from the Turkish airline THY, but this did not result in a sale. BOAC's last commercial Comet 4 service was operated by G-APDM from New Zealand to London, arriving there on 24 November 1965. The last leg, from Damascus to London, was under the command of Captain R.C. Alabaster, the Manager of the Comet

Comet 4 G-APDN at the BOAC engineering base at London Airport in May 1960, in company with another Comet 4 and a Stratocruiser. (Clive Dyball)

Flight. It was he, along with Captain A.M.A. Majendie, who had been in command of BOAC's first Comet 1 service back in 1952. After retirement, G-APDT was sited in the BOAC engineering base at Heathrow as an apprentice-training airframe. As such, it became the only Comet to be repainted in the final BOAC dark blue and gold colour scheme, with 'BOAC Apprentice Training' titles above the cabin windows.

On 8–10 December 1960 BOAC began using Boeing 707s in place of Britannias on a twice-weekly London–New York–San Francisco–Honolulu–Tokyo–Hong Kong service. This connected at Hong Kong with Comet 4 services from London via the Eastern route, and thus completed the first British all-jet Round The World service. The inaugural 707 service, by series 436 G-APFJ, was obliged to make additional stops at Shannon and Wake Island because of adverse headwinds. In command for the transpacific portion were Captains K. Buxton and J.T. Percy (San Francisco–Honolulu), Captain R. Stone (Honolulu–Tokyo) and Captain A. Andrew (Tokyo–Hong Kong). Captain Andrew was also in charge of the first return service out of Hong Kong, operated by the same aircraft on 11 December.

On 26 September 1964 VC-10 services to the Far East were introduced, with flights to Hong Kong and Tokyo via the Eastern route. From January 1965 Singapore had VC-10 services, and on 8 August the type replaced Comet 4s on the London–Colombo route. On 2 April 1966 a weekly VC-10 service to Perth was launched.

It was while operating the Tokyo-Hong Kong leg of the transpacific routing that Boeing 707-436 G-APFE was lost on 5 March 1966. The 707 departed Tokyo (Haneda) for Hong Kong as flight BA911 at 1358hrs. After take-off the aircraft flew over Gotemba City, in the vicinity of Mount Fuji, at an altitude of approximately 4,900 metres. It was observed to be trailing white vapour, and suddenly lost altitude over the Takighara area. Parts of the 707 began to break away over Tsuchiyadai and Ichirimatsu. Finally, overhead Tarobo at a height of approximately 2,000 metres, the forward fuselage broke away. The mid-aft fuselage and the wing, making a slow flat spin to the right, crashed into a forest. The forward fuselage crashed about 300 metres to the west and caught fire. All 113 passengers and eleven crew were killed. The enquiry into the accident concluded that the aircraft suddenly encountered abnormally severe turbulence over Gotemba City, which imposed a gust load considerably in excess of the design limit.

In 1967 the Japanese Agreement was completely renegotiated, permitting BOAC to operate services to Japan via the Polar Route and/or via Siberia, as well as via the existing Eastern and transpacific routings.

Boeing 707-465 G-ARWD in its original BOAC colour scheme. (The A.J. Jackson Collection)

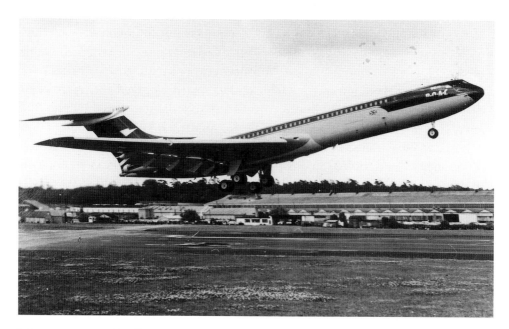

VC-10 G-ARVM on take-off. VC-10 services to Hong Kong and Tokyo commenced in September 1964. (Air-Britain)

Boeing 707-336C G-ATWV in the later BOAC livery. (Air-Britain)

At the beginning of 1968 Boeing 707 equipment was in use on daily services to Tokyo via the Eastern Hemisphere routing, with en route stops at all the major Far East cities. All-cargo flight BA950 operated on Mondays from London to Hong Kong via Bahrain and Karachi, and returned on Wednesdays as flight BA951 with just one stop en route at Karachi. Australia was served by two 707 flights each week on the Eastern Hemisphere routing. BA718 departed London on Thursdays and called at Zurich, Rome, Delhi, Bangkok, Singapore, Darwin and Sydney, while BA722 on Saturdays went via Zurich, Rome, Karachi, Calcutta, Kuala Lumpur, Singapore and Perth to Sydney. On three days each week there was also a Transpacific 707 service to Australia, when flight BA531 flew from London to Sydney via New York, San Francisco, Honolulu and Nandi.

On 8 April 1968 Boeing 707-465 G-ARWE , under the command of Captain Charles Taylor, departed Heathrow's runway 28L at 1527hrs for Zurich, on the first leg of flight BA712 to the Far East. On board was a check pilot, assigned to carry out a routine check on the pilot-in-command. Twenty seconds after take-off, just before the time for a noise abatement power reduction, the flight crew felt and heard a combined shock and bang. The thrust lever for the no.2 engine kicked towards the closed position, and at the same time the instruments showed that the engine was running down. The Captain ordered the engine-failure drill. Because the undercarriage was retracted, the warning horn sounded when the flight engineer fully retarded the thrust lever; the check pilot and the flight engineer simultaneously went for and pulled the horn cancel switch on the pedestal, while the co-pilot instinctively but in error pressed the fire bell cancel button. In front of him, the flight engineer went for the engine fire shut-off handle but did not pull it. The check pilot then reported seeing a serious fire in the no.2 engine. Having initially started an engine-failure drill the flight engineer changed directly to the engine-fire drill. Air Traffic Control originally offered the pilot-in-command a landing back on runway 28L and alerted the fire services, but after a Mayday call flight 712 was offered runway 05R, which was accepted as it would result in a shorter flight path. About 1.5 minutes after the start of the fire no.2 engine, together with part of its pylon, became detached and fell into a water-filled gravel pit. At about the time that the engine fell away, the undercarriage was lowered and full flap was selected. The undercarriage locked down normally, but the hydraulic pressure and contents were seen to fall, and the flaps stopped extending at 47 degrees, about three degrees short of their full range of travel. The approach to runway 05R was made from a difficult position, the aircraft being close to the runway and having reached a height of about 3,000ft and a speed of 225 knots. There was no glide-slope guidance to this runway, but the approach was well judged and touchdown was achieved at approximately 400 yards past the threshold. The aircraft came to a stop just left of the runway centre-line, about 1,800 yards from the threshold. After the aircraft came to rest the flight engineer commenced the engine shutdown drill and closed the start levers.

Almost simultaneously the pilot-in-command ordered the fire drill on the remaining engines. Before this could be carried out there was an explosion from the port wing which increased the intensity of the fire and blew fragments of the wing over to the starboard side of the aircraft. The pilot-in-command then ordered immediate evacuation of the flight deck. The engine fire shut-off handles were not pulled and the fuel booster pumps and main electrical supply were not switched off. There were more explosions, and fuel which was released from the port tanks spread underneath the aircraft and greatly enlarged the area of the fire. The cabin crew had made preparations for an emergency landing, and as the aircraft came to a stop they opened the emergency exits and started rigging the escape chutes. The passengers commenced evacuation from the two starboard overwing exits, and shortly afterwards, when the escape chutes had been inflated, from the rear starboard galley door and then the forward starboard galley door. However, because of the spread of the fire under the rear of the fuselage, the escape chute at the rear galley door soon burst, and following the first explosion the overwing escape route also became unusable. The great majority of the survivors left the aircraft via the forward galley door escape chute. However, out of the 116 passengers and eleven crew aboard, four passengers lost their lives, and stewardess Barbara Jane Harrison was killed when she was overcome in the cabin while trying to save an elderly crippled passenger. For her courage and devotion to duty she was posthumously awarded the George Cross. The enquiry into the accident concluded that 'the accident resulted from an omission to close the fuel shut-off valve when no.2 engine caught fire following the failure of its no.5 low-pressure compressor wheel. The failure of the wheel was due to fatigue.'

A new routing to the Far East was inaugurated on 5 May 1969, when BOAC commenced Boeing 707 services on the transpolar routing from London to Tokyo and Osaka via Anchorage in Alaska. On 28 October 1969 BOAC's first transpacific VC-10 service to Australia via Los Angeles arrived at Sydney, and during that month the BOAC board approved the purchase of two Boeing 707-336Bs in non-convertible all-passenger configuration. This purchase was specifically linked to the airline's plans to operate to Tokyo via Moscow from the summer of 1971. The long Moscow-Tokyo sector was demanding in range, and the convertible Boeing 707-336C, with its strengthened floor and subsequent higher weight, did not provide an adequate payload, hence the need for the lighter series 336Bs for the route. Permission to operate on the routing was received in 1970, and the inaugural London–Moscow–Tokyo service took place on 2 June 1970. The 707s used were among the first BOAC aircraft to be fitted with an in-flight entertainment system, designed for use on long daylight sectors. By the early summer of 1971 the fleet of Boeing 707-336Bs/Cs had grown to nine examples. They were in service on the Polar Route to Tokyo and Osaka via Anchorage, as well as operating through to Japan via the eastern hemisphere. This routing took the aircraft to Frankfurt, then to Rome or Tehran, Delhi, Bangkok,

Hong Kong and Tokyo. The return fare to Tokyo via either routing was £938.10 in First Class or £564.70 in Economy Class. The 707s also flew to Australia and New Zealand, the Auckland service involving stops en route at Zurich, Rome, Karachi, Calcutta, Singapore, Darwin and Sydney. VC-10s were still serving the Far East routes, one such flight routing London–Tehran–Colombo–Kuala Lumpur–Singapore. On 3 July 1971 VC-10s inaugurated flight BA051, a new route from London to the Seychelles, and from February 1972 a stop at the Seychelles was to be incorporated into the Tokyo-Hong Kong-Johannesburg route. On 1 November 1971 G-ARRC operated flight BA713 from Sydney to Heathrow via Brisbane. This was BOAC's last 707 service on the route, which was then taken over by Super VC-10s. The round-trip fare to Sydney was £910.10 in First Class or £578.70 in Economy Class.

In the summer of 1972 BOAC 707s opened the airline's Trans-Russia route to Tokyo via Moscow, as well as operating services to Japan via the eastern hemisphere and on the Polar Route via Anchorage. VC-10s still operated through to Singapore via the Middle East and India, and the Boeing 747 had entered service on Australian services, routing London–Tel Aviv–Tehran–Bangkok–Hong Kong–Darwin–Sydney.

Boeing 707-436s were still operating to the Far East in early 1973, and on 3 April G-APFP took off for Singapore to mark its return to service after a remarkable repair operation. On 15 January 1973 this aircraft had suffered a fire in its port outer engine while on the ground at Heathrow. The port wing was completely burnt through in the vicinity of this engine, and the engine and outer wing broke away from the aircraft. Boeing devised a repair scheme that involved the grafting on of a replacement mid-section from a damaged TWA 707, plus a new outer section. The repair operation, known as 'Operation Wing Graft' was carried out at Heathrow by a team of 42 BOAC engineers using a modified version of the Boeing scheme, and was described by Boeing as the most sophisticated repair job ever carried out on one of its products. The work commenced on 27 February 1973 and took 16,500 man-hours over a five-week period. On 2 April the Boeing was subjected to a five-hour Certificate of Airworthiness renewal check flight, and pronounced fit for service once more.

The summer 1973 BOAC timetable featured VC-10 services to the Seychelles via two routings. One was with just one stop at Nairobi, and the other was via Nicosia and Addis Ababa. From the Seychelles, a joint BOAC/Air Mauritius service offered onward connections to Mauritius. 747s were now operating to Sydney with the stop at Darwin deleted, and VC-10s were still maintaining the multi-stop flights through the Middle and Far East to Tokyo and Australia.

On 3 March 1974 Super VC-10 G-ASGO was on the last leg of a Bombay–Bahrain–Beirut–London flight when it was hijacked over Rhodos by two men. The flight was diverted to Amsterdam, where all 100 passengers and ten crew members were released. The hijackers then threw inflammable liquids around the cabin and set the aircraft on fire. They were captured running away from the burning aircraft. One of the fuselage windows and part of its surrounding structure were salvaged and displayed at the Aviodrome museum at Schipol Airport, Amsterdam.

While on a night flight over the South China Sea in 1974, Super VC-10 G-ASGL suffered a fuel transfer error that caused all four engines to run down. In order to correct a fuel imbalance the Flight Engineer had had all four engines feeding from one main fuel tank, but forgot about the situation when he briefly left his station. The engine rundown occurred while he was away. On his return he restarted the engines, and after a few minutes all four were performing normally. However, as the generators had dropped off-line, the ELRAT (electrical ram air turbine) had quickly been deployed automatically to restore electrical power to the flight controls. The ELRAT could only be re-stowed once the aircraft was on the ground, as it was designed for emergency use only. Continued exposure to the airstream during the remainder of the flight caused it to overspeed and fail completely before landing.

The standard VC-10s were withdrawn from service by British Airways soon after the merger in 1974, but the Super VC-10 fleet continued to serve with them until 1981.

15

The Concorde Order

Under its Terms of Reference laid down in 1964 BOAC was bound to act on normal commercial and financial principles, and because it did not anticipate being able to operate Concorde profitably this appeared to be a bar to the airline acquiring the supersonic airliner. In 1965 Beverly Shenstone, Technical Director of BOAC, described Concorde as the largest, most expensive and most dubious project ever undertaken in the development of civil aircraft. However, lengthy discussions were held with the Department of Trade and Industry and it became clear that BOAC was expected to order Concorde 'in the national interest'. On 29 July 1972 BOAC signed an agreement with the British Aircraft Corporation to purchase five Model 5102 Concordes at a basic contract price of £13,272,286 per aircraft, excluding spares. These were intended for initial operations from London to New York, Sydney, Johannesburg and Tokyo. The order was later increased to seven examples, and the special out-of-sequence registrations G-BOAA to G-BOAG were reserved for them. The Concorde order was subsequently taken over by British Airways at the time of the merger of BOAC and BEA.

Advertisement for forthcoming BOAC Concorde services, previewed in *BOAC News*, 26 May 1972. (via Author)

16

BOAC Crew Training

During the Second World War the BOAC Development Flight was formed jointly by the Air Ministry, the Ministry of Aircraft Production and BOAC to test new equipment intended for use in the projected post-war generation of civil airliners then under design in accordance with the guidelines of the Brabazon Committee, and in particular the Avro Tudor, which was to be BOAC's new airliner. The Development Flight was set up at Hurn in October 1943, and among its first equipment was Lancaster 1 G-AGJI, which was delivered on 20 January 1944 and returned to the RAF in December 1947. This was used to gain experience of operating the Rolls Royce Merlin engine under civil operating conditions in preparation for the anticipated introduction of the Avro Tudor. The first Avro-built Lancastrian conversion, VB873, was delivered to the Development Flight, and between 23 and 27 April 1945 made a record-breaking, four-and-a-half-day proving flight to Auckland. In June 1945 the former Bomber Command airfield at Ossington, near Newark-on-Trent, was handed over to RAF Transport Command, and the existing Operational Training Unit was replaced by 6 LFS, a joint Transport Command and BOAC unit set up to train crews on the Avro Lancastrian.

On 9 May 1946 BOAC opened its new training headquarters at the former wartime USAAF airfield at Aldermaston in Berkshire. Dakotas and Airspeed Oxfords from Whitchurch, and Yorks from Ossington were brought in, to be joined later by Halifaxes, Haltons and Vikings. At the end of 1946 a proposal was put forward to transfer the training headquarters from Aldermaston to Hurn. However, BOAC's Chief Instructor at Aldermaston raised objections to this on the grounds that it would be impossible to carry out the training syllabus without either overflying densely populated areas around Bournemouth, or revising the circuit to avoid this and ending up with a situation whereby only one landing per hour per aircraft could be fitted in. On 1 January 1947 Aldermaston was loaned to the Ministry of Civil Aviation as a temporary civil airport, and on 1 May 1947 Airways Training Ltd was formed jointly by BOAC and BEA to train aircrews for

Dove 1 G-AKCF was used for training and communications work. (Air-Britain)

both airlines. By the end of 1947 aircraft movements had reached almost 10,000 per month, but, with a financial crisis looming, the school at Aldermaston was closed down in November 1948. The site at Aldermaston was later to be used as an atomic energy research centre.

On 23 March 1951 the second prototype Comet 1 G-ALZK was delivered on loan to the BOAC Comet Unit at Hurn, which had been set up by Captain M.R.J. Alderson in September 1950. From Hurn, a programme of route proving and crew training was carried out until 24 October 1951, when Comet crew training was transferred to London Airport after an initial period at the manufacturer's airfield at Hatfield. BOAC also used De Havilland Doves for crew training and miscellaneous purposes. On 22 June 1955 G-ALTM was on a photographic sortie when it lost most of the power from the starboard engine. To compound the problem, the port engine was shut down in error. The ailing starboard engine failed completely while the aircraft was on approach to London Airport, and the Dove crashed at 2152hrs, tearing off the wings and buckling the nose. Captain H. Almond, the co-pilot, and the two BOAC photographers aboard escaped with minor injuries. In January 1956 Britannia

102 crew training was transferred to Hurn from London Airport. The arrival of Comet 4s also meant the introduction of flight simulators, and a Redifon Comet 4 simulator was purchased and installed in a new BOAC training building at Cranebank, near Heathrow. This was used solely for instrument flying training, and by July 1961 over 4,000 hours had been accumulated, at a 99.8 per cent serviceability rate.

17

Royal Flights

As Britain's state airline, BOAC regularly received Royal patronage. On 8 October 1951 Their Royal Highnesses Princess Elizabeth and the Duke of Edinburgh flew from London to Montreal in Stratocruiser G-AKGK 'Canopus', commanded by the legendary Captain O.P. Jones, at the start of their Royal Tour of Canada. This was the first Royal Tour to commence at London Airport, and the first occasion that members of the British Royal Family had crossed the Atlantic by air.

One of the most famous Royal usages of BOAC aircraft commenced at the beginning of February 1952, when HRH Princess Elizabeth and the Duke of Edinburgh set off from London Airport in Argonaut G-ALHK 'Atalanta' on the first stage of their Royal Tour to Australia. They were seen off at the airport by His Majesty King George VI, and flew to Nairobi via El Adem. After a stopover in Kenya they were due to continue onwards to Australia by sea, but it was while they were in Kenya that they were notified of the death of the King. The couple returned from Entebbe to London aboard the same Argonaut, and at 1630hrs on 7 February 1952 the former Princess Elizabeth set foot on British soil for the first time as Her Majesty Queen Elizabeth II.

On 23 November 1953 HM the Queen and the Duke of Edinburgh left London Airport in Stratocruiser G-AKGK 'Canopus', heading for Jamaica via Bermuda on the first leg of their Commonwealth Tour. In 1954, during the final stages of that year's Commonwealth Tour, the Queen and the Duke of Edinburgh flew from Aden to Entebbe on 28 April, and from Entebbe to Tobruk (El Adem) on 30 April, in Argonaut G-ALHD 'Ajax', commanded by Captain F.A. Taylor. During May 1953, after a request from Buckingham Palace, a special Comet 1 demonstration flight around Europe was arranged for the HM Queen Mother and HRH Princess Margaret. On board the Comet during the four-hour flight were Sir Geoffrey and Lady De Havilland.

On 31 January 1955 Stratocruiser G-AKGK 'Canopus' again received Royal patronage. This time the Royal passenger was HRH Princess Margaret, at the

HM Queen Elizabeth II descends the steps of Argonaut G-ALHK at London Airport on 7 February 1952 to set foot on British soil for the first time as Monarch. (Heathrow Airport PLC)

commencement of her Caribbean Tour. Under the command of Captain P.C. Fair, the Stratocruiser departed London at 1500hrs and flew the 3,309 miles to Montreal (Dorval) non-stop. After refuelling at Dorval the aircraft flew onwards to Montego Bay, Kingston and Port of Spain.

In 1958 HM the Queen Mother was due to make a Royal visit to New Zealand, flying to Auckland via Vancouver and Fiji. The Douglas DC-7C was selected as BOAC for the journey, as it had the long range necessary for the transpacific legs, and because it would have relatively easy access to the Douglas plant in California should spares be needed during the trip. The Royal flight left London on 28 January 1958, but while it was en route word was received that the clearance to land at Whenuepai Airport at Auckland had been withdrawn.

The runway there was of unusual construction, being made of hexagonal concrete blocks, and the weather had caused some of the blocks to suffer subsidence. This would not hamper most types of aircraft, but the subsidence was judged to be marginally too much for the hard tyres of the DC-7C to cope with. Fortunately, the British Prime Minister Harold Macmillan was in Australia at the time, using a chartered BOAC Britannia for his transport. This was borrowed from him for a couple of days and positioned to Fiji in time for the Queen Mother to use it for her flight to Auckland without disrupting her schedule.

On 19 April 1958 Britannia 312 G-AOVF was used to carry HRH Princess Margaret on her Royal Tour to the West Indies. On 20 January 1959 HRH the Duke of Edinburgh left London in BOAC Comet 4 G-APDE on the first stages of his Commonwealth Tour. This was to end on 30 April, when he arrived back at London from Bermuda, having flown that stage in a Britannia under the command of Captain Stead. Another Britannia, this time series 312 G-AOVN under the command of Captain R.H. Tapley, carried HRH Princess Alexandra to Nigeria on 25–26 November 1960 to attend that country's independence celebrations. The London–Lagos flight of 3,180 statute miles was accomplished non-stop in 10hrs 30mins, and was believed to have been the first non-stop flight over the route by a commercial aircraft.

Between 20 January and 6 March 1961 HM the Queen and HRH the Duke of Edinburgh undertook a State Visit to India, Pakistan, Nepal and Iran. The was the most comprehensive royal trip that BOAC had been asked to arrange, involving stops at twenty-three airports. BOAC supplied a Britannia 312 for the Royal couple, and a Britannia 102 support aircraft. The tour also utilised two Queens Flight Herons, and aircraft of the RAF, Indian Air Force and Pakistan Air Force for local flights. All the flights were operated without a hitch and on schedule.

In February 1965 the first Royal flight by a VC-10 was operated by G-ARVL, carrying HM the Queen and the Duke of Edinburgh on a tour of Ethiopia and Sudan, and in March 1965 HRH Princess Margaret and Lord Snowdon also used a VC-10 for a visit to Uganda.

18

The British Airways Merger

In May 1969 the Edwards Committee, which had been appointed to look into the organisation of Britain's airline industry, published its report. Among its recommendations was the formation by mergers of a powerful independent 'second force' airline to provide effective British competition for BOAC and BEA. This led to the merger of British United Airways and Caledonian Airways (Prestwick) to form what was eventually named British Caledonian Airways. Another of its recommendations was that BOAC and BEA should become responsible to a single holding board, with a view to increasing co-operation between them and reducing wasteful duplication of resources and facilities. The British Airways Board was established on 1 April 1972 to take control of BEA and BOAC and their subsidiaries, and to bring them together as the British Airways Group with effect from 1 September 1972. Full amalgamation of the two companies was not fully implemented until 1 April 1974, although the trading name British Airways had been adopted on 1 September 1973, with BOAC then becoming the British Overseas Airways Division of British Airways. On the 1 April 1974 24,646 BOAC staff moved over to British Airways. The operating fleet of the former BOAC on that date comprised nine standard VC-10s, fifteen Super VC-10s, eleven Boeing 707-436s, eleven Boeing 707-336Bs/336Cs, and fifteen Boeing 747-136s, with five Concordes on order. The new British Airways aircraft colour scheme had been decided on in July 1973, and the first aircraft to appear in the new livery was Boeing 707-336B G-AXXY, which operated the first service in the new colour scheme when it took off from London for Tokyo and Osaka via Anchorage as flight BA850 in September 1973. Among its passengers were the Duke and Duchess of Kent, on a State Visit to Japan. The first Boeing 747 to be repainted in the full British Airways livery was G-AWNN. By the full amalgamation date of 1 April 1974 many other aircraft in the fleet had been repainted, but some continued to wear the basic BOAC livery with British Airways titles for some time afterwards. The last BOAC tail fin disappeared in February 1977, when Boeing 747-136 G-AWNC was stripped and resprayed in the full British Airways colours.

Appendix 1

An Extract from the
British Overseas Airways Act 1939

An Act to provide for the establishment of a corporation to be known as the British Overseas Airways Corporation; to facilitate the acquisition by that Corporation of certain air transport undertakings; to make further and better provision for the operation of air transport services, and for purposes connected with the matters aforesaid. (4 August 1939.)

Constitution and Functions of the British Overseas Airways Corporation.

Section 1

1 So soon as may be after the passing of this Act, there shall be established for the purposes thereof a corporation to be known as the British Overseas Airways Corporation (hereafter in this Act referred to as the Corporation).

2 The Corporation shall consist of a chairman, deputy chairman and such number of other members, not being less than nine nor more than fifteen, as the Secretary of State may from time to time think fit: Provided that the Corporation shall be deemed to have been established when the chairman, deputy-chairman and five other members have been appointed, and the proceedings of the Corporation shall not be affected by any vacancy among the members thereof or by any defect in the appointment of a member.

3 The members of the Corporation shall be appointed by the Secretary of State, who shall also appoint two of the members to be chairman and deputy chairman respectively.

4 The Corporation may appoint a member, not being either the chairman or deputy chairman, to be chief executive member of the Corporation.

5 The Corporation shall pay to each member thereof, in respect of his office as such, such remuneration as may be determined by the Secretary of State with the approval of the Treasury, and shall pay to the chairman and deputy-chairman thereof, in respect of his office as such, such remuneration (in addition to any remuneration to which he may be entitled in respect of his office as a member) as may be so determined.

6   The Corporation may pay to the chief executive member thereof, in respect of his office as such, such remuneration (in addition to any remuneration to which he may be entitled in respect of his office as a member) as the Corporation may determine.

7   The supplementary provisions contained in the First Schedule to this Act shall have effect in relation to the Corporation.

Section 2

1   It shall be the duty of the Corporation, subject as hereinafter provided, to secure the fullest development, consistent with economy, of efficient overseas air transport services to be operated by the Corporation and to secure that such services are operated at reasonable charges.

2   The Corporation shall have power, subject as hereinafter provided, either in connection with the discharge of their duty under the preceding subsection or as an independent activity

(a)   to operate internal air transport services;

(b)   to undertake flights on charter terms;

(c)   to undertake flights for the purposes of aerial survey;

(d)   to make arrangements for the instruction and training in matters connected with aerial navigation of persons employed, or desirous of being employed, whether as pilots or in any other capacity, either by the Corporation or by other persons; and

(e)   to carry out repairs to aircraft.

3   The Corporation shall have power, subject as hereinafter provided, to do anything which is calculated to facilitate the discharge of the functions conferred on them by the preceding provisions of this section or is incidental or conducive thereto, including in particular, but without prejudice to the generality of this provision, power

(a)   to acquire aircraft, parts of aircraft and aircraft equipment and accessories;

(b)   to acquire or construct aerodromes, buildings and repair shops;

(c)   to acquire lights, beacons, wireless installations and other plant and equipment;

(d)   to manufacture parts of air-frames and of aero-engines and aircraft equipment and accessories;

(e)   to sell, let, or otherwise dispose of any property belonging to them and not in their opinion required for the proper discharge of their functions;

(f)   to enter into any arrangement for establishing or maintaining air transport services to be operated, in collaboration with the Corporation or otherwise, by other persons, or any arrangement for the pooling of receipts or profits with other persons operating air transport services;

(g)   to act as agents for any other undertaking engaged in the provision of air transport services, or in other activities of a kind which the Corporation have power to carry on;

(h)   to provide accommodation, in hotels or otherwise, for passengers, and facilities for the transport of passengers to or from aerodromes and for the collection, delivery and storage of baggage and freight;

(i) to make, with persons carrying on a business of providing any facilities for passengers or freight in connection with air transport services, arrangements for the provision of such facilities;

(j) to acquire any undertaking engaged in the provision of air transport services or in other activities of a kind which the Corporation have power to carry on, or to acquire, hold or have any shares or stock of, or any financial interest in, any such undertaking;

(k) to lend money to, or enter into guarantees on behalf of, any such undertaking as is mentioned in the last preceding paragraph;

(l) to carry out experimental work, and conduct, promote and encourage education and research in matters connected with any of their functions;

(m) to appoint such advisory boards or committees, and such local boards or committees, with such executive or other functions and upon such terms as to remuneration and otherwise, as they may deem expedient;

(n) to enter into agreements with the Government of any country; and

(o) to promote Bills in Parliament.

Appendix 2

BOAC/BSAAC Movements
at London Airport in 1948

(Reproduced by permission from *ABC of Airports and Airliners*, by Owen G. Thetford, published by Ian Allan Ltd 1948, reprinted 1998.)

Mondays

Arrivals	Departures
0745 BOAC York from Calcutta	0815 BOAC York to Nairobi
1035 BOAC York from Accra	1000 BOAC Dakota to Cairo
1535 BSAAC York from Buenos Aires	1025 BSAAC York to Buenos Aires
1700 BOAC Dakota from Cairo	1345 BOAC York to Accra
	1900 BOAC Constellation to New York

Tuesdays

Arrivals	Departures
1035 BOAC York from Accra	0815 BOAC York to Nairobi
1445 BOAC Liberator from Montreal	0830 BOAC York to Tanganyika
1515 BOAC Constellation from New York	1000 BOAC Dakota to Cairo
1700 BOAC Dakota from Cairo	1255 BSAAC Lancastrian to Havana
1900 BSAAC Lancastrian from Santiago, Chile	1345 BOAC York to Accra
1925 BOAC York from Tanganyika	1445 BOAC York to Delhi
2015 BOAC Lancastrian Freighter from Johannesburg	1900 BOAC Constellation to New York
	2200 BOAC Constellation to Montreal

Wednesdays

Arrivals	Departures
0745 BOAC York from Calcutta	1000 BOAC Dakota to Cairo
1700 BOAC Dakota from Cairo	1025 BSAAC York to Buenos Aires
1925 BOAC York from Nairobi	1345 BOAC York to Accra
	1445 BOAC York to Calcutta
	1700 BOAC Liberator to Montreal
	1900 BOAC Constellation to New York

Thursdays

Arrivals	Departures
1035 BOAC York from Accra	0830 BOAC York to Tanganyika
1445 BOAC Liberator from Montreal	1000 BOAC Dakota to Cairo
1535 BSAAC York from Buenos Aires	1025 BSAAC Lancastrian to Nassau
1700 BOAC Dakota from Cairo	2200 BOAC Constellation to Montreal
1830 BOAC Constellation from Montreal	

Fridays

Arrivals	Departures
0745 BOAC York from Calcutta	1000 BOAC Dakota to Cairo
1035 BOAC York from Accra	1025 BSAAC York to Buenos Aires
1445 BOAC Liberator from Montreal	1045 BOAC Dakota to Cairo
1515 BOAC Constellation from New York	1345 BOAC York to Accra
1700 BOAC Dakota from Cairo	1445 BOAC York to Calcutta
1925 BOAC York from Nairobi	1900 BOAC Constellation to New York

Saturdays

Arrivals	Departures
0730 BOAC Lancastrian Freighter from Sydney	0815 BOAC York to Nairobi
0730 BOAC York from Colombo	1000 BOAC Dakota to Cairo
0745 BOAC York from Delhi	1025 BSAAC Lancastrian to Santiago, Chile
1035 BOAC York from Accra	1345 BOAC York to Accra
1445 BOAC Constellation from New York	1700 BOAC Liberator to Montreal
1535 BSAAC York from Buenos Aires	1715 BOAC York to Colombo
1635 BOAC Dakota from Tehran	1900 BOAC Constellation to New York
1700 BOAC Dakota from Cairo	2200 BOAC Constellation to Montreal
1830 BOAC Constellation from Montreal	
1925 BOAC York from Nairobi	
2100 BSAAC Lancastrian from Havana	

Sundays

Arrivals	Departures
0730 BOAC York from Colombo	0920 BOAC Dakota to Teheran
1535 BSAAC York from Rio De Janeiro	1000 BOAC Dakota to Cairo
1730 BOAC Dakota from Cairo	1445 BOAC York to Calcutta
1900 BSAAC Lancastrian from Nassau	1700 BOAC Lancastrian Freighter to Johannesburg
1925 BOAC York from Tanganyika	1900 BOAC Constellation to New York
	1945 BOAC Lancastrian Freighter to Sydney

Appendix 3

The Development of BOAC
Services Worldwide, 1949–1954

This page and following two pages:

BOAC and Associate Companies route map 31 March 1949

BOAC and subsidiary companies route map 31 March 1952

BOAC and Associate Companies route map May 1954

(All courtesy British Airways Archives.)

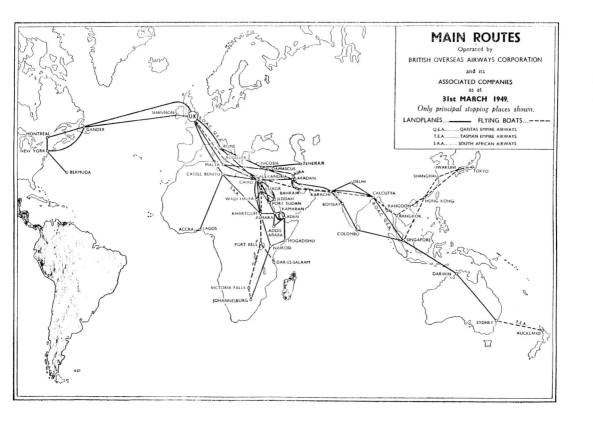

MAP OF WORLD ROUTES

as at 31st. March 1952.

IN ASSOCIATION WITH QANTAS EMPIRE AIRWAYS LTD · SOUTH AFRICAN AIRWAYS · TASMAN EMPIRE AIRWAYS LTD

BRITISH COMMONWEALTH PACIFIC AIRLINES LTD & WHOLLY OWNED SUBSIDIARIES BRITISH WEST INDIAN AIRWAYS LTD · BAHAMAS AIRWAYS LTD & ADEN AIRWAYS LTD

MAIN ROUTES ———○———   SUBSIDIARY ROUTES ———

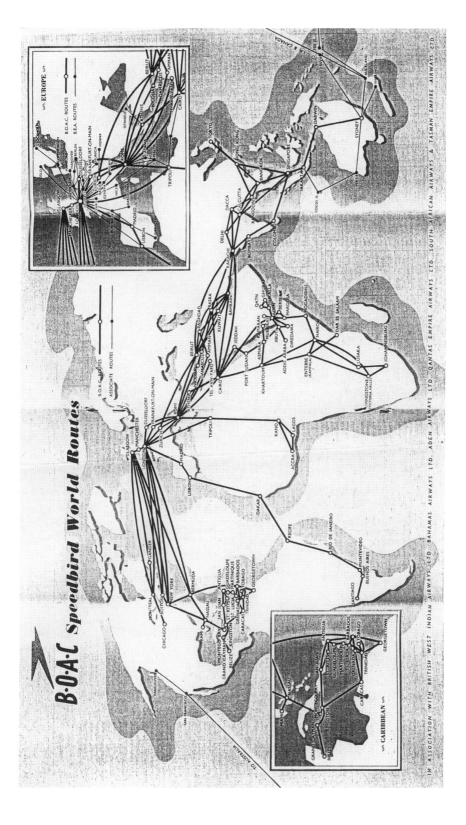

B·O·A·C Speedbird World Routes

EUROPE

B.O.A.C. ROUTES
B.E.A. ROUTES

B.O.A.C. ROUTES
ASSOCIATE ROUTES

CARIBBEAN

IN ASSOCIATION WITH BRITISH WEST INDIAN AIRWAYS LTD. BAHAMAS AIRWAYS LTD. ADEN AIRWAYS LTD. QANTAS EMPIRE AIRWAYS LTD. SOUTH AFRICAN AIRWAYS & TASMAN EMPIRE AIRWAYS LTD.

Appendix 4

Seating Layouts Applicable to Various BOAC Aircraft Types

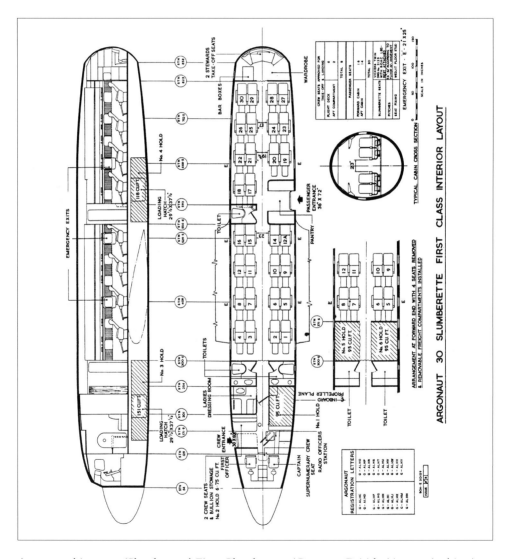

Argonaut thirty-seat 'Slumberette' First-Class layout. (Courtesy British Airways Archives)

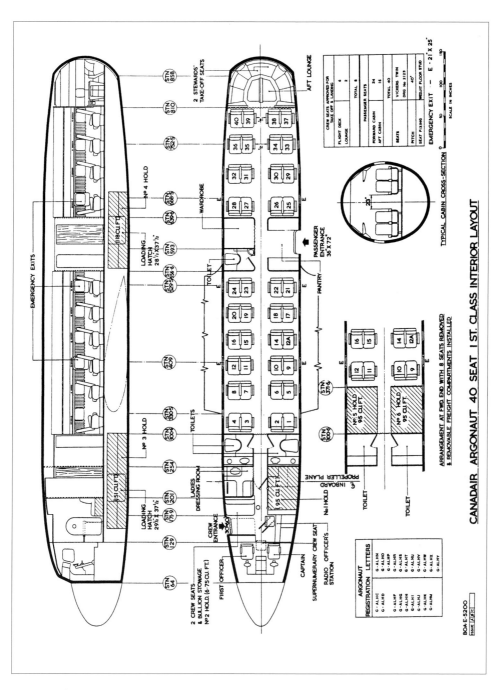

Argonaut forty-seat First-Class layout. (Courtesy British Airways Archives)

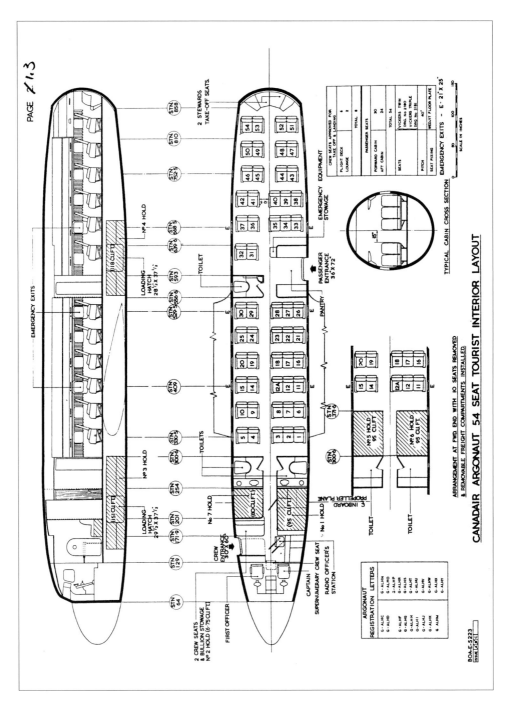

CANADAIR ARGONAUT 54 SEAT TOURIST INTERIOR LAYOUT

Argonaut fifty-four-seat Tourist-Class layout. (Courtesy British Airways Archives)

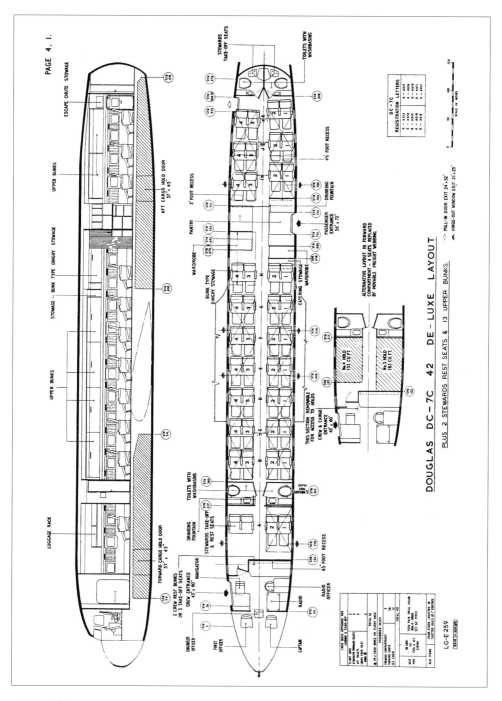

DC-7C 42-seat De Luxe Layout. (Courtesy British Airways Archives)

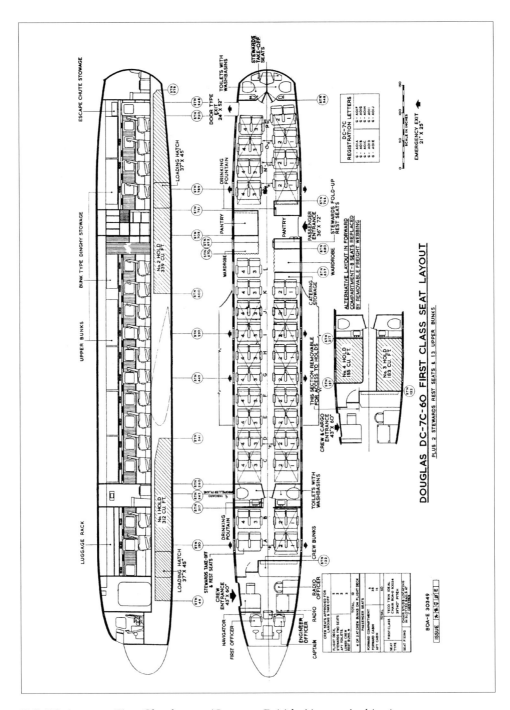

DC-7C sixty-seat First-Class layout. (Courtesy British Airways Archives)

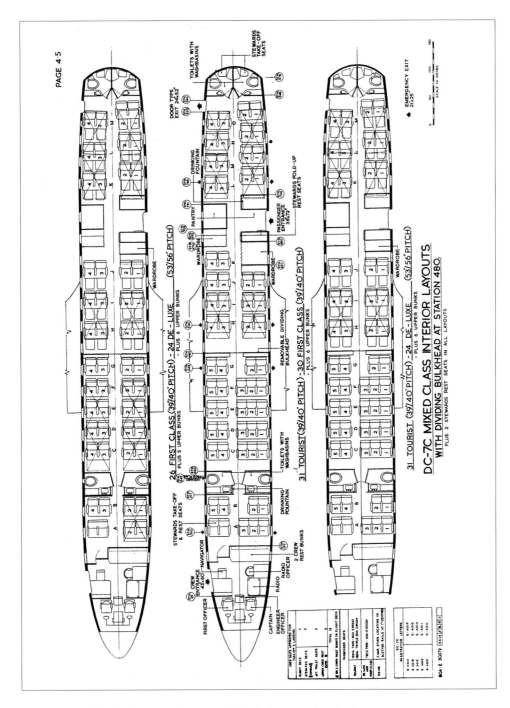

DC-7C Mixed Class layouts. (Courtesy British Airways Archives)

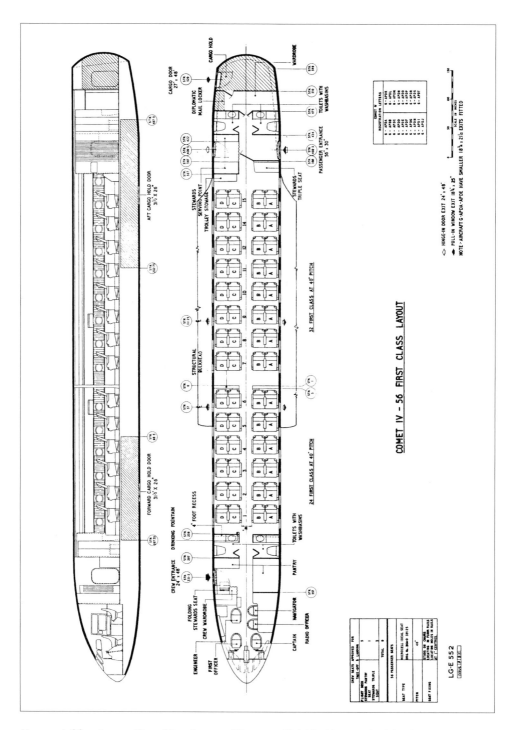

Comet 4 fifty-six-seat First-Class layout. (Courtesy British Airways Archives)

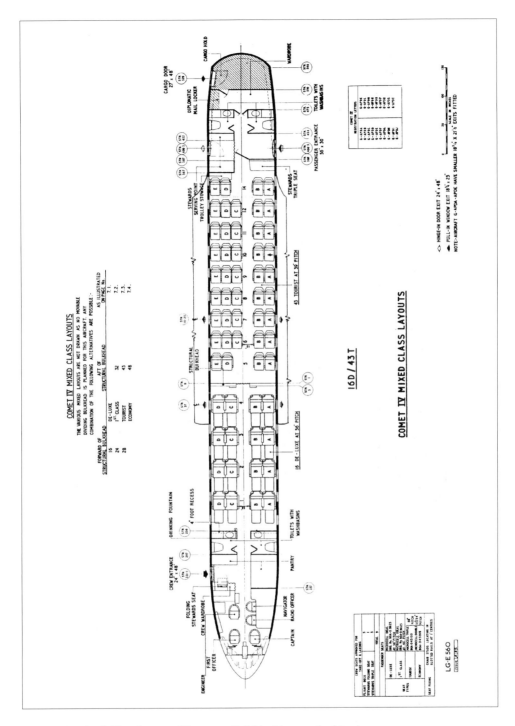

Comet 4 Mixed Class layout. (Courtesy British Airways Archives)

Appendix 5

A Miscellany of Advertisements and Promotional Literature

NOW *double door*

DC7 Freighters speed your cargo across the Atlantic

14 tons of cargo. Big bulky cargo. Loaded into the massive hold of the DC7 Freighter.

Convenient, late-night departures from London, Manchester, Glasgow and New York.

These new regular all-cargo services augment the

cargo capacity on B.O.A.C's many passenger flights between

Europe, Canada and the United States.

More space-more often-for more bulky goods

ARMS

Azure a lion's face winged the wings enfiled with
an astral crown or.

CREST

On a wreath of the colours upon a mount vert
a winged lion passant or collared of the first the
tips of the wings enveloped in clouds proper.

SUPPORTERS

On the dexter side a winged lion and on the
sinister side a winged sea-lion both or and each
gorged with a collar vert.

BRITISH OVERSEAS
AIRWAYS CORPORATION

GREAT BRITAIN · U.S.A. · CANADA · MIDDLE EAST · WEST AFRICA · EAST AFRICA · SOUTH AFRICA (with S.A.A.)
PAKISTAN · INDIA · CEYLON · AUSTRALIA (with Q.E.A.) · NEW ZEALAND (with T.E.A.L.) · FAR EAST · JAPAN

48/2027/55   International Who's Who   1949   8¼ x 5½   Final Proof 20/8/48   EE/654   8L884   Printed in Great Britain

Experienced travellers fly B.O.A.C. every time

WHY? Because they've learned that only B.O.A.C. can offer them *everything* that's required for the perfect journey. They know they'll travel in the world's finest, fastest airliners, relax in wonderful comfort, enjoy magnificent food. And they know they'll receive friendly, personal attention, making them feel at home though thousands of miles away. Fly B.O.A.C. yourself — to any one of 51 countries — and see how B.O.A.C. takes good care of *you*.

World leader in air travel

B·O·A·C

takes good care of you

BRITISH OVERSEAS AIRWAYS CORPORATION WITH S.A.A., C.A.A., QANTAS AND TEAL

No. 128]   FEBRUARY 15th to MARCH 14th 1952   [Price 5/- net

OFFICIAL   EVERY MONTH

BY APPOINTMENT
PUBLISHERS OF BRADSHAW'S GUIDES
TO HIS MAJESTY THE KING
HENRY BLACKLOCK & CO LTD., PROPRIETORS & PUBLISHERS OF

BRADSHAW'S
INTERNATIONAL
AIR GUIDE

BRADSHAW HOUSE, SURREY STREET, LONDON, W.C.2   CONTENTS, see page 3

B.O.A.C. flies to 51 countries

on all 6 continents

EUROPE · ASIA · AFRICA · AUSTRALIA
N. AMERICA · S. AMERICA

Planning to travel this year? Then fly by B.O.A.C. and give yourself *extra* time for more business or a longer holiday. By B.O.A.C. most places are only a matter of hours away. Four-engined, fully-pressurized airliners speed you there swiftly, smoothly—you arrive, rested and refreshed! First Class or "low budget" Tourist Class services. Complimentary meals. No tips or extras.

FLY BY **B·O·A·C**

Consult your local B.O.A.C. Travel Agent or office

B·O·A·C
TO ALL
SIX CONTINENTS

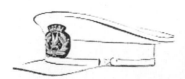

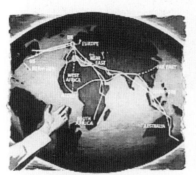

B·O·A·C

BALTIMORE - BERMUDA

NOVEMBER, 1946

...and Across the World

SPEEDBIRD SERVICE... Over the Atlantic...

BRITISH OVERSEAS AIRWAYS CORPORATION

B·O·A·C
to all six
continents

FLY BRITISH BY **B·O·A·C**

BRITISH OVERSEAS AIRWAYS CORPORATION, AIRWAYS TERMINAL
BUCKINGHAM PALACE ROAD, LONDON, S.W.1 TEL: VICTORIA 2323

B·S·A·A

SCHEDULES

SOUTH AMERICAN
(EAST AND WEST COAST)

A N D

C A R I B B E A N

S E R V I C E S

VALID

FROM APRIL, 1948

THIS TIME TABLE IS SUBJECT TO
ALTERATION WITHOUT NOTICE

BRITISH SOUTH AMERICAN AIRWAYS

Appendix 6

BOAC Fleet List

Author's Note

This list is in alphabetical order by manufacturer. It is intended to be a record of the aircraft operated by BOAC throughout its history. Where possible, constructors' numbers, delivery dates etc. are included, but I do not claim to be an expert on individual airframe histories, and there are gaps. Help from readers in filling these in is always welcome.

Abbreviations

BUA	British United Airways
c/n	constructors/construction number
Cnvtd	Converted
Dbr	Damaged beyond repair.
EAAC	East African Airways Corporation.
LAC	Lancashire Aircraft Corporation
MCA	Ministry of Civil Aviation
MoS	Ministry of Supply
MOD (PE)	Ministry of Defence (Procurement Executive)
RAAF	Royal Australian Air Force.
Regd	Date of civil registration (used sometimes in lieu of delivery date)
TEAL	Tasman Empire Airways Ltd
Wfu	Withdrawn from use
w/o	written off

Airspeed AS 10 Oxford

G-AIAV ex NM536 RAF. Used for crew training in 1947
G-AIAY ex DF521 RAF. Used for crew training in 1947
Plus the following RAF examples used by BOAC: P1895,
P8996, R6263, R6070, T1379, W6626, AP474,
AS964, BF988, BG543, ED141, HM832, HM914,
LB523, PG933, PG950, PH239.

Armstrong Whitworth AW 27 Ensign

G-ADSR c/n 1156 'Ensign'. Scrapped Almaza 3.1.45
G-ADSS c/n 1157 'Egeria'. Wfu 13.4.47 Hamble
G-ADST c/n 1158 'Elsinore'. Wfu 19.2.46 Hamble
G-ADSU c/n 1159 'Euterpe'. Wfu 15.2.46 Almaza
G-ADSV c/n 1160 'Explorer'. Scrapped 23.3.47 Hamble
G-ADSW c/n 1161 'Eddystone'. Wfu 21.4.47
G-ADSX c/n 1162 'Ettrick'. Abandoned 1.6.40 Paris
G-ADSY c/n 1163 'Empyrean'. Wfu 14.1.46 Hamble
G-ADSZ c/n 1164 'Elysian'. w/o in air raid 23.5.40
Merville, France
G-ADTA c/n 1165 'Euryalus'. Scrapped Lympne 14.11.41
after being shot up by German fighters 23.5.40
G-ADTB c/n 1166 'Echo'. Wfu 28.4.46
G-ADTC c/n 1167 'Endymion'. w/o in air raid
Whitchurch 24.11.40
All above examples taken over from Imperial Airways
1.4.40
G-AFZU c/n 1821 Ensign Mk II. 'Everest'. Delivered
24.6.41. Scrapped Hamble 16.4.47
G-AFZV c/n 1822 Ensign Mk II. 'Enterprise'. Delivered
28.10.41.Forced down in desert during delivery
flight to Middle East. Abandoned, but seized by
French and repaired.

Armstrong Whitworth AW 38 Whitley V

G-AGCF c/n 2694. ex RAF BD360.Regd 16.4.42.
Returned to RAF 26.8.43
G-AGCG c/n 2695.ex RAF BD361. Regd 16.4.42.
Returned to RAF 22.7.43
G-AGCH c/n 2696. ex RAF BD362. Regd 16.4.42.
Returned to RAF 5.3.43
G-AGCI c/n 2716. ex RAF BD382. Regd 16.4.42.
Ditched Gibraltar 29.9.42
G-AGCJ c/n 2717. ex RAF BD383. Regd 16.4.42.
Returned to RAF 17.10.43
G-AGCK c/n 2717.ex RAF BD384. Regd 16.4.42.
Returned to RAF 16.10.43
G-AGDU c/n S4/VA/1126. ex RAF Z9208. Regd 17.3.42.
Returned to RAF 15.4.42. Returned to BOAC
27.6.42. Dbr 12.8.42.
G-AGDV c/n S4/VA/1134. ex RAF Z9216. Regd 17.3.42.
Returned to RAF 15.4.42
G-AGDW c/n S4/VA/886. ex RAF Z6660. Regd 17.3.42.
Returned to RAF 15.4.42
G-AGDX c/n 2719. ex RAF BD385. Regd 16.4.42.
Returned to RAF 22.7.43
G-AGDY c/n 2720. ex RAF BD386. Regd 16.4.42.
Returned to RAF 20.4.43
G-AGDZ c/n 2721. ex RAF BD387. Regd 16.4.42.
Returned to RAF 27.1.43

G-AGEA c/n 2722. ex RAF BD388. Regd 16.4.42.
Returned to RAF 27.1.43
G-AGEB c/n 2723. ex RAF BD389. Regd 16.4.42.
Returned to RAF 27.1.43
G-AGEC c/n 2724. ex RAF BD390. Regd 16.4.42.
Returned to RAF 22.7.43

ARMSTRONG WHITWORTH AW 41 ALBERMARLE 1
P1454. Loaned by RAF for evaluation 11.42-3.43.

Avro 652A Anson

G-AGGJ to G-AGGP inclusive, and G-AGGR to G-AGHD
inclusive
Regd to BOAC solely for ferry flights UK–Takoradi–Cairo
5.43

Avro 683 Lancaster B. Mk 1

G-AGJI ex RAF DV379.Delivered 9.11.43 on loan to
BOAC Development Flight, Hurn Returned to RAF
24.12.46
G-AGUM ex RAF PP751. Regd 27.10.45. Loaned to
BSAA 25.1.46 and re-acquired on take-over 30.7.49.
To R.J. Coley for scrap 12.49
G-AGUN/G-AHVN ex RAF PP744. Regd as G-AGUN to
Ministry of Supply 27.10.45. Loaned to BSAA
7.2.46. Returned to RAF 17.5.46. Loaned to BOAC
Development Flight as PP744 2.7.46. Regd to BOAC
as G-AHVN 17.7.46. Transferred to Ministry of
Supply 17.8.48 but remained on loan to BOAC until
23.2.49
PP741/G-AJWM Leased to BOAC as PP741 6.5.47-
28.5.47. Regd. to BEA as G-AJWM 4.6.47

Avro 691 Lancastrian C. Mk 1

VB873/G-AGLF c/n 1172. Prototype Lancastrian 1.
Handed over to BOAC Development Flight at Hurn
as VB873 18.2.45. Regd as G-AGLF 5.45. Sold
10.5.46
G-AGLS c/n 1173 'Nelson'. ex VD238. Delivered
10.5.45. Wfu 10.9.50
G-AGLT c/n 1174 'Newcastle'. ex VD241. Delivered
21.3.45. Sold for scrap 14.12.49
G-AGLU c/n 1175 . ex VD253. Delivered 5.4.45. Dbr
Hurn 15.8.46
G-AGLV c/n 1176. ex VF163. Delivered 19.4.45. Sold
8.4.46
G-AGLW c/n 1177. 'Northampton'. ex VF164. Delivered
27.4.45. Wfu 1.9.50
G-AGLX c/n 1178. ex VF165. Delivered 18.5.45.
Disappeared, Indian Ocean 23/24.3.46.
G-AGLY c/n 1179. 'Norfolk'. ex VF166. Delivered 8.6.45.
Scrapped 1.51
G-AGLZ c/n 1180. 'Nottingham'. ex VF167. Delivered
8.6.45. Sold 3.10.47
G-AGMA c/n 1181. 'Newport'. ex VF152. Delivered
13.6.45. Scrapped 13.1.51
G-AGMB c/n 1182 'Norwich'. ex VF153. Delivered
18.6.45. Crashed Singapore 27.8.48
G-AGMC c/n 1183 . ex VF154. Delivered 23.6.45. w/o

Sydney 2.5.46

G-AGMD c/n 1184 'Nairn'. ex VF155. Delivered 2.7.45.
Sold 16.7.47

G-AGME c/n 1185 'Newhaven'. ex VF156. Delivered
5.7.45. Scrapped Hurn 12.49

G-AGMF c/n 1186. ex VF160. Delivered 26.7.45.
Crashed nr Rouen 20.8.46

G-AGMG c/n 1187 'Nicosia'. ex VF161. Delivered
23.8.45. Scrapped Hurn 11.50

G-AGMH c/n 1188. ex VF162. Delivered 31.8.45. w/o
Mauripur, India 17.5.46

G-AGMJ c/n 1189 'Naseby'. ex VF145. Delivered
12.9.45. Scrapped 15.1.51

G-AGMK c/n 1190 'Newbury'. ex VF146. Delivered
24.9.45. Scrapped 15.1.51

G-AGML c/n 1191 'Nicobar'. ex VF147. Delivered
28.9.45. Sold 15.8.47

G-AGMM c/n 1192 'Nepal'. ex VF148. Delivered
9.10.45. w/o Castel Benito 7.11.49

G-AHCD Lancastrian C. Mk II.. c/n Set 81. Leased from
BSAA for Alitalia crew training 16.4.47-6.6.47 and
16.7.47–24.7.47.

G-AKPY Lancastrian C. Mk II.. 'Natal'. ex VL971. Regd
19.1.48. Scrapped 14.12.49

G-AKPZ Lancastrian C. Mk II. 'Nile'. ex VL972. Regd
19.1.48. Scrapped 14.12.49

G-AKRB Lancastrian C. Mk II. c/n Set 41. 'Nyanza''. ex
VM737. Regd 19.1.48. Scrapped 14.12.49.

G-AGMN to G-AGMP inclusive, and G-AGMR to G-
AGMY inclusive. Regd to BOAC 1.12.44 but not
completed.

G-AGPK to G-AGPP inclusive, and G-AGPR. Regd to
BOAC 1.8.45 but not completed

Avro 688 Tudor

G-AGRF Tudor 2. c/n 1254. Delivered to BOAC 21.1.47
for trials. Named 'Elizabeth of England', but rejected
and returned to Avro 11.4.47. Converted to Tudor
4B 48. Sold to BSAA 12.12.48. Re-acquired by
BOAC on take-over 9.49. Wfu and stored Hurn 52.
Sold to Aviation Traders Ltd 9.53

G-AGRG Tudor Freighter 2. c/n 1255. Leased from MCA
14.7.48. Subleased to BSAA 49. Re-acquired on
take-over 9.49. Sold to Aviation Traders Ltd 2.9.53

G-AGRH Tudor 2. c/n 1256. Leased from MCA 6.48.
Converted to Tudor Freighter 2. Leased to BSAA 49.
Re-acquired on take-over 9.49. Sold to Aviation
Traders Ltd 2.9.53

G-AGRJ Tudor 2. c/n 1258. Leased from MCA 5.48.
Subleased to BSAA 49. Re-acquired on take-over
9.49. Sold to Aviation Traders Ltd 14.9.53

G-AHNJ Tudor 1. c/n 1343. Acquired from BSAA on
take-over 9.49. Wfu and stored Ringway 3.50. To
MCA 12.10.51

G-AHNK Tudor 1. c/n 1344. Acquired from BSAA on
take-over 9.49. Wfu and stored Ringway 3.50. To
MCA 12.10.51

G-AHNN Tudor 1. c/n 1347. Acquired from BSAA on
take-over 9.49. Wfu and stored Ringway 3.50. To

MCA 12.10.51

G-AKBZ Tudor 5. c/n 1418. Acquired from BSAA on
take-over 9.49. Wfu and stored Woodford 49.
Broken up Stansted 7.59.

G-AKCA Tudor 5. c/n 1419. Acquired from BSAA on
take-over 9.49. Wfu and stored Ringway 3.50. To
Surrey Flying Services Ltd 5.10.51

G-AKCB Tudor 5. c/n 1420. Acquired from BSAA on
take-over 9.49. Wfu and stored Ringway 3.50. To
MCA 12.10.51

G-AKCC Tudor 5. c/n 1421. Acquired from BSAA on
take-over 9.49. Wfu and stored Ringway 3.50. To
William Dempster Ltd 5.4.50

G-AKCD Tudor 5. c/n 1422. Acquired from BSAA on
take-over 9.49. Wfu and stored Ringway 3.50. To
William Dempster Ltd 5.4.50

Avro 685 York

5958M. ex RAF MW250. Supplied to BOAC training
school at White Waltham for ground instruction
17.6.46 after being dbr Stradishall 28.5.46. Broken
up

MW106 Leased from MoS 21.4.47-14.7.47 and 21.3.49-
22.4.49 Purchased from Mos 1.51 Broken up for
spares

MW122 Leased from Mos 9.4.47-26.2.48

MW167 Leased from Mos 9.5.47-28.1.48

MW181 Leased from MoS 9.5.47-10.12.47

MW103/G-AGJA c/n 1207 'Mildenhall'. Delivered
31.2.44. Sold to BSAA 18.5.49. Re-acquired on
takeover 9.49 and renamed 'Kingston'. Sold to LAC
29.5.51

NW108/G-AGJB c/n 1208 'Marathon'. Delivered
19.4.44. Sold to Aviation Traders 5.11.53

MW113/G-AGJC c/n 1209 'Malmesbury'. Delivered
30.5.44. Sold to Skyways 22.11.57

MW121/G-AGJD c/n 1210 'Mansfield'. Delivered
31.7.44 Crashed Castel Benito 1.2.49

MW129/G-AGJE c/n 1211 'Middlesex'. Delivered
26.9.44. Sold to BSAA 6.5.49. Re-acquired on
takeover 9.49 and renamed 'Panama'.Sold to LAC
31.7.51

N.B. G-AGJA-E were operated during wartime under RAF
Transport Command control

G-AGNL c/n 1213 'Mersey'. Delivered 30.1.46. Sold to
LAC 3.6.52

G-AGNM c/n 1215 'Murchison'. Delivered 28.12.45.
Sold to Eagle Aviation 17.10.49

G-AGNN c/n 1216 'Madras'. Delivered 10.10.45. Leased
to SAA as ZS-BGU 19.5.47-12.9.47

Sold to BSAA 6.7.48. Re-acquired on takeover 9.49.
Renamed 'Atlantic Trader'. Sold to Skyways 4.4.57

G-AGNO c/n 1217 'Manton'. Delivered 31.8.45. Sold to
LAC 5.6.51

G-AGNP c/n 1218 'Manchester'. Delivered 14.9.45.
Leased to SAA as ZS-BRA 10.5.47-19.9.47. Sold to
Air Freight 20.8.52

G-AGNR c/n 1219 'Moira'. Delivered 22.9.45. Leased to
SAA as ZS-ATP 4.47-5.47. Crashed Nr Basra 16.7.47

G-AGNS c/n 1220 'Melville'. Delivered 20.10.45. Leased
to SAA as ZS-BTT 16.4.47-17.9.47 Sold to BSAA
30.5.49. Re-acquired on takeover 9.49.Renamed
'Pacific Trader'. Dbr Idris, Libya 22.4.56

G-AGNT c/n 1221 'Mandalay'. Delivered 31.10.45.
Leased to SAA as ZS-ATU 21.6.47-3.10.47. Sold to
Air Freight Ltd 20.8.52

G-AGNU c/n 1222 'Montgomery'. Delivered 14.12.45.
Leased to SAA as ZS-ATR 10.1.46-24.9.47. Sold to
BSAA 26.7.49. Re-acquired on takeover 9.49. Sold
to Air Charter 29.8.52

G-AGNV c/n 1223 'Morville' Delivered 9.12.45.
Renamed 'Middlesex'. Sold to Skyways 30 3.55

G-AGNW c/n 1224 'Morecambe'. Delivered 24.1.46.
Leased to SAA as ZS-ATS 27.3.46–10.9.47. Renamed
'Caribbean Trader'. Sold to LAC 5.6.51

G-AGNX c/n 1225 'Moray'. Delivered 6.2.46. Sold to
BSAA 26.7.49. Re-acquired on takeover 9.49. Sold
to LAC 29.5.51

G-AGNY c/n 1226 'Melrose'. Delivered 23.2.46. Sold to
Eagle Aviation 17.10.49

G-AGNZ c/n 1227 'Monmouth'. Delivered 7.6.46.
Leased to SAA as ZS-BRB 5.47-6.47. Sold to Eagle
Aviation 12.10.49

G-AGOA c/n 1228 'Montrose'. Delivered 28.8.46. Sold
to LAC 5.6.51

G-AGOB c/n 1229 'Milford'. Delivered 22.6.46. Sold to
LAC 5.6.51

G-AGOC c/n 1230 'Malta'. Delivered 19.4.46. Sold to
BSAA 9.5.49. Re-acquired on takeover 9.49. Wfu
and broken up Hurn 11.49

G-AGOD c/n 1231 'Midlothian'. Delivered 2.7.46. Sold
to LAC 5.8.52

G-AGOE c/n 1232 'Medway'. Delivered 17.7.46. Sold to
LAC 5.8.52

G-AGOF c/n 1233 'Macduff'. Delivered 16.9.46. Leased
to SAA as ZS-ATT 4.47-9.47. Sold to LAC 5.3.52

G-AGSL c/n 1236 'Morley'. Delivered 25.10.46. Sold to
LAC 5.6.51

G-AGSM c/n 1237 'Malvern'. Delivered 8.10.46. Sold to
LAC 5.6.51

G-AGSN c/n 1238 'Marlow'. Delivered 8.11.46. Sold to
LAC 3.8.51

G-AGSO c/n 1239 'Marston'. Delivered 2.5.46. Sold to
Skyways 22.11.57

G-AGSP c/n 1240 'Marlborough'. Delivered 11.5.46.
Renamed 'Santiago'. Wfu and broken up London
Airport 5.55

G-AHEY c/n 1302. Acquired from BSAA on takeover
9.49. Sold to LAC 8.4.52

G-AHFA c/n 1304. Acquired from BSAA on takeover
9.49. Sold to LAC 11.12.51

G-AHFB c/n 1305. Acquired from BSAA on takeover
9.49. Sold to LAC 27.9.51

G-AHFC c/n 1306. Acquired from BSAA on takeover
9.49. Sold to LAC 3.4.52

G-AHFD c/n 1307. Acquired from BSAA on takeover
9.49. Sold to LAC 5.11.51

G-AHFE c/n 1308. Acquired from BSAA on takeover

9.49. Sold to LAC 7.8.51

G-AHFF c/n 1309. Acquired from BSAA on takeover
9.49. Sold to LAC 16.1.52

G-AHFG c/n 1310. Acquired from BSAA on takeover
9.49. Sold to LAC 14.9.51

G-AHFH c/n 1311. Acquired from BSAA on takeover
9.49. Sold to LAC 22.11.51

Beechcraft AT-7

42-2509 Loaned by US Navy for training

Boeing 314A

G-AGBZ c/n 2081 'Bristol'. Delivered 5.41. Returned to
USA.

G-AGCA c/n 2082 'Berwick'. Delivered 41. Returned to
USA.

G-AGCB c/n 2083 'Bangor'. Delivered 41. Returned to
USA.

Boeing 377 Stratocruiser

G-AKGH c/n 15974 'Caledonia'. Delivered 16.11.49.
Sold to Transocean Air Lines 4.8.58

G-AKGI c/n 15975 'Caribou''. Delivered 10.1.50. Sold to
Transocean Air Lines 8.1.59

G-AKGJ c/n 15976 'Cambria'. Delivered 7.2.50. Sold to
Transocean Air Lines 21.1.59

G-AKGK c/n 15977 'Canopus'. Delivered 17.2.50. Sold
to Transocean Air Lines 12.3.59

G-AKGL c/n 15978 'Cabot'. Delivered 25.1.50. Sold to
Transocean Air Lines 12.9.58

G-AKGM c/n 15979 'Castor'. Delivered 24.3.50. Sold to
Transocean Air Lines 12.9.58

G-ALSA c/n 15943 'Cathay'. Delivered 12.10.49.
Crashed Prestwick 25.12.54

G-ALSB c/n 15944 'Champion'. Delivered 24.10.49. Sold
to Transocean Air Lines 3.2.59

G-ALSC c/n 15945 'Centaurus'. Delivered 2.12.49. Sold
to Transocean Air Lines 18.12.58

G-ALSD c/n 15946 'Cassiopeia'. Delivered 16.12.49.
Sold to Transocean Air Lines 7.9.58

G-ANTX c/n 15965 'Cleopatra'. ex United Airlines
29.12.54. Sold to Transocean Air Lines 27.7.59

G-ANTY c/n 15966 'Coriolanus'. ex United Airlines
27.10.54. Sold to Transocean Air Lines 31.7.59

G-ANTZ c/n 15967 'Cordelia'. ex United Airlines
16.12.54. Sold to Transocean Air Lines 10.5.59

G-ANUA c/n 15968 'Cameronian'. ex United Airlines
30.12.54. Sold to Transocean Air Lines 8.8.59

G-ANUB c/n 15969 'Calypso'. ex United Airlines 2.9.54.
Wfu and stored Stansted 1.60. Broken up

G-ANUC c/n 15971 'Clio'. ex United Airlines 1.12.54.
Wfu and stored Stansted 1.60. Broken up

G-ANUM c/n 15927 'Clyde'. ex Pan American Airways
26.8.54. Sold to Transocean Air Lines 7.7.58

Boeing 707

G-APFB srs 436. c/n 17703. Delivered 5.60. Leased to
Syrian Arab Airways 3.74

G-APFC srs 436. c/n 17704. Delivered 5.60. Transferred

to British Airways

G-APFD srs 436. c/n 17705. Delivered 4.60. Sold to BEA
  Airtours 2.73

G-APFE srs 436. c/n 17706. Delivered 4.60. Crashed
  5.3.66 Mount Fuji, Japan

G-APFF srs 436. c/n 17707. Delivered 5.60.
  Transferred to British Airways

G-APFG srs 436. c/n 17708. Delivered 6.60. Sold to BEA
  Airtours 3.73

G-APFH srs 436. c/n 17709. Delivered 7.60. Sold to BEA
  Airtours 1.72

G-APFI srs 436. c/n 17710. Delivered 7.60. Transferred
  to British Airways

G-APFJ srs 436. c/n 17711. Delivered 9.60. Transferred
  to British Airways

G-APFK srs 436. c/n 17712. Delivered 9.60. Sold to BEA
  Airtours 12.71

G-APFL srs 436. c/n 17713. Delivered 10.60. Sold to
  BEA Airtours 12.72

G-APFM srs 436. c/n 17714. Delivered 11.60.
  Transferred to British Airways

G-APFN srs 436. c/n 17715. Delivered 11.60. Transferred
  to British Airways

G-APFO srs 436. c/n 17716. Delivered 12.60. Sold to
  BEA Airtours 11.72

G-APFP srs 436. c/n 17717. Delivered 12.60. Transferred
  to British Airways

G-ARRA srs 436. c/n 18411. Delivered 2.62. Transferred
  to British Airways

G-ARRB srs 436. c/n 18412. Delivered 2.63. Transferred
  to British Airways

G-ARRC srs 436. c/n 18413. Delivered 3.63. Transferred
  to British Airways

G-ARWD srs 465. c/n 18372. Delivered 9.62. Sold to
  BEA Airtours 1.73

G-ARWE srs 465. c/n 18373. Delivered 62. Burnt out
  Heathrow 8.4.68

G-ASZF srs 379C. c/n 18924. Delivered 12.65.
  Transferred to British Airways

G-ASZG srs 336C. c/n 18925. Delivered 12.65.
  Transferred to British Airways

G-ATZD srs 365C. c/n 19590. Delivered 5.69.
  Transferred to British Airways

G-ATWV srs 336C. c/n 19498. Delivered 11.67.
  Transferred to British Airways

G-AVPB srs 336C. c/n 19843. Delivered 8.68.
  Transferred to British Airways

G-AWHU srs 379C. c/n 19821. Delivered 6.68.
  Transferred to British Airways

G-AXGW srs 336C. c/n 20374. Delivered 3.70.
  Transferred to British Airways

G-AXGX srs 336C. c/n 20375. Delivered 3.70.
  Transferred to British Airways

G-AXXY srs 336C. c/n 20456. Delivered 2.71.
  Transferred to British Airways

G-AXXZ srs 336C. c/n 20457. Delivered 4.71.
  Transferred to British Airways

G-AYLT srs 336C. c/n 20517. Delivered 5.71. Transferred
  to British Airways

Boeing 747-136

G-AWNA c/n 19761. Delivered 22.4.70

G-AWNB c/n 19762. Delivered 22.5.70

G-AWNC c/n 19763. Delivered 29.6.70

G-AWND c/n 19764. Delivered 28.2.71

G-AWNE c/n 19765. 'City of Southampton'. Delivered
  5.3.71

G-AWNF c/n 19766. Delivered 14.3.71

G-AWNG c/n 20269. Delivered 8.9.71

G-AWNH c/n 20270. Delivered 23.11.71

G-AWNI c/n 20271. Delivered 7.1.72

G-AWNJ c/n 20272. Delivered 21.3.72

G-AWNK c/n 20273. Delivered 24.3.72

G-AWNL c/n 20284. Delivered 19.4.72

G-AWNM c/n 20708. Delivered 3.5.73

G-AWNN c/n 20809. Delivered 7.11.73

G-AWNO c/n 20810. Delivered 7.12.73

All above examples transferred to British Airways.

Bristol Britannia srs 102

G-ANBA c/n 12902. Delivered 22.8.57. Lsd to Nigerian
  Airways 13.4.59-1960. Lsd to Malayan Airways
  19.12.61-17.1.62. Wfu and stored Cambridge 11.62

G-ANBB c/n 12903. Delivered 18.6.57. Lsd to Nigerian
  Airways 6.59-1960. Lsd to Cathay Pacific 1961-1.63.
  Wfu and stored Cambridge 1.63

G-ANBC c/n 12904. Delivered 30.12.55. Lsd to Ghana
  Airways during 1960. Dbr Khartoum 11.11.60

G-ANBD c/n 12905. Delivered 30.12.55. Wfu and stored
  Cambridge 1.63

G-ANBE c/n 12906. Delivered 2.3.56. Lsd to Nigerian
  Airways 4.58-1959. Lsd to Ghana Airways 60. Wfu
  and stored Cambridge 4.63

G-ANBF c/n 12907. Delivered 14.3.56. Lsd to Malayan
  Airways 10.61-14.11.61. Wfu and stored Cambridge
  1.63

G-ANBG c/n 12908. Delivered 8.5.56. Re-registered as
  G-APLL 19.3.58. Lsd to Nigerian Airways 59-60. Lsd
  to Malayan Airways 10.5.62-6.6.62 and 3.7.62-
  1.8.62. Wfu and stored Cambridge 1.63

G-ANBH c/n 12909. Delivered 24.7.57. Wfu and stored
  Cambridge 11.62

G-ANBI c/n 12910. Delivered 29.6.56. Lsd to Ghana
  Airways 60. Lsd to Malayan Airways 12.4.62-9.5.62.
  Wfu and stored Cambridge 1.63

G-ANBJ c/n 12911. Delivered 22.11.56. Lsd to Malayan
  Airways 8.2.62-7.3.62 and 6.62-4.7.62. Wfu and
  stored Cambridge 11.62

G-ANBK c/n 12912. Delivered 12.2.57. Lsd to Nigerian
  Airways 61-62. Wfu and stored Cambridge 12.62

G-ANBL c/n 12913. Delivered 2.3.57. Lsd to Cathay
  Pacific 12.12.60-31.1.61. Wfu and stored
  Cambridge 11.62

G-ANBM c/n 12914. Delivered 11.3.57. Lsd to Nigerian
  Airways 10.59-1960. Lsd to Malayan Airways
  15.11.61-18.12.61 and 18.1.62-7.2.62 and 25.9.62-
  24.10.62.Wfu and stored Cambridge 12.62

G-ANBN c/n 12915. Delivered 4.5.57. Lsd to Nigerian
  Airways 1.10.60-1961. Leased to Malayan Airways

8.3.62–11.4.62 and 28.8.62–26.9.62 and
23.10.62–15.1.63. Wfu and stored Cambridge 1.63

G-ANBO c/n 12916. Delivered 31.5.57. Lsd to Cathay
Pacific 24.1.61–1961. Leased to Malayan Airways
2.9.61–10.61 and 31.7.62–29.8.62. Wfu and stored
Cambridge 12.62

Bristol Britannia srs 312

G-AOVA c/n 13207. Lsd from Bristol Aircraft Ltd.
15.7.57–30.7.57

G-AOVB c/n 13230. Delivered 10.9.57. Lsd to British
Eagle 15.10.63–6.11.68. Sold to Aerotransportes
Entres Rios 3.10.69

G-AOVC c/n 13231. Delivered 15.11.57. Lsd to British
Eagle 15.5.64–6.11.68. Lsd to Donaldson
International 20.5.69. Wfu 16.11.70

G-AOVD c/n 13235. Delivered 6.12.57. Crashed Sopley
Farm 24.12.58

G-AOVE c/n 13236. Delivered 21.12.57. Lsd to BUA
27.9.61–21.5.64. Lsd to British Eagle 6.6.64. Sold to
British Eagle 30.11.66

G-AOVF c/n 13237. Delivered 2.1.58. Lsd to British
Eagle 4.3.64–6.11.68. Sold to Monarch Airlines
22.1.70

G-AOVG c/n 13238. Delivered 19.3.58. Lsd to BEA
4.61–5.61. Lsd to British Eagle 3.4.65–6.11.68. Sold
to Monarch Airlines 10.10.69

G-AOVH c/n 12925. Delivered 11.2.58. Lsd to British
Eagle 6.11.64–2.65. Lsd to Caledonian Airways
7.3.65–1.4.68. Sold to Monarch Airlines 1.4.68

G-AOVI c/n 12926. Delivered 26.2.58. Lsd to BUA
21.9.61–1.7.64. Lsd to Caledonian Airways
18.12.64. Sold to Caledonian Airways 4.65

G-AOVJ c/n 13418. Delivered 23.4.58. Lsd to BWIA
11.60–61. Lsd to Caledonian Airways 28.4.65. Sold
to Caledonian Airways 12.11.69

G-AOVK c/n 13419. Delivered 11.5.58. Lsd to British
Eagle 30.4.65. Sold to British Eagle 1.12.67

G-AOVL c/n 13420. Delivered 20.5.58. Lsd to British
Eagle 30.4.65. Sold to British Eagle 18.4.68

G-AOVM c/n 13421. Delivered 10.6.58. Lsd to British
Eagle 29.3.64–6.11.68. Sold to Air Spain 6.3.69

G-AOVN c/n 13422. Delivered 4.7.58. Lsd to British
Eagle 2.6.64–6.11.68. Sold to Monarch Airlines
6.3.69

G-AOVO c/n 13423. Delivered 4.9.58. Lsd to British
Eagle 17.1.64. Crashed nr Innsbruck while on lease
29.2.64.

G-AOVP c/n 13424. Delivered 15.9.58. Lsd to BEA 4.61–
5.61. Lsd to Lloyd International Airways 15.4.65.
Sold to International Aviation Services (UK) 10.7.73

G-AOVR c/n 13429. Delivered 3.10.58. Lsd to British
Eagle 22.2.63. Sold to British Eagle 17.10.66

G-AOVS c/n 13430. Delivered 29.10.58. Lsd to Lloyd
International Airways 4.7.65. Sold to Lloyd
International Airways 1.69

G-AOVT c/n 13427. Delivered 1.1.59. Lsd to BEA 4.61–
5.61. Lsd to British Eagle 13.9.63. Sold to Monarch
Airlines 18.8.68

CANADAIR C-4 ARGONAUT

G-ALHC c/n 145. 'Ariadne' Delivered 29.3.49. Sold to
Royal Rhodesian Air Force 14.1.60

G-ALHD c/n 146 'Ajax'. Delivered 10.5.49. Lsd to East
African Airways Corp. as VP-KOY 25.2.49. Sold to
Overseas Aviation 22.5.59

G-ALHE c/n 151 'Amazon'. Delivered 15.6.49. Renamed
'Argo'. Crashed Kano 24.6.56

G-ALHF c/n 152 'Atlas'. Delivered 25.6.49. Sold to East
African Airways Corp. 25.8.57

G-ALHG c/n 153 'Aurora'. Delivered 5.7.49. Sold to
Overseas Aviation 14.4.60

G-ALHH c/n 154 'Attica'. Delivered 15.7.49. Sold to
Royal Rhodesian Air Force 23.2.60

G-ALHI c/n 155 'Antares'. Delivered 21.7.49. Sold to
Royal Rhodesian Air Force 28.3.60

G-ALHJ c/n 156 'Arcturus'. Delivered 27.7.49. Lsd to East
African Airways Corp as VP-KOT 2.58–61. Wfu and
used for apprentice training at Heathrow 61–66. To
Airport Fire Service at Heathrow 70–82. Broken up

G-ALHK c/n 157 'Atalanta'. Delivered 3.8.49. Sold to
Overseas Aviation 23.3.59

G-ALHL c/n 158 'Altair'. Delivered 9.8.49. Crashed Idris
21.9.55

G-ALHM c/n 159 'Antaeus'. Delivered 15.8.49. Sold to
East African Airways Corp 30.8.57

G-ALHN c/n 160 'Argosy'. Delivered 19.8.49. Sold to
Overseas Aviation 1.2.60

G-ALHO c/n 161 'Althea'. Delivered 29.8.49. Sold to
East African Airways Corp 29.3.57

G-ALHP c/n 162 'Aethra'. Delivered 2.9.49. Sold to
Overseas Aviation 12.6.59

G-ALHR c/n 163 'Antiope'. Delivered 14.9.49. Sold to
Aden Airways 17.2.60

G-ALHS c/n 164 'Astra'. Delivered 20.9.49. Sold to
Overseas Aviation 17.2.60

G-ALHT c/n 165 'Athena'. Delivered 28.9.49. Sold to
Overseas Aviation 31.10.58

G-ALHU c/n 166 'Artemis'. Delivered 24.10.49. Lsd to
Kuwait Airways 58–1.59. Sold to Overseas Aviation
30.1.59

G-ALHV c/n 167 'Adonis'. Delivered 7.10.49. Sold to
Aden Airways 6.60

G-ALHW c/n 168 'Aeolus'. Delivered 18.10.49. Sold to
Royal Rhodesian Air Force 15.12.59

G-ALHX c/n 169 'Astraea'. Delivered 27.10.49. Sold to
Aden Airways 4.60

G-ALHY c/n 170 'Arion'. Delivered 11.11.49. Sold to
Overseas Aviation 9.3.60

Consolidated OA-10A Canso

44-33965. Loaned by USAAF for training at Baltimore
5.45

Consolidated PB2Y-3B Coronado

JX470

JX471

JX472

JX486

JX490
JX494
JX495
JX496
JX498
JX501

Consolidated 28 Catalina PBY-2/5/5B

G-AGBJ c/n C-3. To RAF 1.44
G-AGDA c/n 122. Written off 23.3.43
G-AGFL c/n 808. ex FP221. Scuttled Australia 45/46
G-AGFM c/n 831. ex FP244. Scuttled Australia 45/46
G-AGID c/n 1109. ex JX575. Scuttled Australia 45/46
G-AGIE c/n 1111. ex JX577. Scuttled Australia 45/46
G-AGKS. ex JX287. Scuttled Australia 45/46

Consolidated 32 Liberator I and II

G-AGFZ
G-AGGA
G-AGGB
G-AGGC
G-AGGE
G-AGHB
AL504. Liberator II
AL507/G-AHYC c/n 5. Liberator II. Dbr Heathfields,
    Prestwick 13.11.48
AL512/G-AGEL. Liberator II. Crashed Gander 27.12.43
AL514/G-AGJP. Liberator II
AL516/G-G-AHZP Liberator II
AL522/G-AHYD Liberator II
AL524/G-AGTJ Liberator II
AL528/G-AGEM c/n 26. Liberator II. Crashed
    Charlottetown, PEI, Canada 21.2.46
AL529/G-AHYE Liberator II
AL541/G-AGTI Liberator II
AL547/G-AGKU Liberator II
AL552/G-AHZR Liberator II
AL557/G-AGZI Liberator II
AL559. Liberator II
AL561. Liberator II
AL571/G-AGZH Liberator II
AL578. Liberator II
AL587. Liberator II
AL590. Liberator II
AL591. Liberator II. Crashed on approach to Gander
    9.2.43
AL592/G-AHYF c/n 30. Liberator II. Sold to Scottish
    Airlines 9.46
AL593. Liberator II
AL597. Liberator II
AL603/G-AHYG Liberator II.
AL614. Liberator II
AL619/G-AGKT Liberator II
AL625. Liberator II
AL627/G-AHYJ Liberator II.
AM258
AM259/G-AGDD
AM260
AM261

AM262/G-AGHG
AM912
AM914
AM915
AM918/G-AGDR. Shot down in error off Eddystone
    15.2.42
AM920/G-AHYB

Consolidated 32 Liberator III

G-AGFN ex FI909
G-AGFO ex FL915
G-AGFP ex FL917
G-AGFR ex FL918
G-AGFS ex FL920

Curtiss-Wright CW.20 Commando

G-AGDI c/n 101. Wfu 2.43. To Bristol Aeroplane Company.

DE HAVILLAND DH.86 EXPRESS

G-ACPL c/n 2300 'Delphinus'. Impressed into RAF as
    HK844 13.12.41
G-ACWC c/n 2304 'Delia'. Written off Minna, Nigeria
    17.6.41
G-ACWD c/n 2305 'Dorado'. Impressed into RAF as
    HK829 22.11.41
G-ADFF c/n 2328 'Dione'. Impressed into RAF as AX760
    15.8.41
G-ADUE c/n 2333 'Dardanus'. Impressed into RAF as
    AX762 20.9.41
G-ADUF c/n 2334 'Dido'. Impressed into RAF as HK828
    5.11.41
G-ADUG c/n 2335 'Danae'. Impressed into RAF as
    HK831 5.11.41
G-ADUI c/n 2337 'Denebola'. Impressed into RAF as
    HK830 5.11.41
G-AEAP c/n 2349 'Demeter'. Impressed into RAF as
    HK843 22.10.41
All above acquired from Imperial Airways 1.4.40

De Havilland DH.89A Dragon Rapide

G-AFEN c/n 6399. Leased from RAF 7.40–2.42
G-AGNH c/n 6803. Leased from MCA 45. To EAAC as
    VP-KCT 46
G-AGOT c/n 6876. Leased from MCA 45. To EAAC as
    VP-KCX 46
G-AGOU c/n 6875. Leased from MCA 45. To EAAC as
    VP-KCW 46
G-AGOV c/n 6874. Leased from MCA 45. To EAAC as
    VP-KCY 46
G-AGOW c/n 6849. Leased from MCA 45. To EAAC as
    VP-KCV 46
G-AGOX c/n 6848. Leased from MCA 45. To EAAC as
    VP-KCU 46

DE HAVILLAND DH.91 ALBATROSS

G-AEVV c/n 6800 'Faraday'. Impressed into RAF as
    AX903 1.9.40

G-AEVW c/n 6801 'Franklin'. Impressed into RAF as
AX904 1.9.400

G-AFDI c/n 6802 'Frobisher'. Set on fire by saboteur and
written off Whitchurch 20.12.40

G-AFDJ c/n 6803 'Falcon'. Wfu Whitchurch 6.7.43

G-AFDK c/n 6804 'Fortuna'. Written off on mudflats,
River Fergus, Shannon 6.7.43

G-AFDL c/n 6805 'Fingal'. Written off nr Pucklechurch
6.10.40

G-AFDM c/n 6806 'Fiona'. Wfu Whitchurch 6.7.43

All above acquired from Imperial Airways 1.4.40

De Havilland DH.95 Flamingo

G-AFYE c/n 95007 'King Arthur'. Delivered 20.7.40.
Written off 15.2.43

G-AFYF c/n 95009 'King Alfred'. Delivered 1.11.40. Wfu
and sold 45

G-AFYG c/n 95010 'King Harold'. Delivered 14.11.40.
Written off Addis Ababa 18.11.42

G-AFYH c/n 95011 'King William'. Not delivered.
Transferred to Royal Navy

G-AFYI c/n 95012 'King Henry'. Delivered 29.12.40.
Written off Adana 13.9.42

G-AFYJ c/n 95013 'King Richard'. Scrapped 50

G-AFYK c/n 95014 'King James'. Delivered 19.3.41. Wfu
45. Sold 48

G-AFYL c/n 95015 'King Charles'. Delivered 27.5.41.
Wfu 45. Sold 48

G-AGBY c/n 95020 'King William'. Delivered 9.41. Wfu
45. Scrapped 50

De Havilland DH.98 Mosquito Mk.III

HJ985. Loaned from MCA for crew training
28.11.43–26.1.44

LR524. Loaned from MCA for crew training
21.2.44–4.12.44

HJ898. Loaned from MCA for crew training

De Havilland DH.98 Mosquito Mk.IV

G-AGFV c/n 98421. ex DZ411. Delivered 15.12.42.
Written off Stockholm 4.7.44

G-AGGC c/n 98723. ex HJ680. Delivered 16.4.43. Wfu
30.11.44 and returned to RAF

G-AGGD c/n 98730. ex HJ681. Delivered 16.4.43.
Written off Satenas, Sweden 3.1.44

G-AGGE c/n 98740. ex HJ718. Delivered 23.4.43. Wfu
16.6.45 and returned to RAF

G-AGGF c/n 98742. ex HJ720. Delivered 24.4.43.
Written off nr Leuchars 17.8.43

G-AGGG c/n 98743. ex HJ721. Delivered 2.5.43.
Written off Leuchars 25.10.43

G-AGGH c/n 98750. ex HJ723. Delivered 2.5.43.
Returned to RAF 16.6.45

G-AGKO. ex HJ667. Delivered 27.4.44. Returned to RAF
30.11.44

G-AGKP. ex LR296. Delivered 22.4.44. Written off 9.8.44
off Scottish coast.

G-AGKR. ex HJ972. Delivered 11.4.44. Written off over
North Sea 29.8.44

G-AGKS. ex HJ898. Delivered 22.4.45. Written off
Leuchars 12.5.45

De Havilland DH.104 Dove

G-AGUC c/n 04000/P2. Srs 1. 2 prototype Dove.
Delivered to BOAC Development Flight, Hurn,
29.7.46. Crashed Nr Hurn 14.8.46

G-AHRA c/n 04003. Srs 1. Delivered 15.1.47 to BOAC
Development Flight. Crashed 13.3.47

G-AJHL c/n 04043. Srs 1. Delivered 5.9.47. Crashed
Ionian Sea 9.2.48

G-AJPR c/n 04029. Srs 1. Delivered 28.5.47. Lsd to Gulf
Aviation 30.6.52. Sold to Gulf Aviation 1.10.56.

G-AKCF c/n 04030. Srs 1. Delivered 28.7.47. Sold 27.1.60

G-ALTM c/n 04236. Srs 2. Delivered 29.6.49. Crashed nr
London Airport 22.6.55

G-AMZY c/n 04431. Srs 2B. Delivered 30.6.53. Sold
19.2.59

G-AOFI c/n 04477. Srs 2B. Delivered 16.11.56. Sold
13.3.59

De Havilland DH.106 Comet 1

G-ALYP c/n 06003. Delivered 8.4.52. Crashed nr Elba
10.1.54

G-ALYR c/n 06004. Delivered 17.5.52. Crashed Calcutta
25.7.53. Remains to RAE Farnborough

G-ALYS c/n 06005. Delivered 04.2.52. Wfu 4.54. To RAE
Farnborough

G-ALYU c/n 06007. Delivered 6.3.52. Wfu 4.54. To RAE
Farnborough

G-ALYV c/n 06008. Delivered 23.4.52. Crashed nr
Calcutta 2.5.53

G-ALYW c/n 06009. Delivered 14.6.52. Wfu 4.54. To
RAE Farnborough

G-ALYX c/n 06010. Delivered 25.7.52. Sold to MoS/RAE
for structural tests 30.5.55

G-ALYY c/n 06011. Delivered 23.9.52. Crashed nr
Stromboli 8.4.54

G-ALYZ c/n 06012. Delivered 30.9.52. Crashed on take-
off Rome 26.10.52

G-ALZK c/n 06002. Loaned from MoS for route-proving
etc 23.3.51-24.10.51

G-ANAV (srs 1A) c/n 06013. Delivered 12.8.53. Wfu
4.54

G-AOJU (srs 1XB) c/n 06021. Loaned from MoS for crew
training etc 10.4.57-14.10.58

De Havilland DH.106 Comet 2

G-ALYT (srs 2X) c/n 06006. Loaned from MoS
29.7.53–23.9.53

G-AMXA to G-AMXJ c/ns 06023 to 06032. Not
delivered. Order diverted to RAF

G-AMXK c/n 06033. Leased to BOAC for route proving
for Comet 4 26.8.57–1.58

G-AMXL c/n 06034. Not delivered. Order diverted to
RAF

De Havilland DH.106 Comet 4

N.B. Several of these aircraft were leased out at various

times to airlines such as Middle East Airlines and Air
Ceylon, wearing BOAC colours with fuselage
stickers.

G-APDA c/n 6401. Delivered 24.2.59. Leased to
Malaysian Airlines as 9M-AOA 8.12.65, then to
Dan-Air.

G-APDB c/n 6403. Delivered 30.9.58. Leased to
Malaysian Airlines as 9M-AOB 9.9.65, then to Dan-
Air

G-APDC c/n 6404. Delivered 18.11.58. Leased to
Malaysian Airlines as 9M-AOC 13.10.65, then to
Dan-Air.

G-APDD c/n 6405. Delivered 18.11.58. Leased to
Malaysian Airlines as 9M-AOD 6.11.65, then to
Dan-Air.

G-APDE c/n 6406. Delivered 2.10.58. Leased to
Malaysian Airlines as 9M-AOE 4.10.65, then to Dan-
Air.

G-APDF c/n 6407. Delivered 31.12.58. Sold to MoD (PE)
1.3.67 as XV814

G-APDG c/n 6427. Delivered 28.11.59. Leased to Kuwait
Airways as 9K-ACI 15.12.66, then to Dan-Air.

G-APDH c/n 6409. Delivered 8.12.59. Written off
Singapore 22.3.64

G-APDI c/n 6428. Delivered 19.12.59. Sold to AREA
Ecuador as HC-ALT 13.3.66

G-APDJ c/n 6429. Delivered 11.1.60. Leased to Dan-Air
14.4.67. Later sold to Dan-Air

G-APDK c/n 6412. Delivered 12.2.59. Sold to Dan-Air
19.5.66

G-APDL c/n 6413. Delivered 6.5.59. Leased to EAAC as
5Y-ADD 8.10.65, then to Dan-Air

G-APDM c/n 6414. Delivered 16.4.59. Leased to
Malaysian Airlines as 9V-BBJ 20.1.68, then to Dan-
Air.

G-APDN c/n 6415. Delivered 10.6.59. Leased to Dan-Air
10.67. Later sold to Dan-Air

G-APDO c/n 6416. Delivered 14.5.59. Sold to Dan-Air
26.5.66

G-APDP c/n 6417. Delivered 11.6.59. Leased to
Malaysian Airlines as 9V-BBH 30.11.67, then to
Dan-Air.

G-APDR c/n 6418. Delivered 20.7.59. Sold to Mexicana
as XA-NAZ 3.12.64

G-APDS c/n 6419. Delivered 14.8.59. Sold to MoD (PE)
as XW626 30.1.69

G-APDT c/n 6420. Delivered 19.10.59. Leased to
Mexicana as XA-POW 25.11.65. Returned to BOAC
6.12.69 for apprentice training at Heathrow. Then to
Heathrow Fire Service

Douglas DC-2-115L

G-AGBH c/n 1584. ex PH-ALE of KLM. Written off
3.10.46

Douglas DC-3

G-AGBB c/n 1590. ex PH-ALI of KLM. Shot down by
Luftwaffe 1.6.43

G-AGBC c/n 1939. ex PH-ALR of KLM. Written off

Heston 21.9.40

G-AGBD c/n 1980. ex PH-ARB of KLM. Returned to KLM
2.46

G-AGBE c/n 2022. ex PH-ARZ of KLM. Returned to KLM
2.46

G-AGBI c/n 2019. ex PH-ARW of KLM. Dbr in air raid
Whitchurch 24.11.40

G-AGEN c/n 4118. ex RAF. Civilian registration not used.
Returned to RAF

Douglas C-47 Dakota

G-AGFX c/n 6223. Dakota 1. Sold to Westair Transport
(Pty) as ZS-DCZ

G-AGFY c/n 6224. Dakota 1. Sold to Westair Transport
(Pty) as ZS-DAH

G-AGFZ c/n 6225. Dakota 1. Written off Bromma,
Stockholm 21.4.44

G-AGGA c/n 6241. Dakota 1. Sold to Societe Indo-
Chinoise as F-OACA

G-AGGB c/n 6227. Dakota 1. Sold to Westair Transport
(Pty) as ZS-DDJ

G-AGGI c/n 9050. Dakota 1. Sold as ZS-DGY

G-AGHE c/n 9189. Dakota 3. Sold to Malayan Airways
as VR-SCR

G-AGHF c/n 9186. Dakota 3. Sold as N9994F

G-AGHH c/n 9187. Dakota 3. Sold to TAE as SX-BAN

G-AGHJ c/n 9413. Dakota 3. To BEA

G-AGHK c/n 9406. Dakota 3. Crashed Lugo De Lanera,
Spain 17.4.46

G-AGHL c/n 9407. Dakota 3

G-AGHM c/n 9623. Dakota 3

G-AGHN. Sold to Guinea Air Transport as VH-BZB

G-AGHO c/n 9682. Dakota 3. Sold as N9993F

G-AGHP c/n 9408. Dakota 3

G-AGHR c/n 10097. Dakota 3. Crashed on take-off Malta
24.10.45

G-AGHS c/n 10099. Dakota 3

G-AGHT c/n 10103. Dakota 3. Crashed Malta 14.8.46

G-AGHU c/n 9863. Dakota 3. Sold to Hong Kong
Airways as VR-HDQ

G-AGIO c/n 11907. Dakota 3. Sold to Hong Kong
Airways as VR-HDO

G-AGIP c/n 11903. Dakota 3

G-AGIR c/n 11932. Dakota 3. Crashed Atlas Mountains
nr Casablanca 28.8.44

G-AGIS c/n 12017. Dakota 3

G-AGIT c/n 11921. Dakota 3. Sold to Hong Kong
Airways as VR-HDP

G-AGIU c/n 12096. Dakota 3

G-AGIW c/n 12186. Dakota 3

G-AGIX c/n 12053. Dakota 3

G-AGIY c/n 12102. Dakota 3. Written off El Adem
23.1.46

G-AGIZ c/n 12075. Dakota 3

G-AGJR c/n 11995. Dakota 3. To KLM as PH-AZR 2.46

G-AGJS c/n 12173. Dakota 3. To KLM as PH-AZS 2.46

G-AGJT c/n 12172. Dakota 3. To KLM as PH-AZT 2.46

G-AGJU c/n 12169. Dakota 3. Written off Whitchurch
3.1.47

G-AGJV c/n 12195. Dakota 3

G-AGJW c/n 12199. Dakota 3

G-AGJX c/n 12014. Dakota 3. Crashed Stowting, Kent
11.1.47

G-AGJY. Sold to Hong Kong Airways as VR-HDM

G-AGJZ c/n 12054. Dakota 3

G-AGKA c/n 14141. Dakota 4. Sold to Aden Airways as
VR-AAA

G-AGKB c/n 14143. Dakota 4. Sold in USA

G-AGKC c/n 14146. Dakota 4. Sold in Switzerland

G-AGKD c/n 14150. Dakota 4. Written off Malta
23.12.46

G-AGKE c/n 14361. Dakota 4. Sold to Aden Airways as
VR-AAB

G-AGKF c/n 14362. Dakota 4. Sold to Air Nous as F-
BEFQ

G-AGKG c/n 14373. Dakota 4. Sold to Union of Burma
Airways as XY-ACL

G-AGKH c/n 14365. Dakota 4. Sold to Aden Airways as
VR-AAC

G-AGKI c/n 14654. Dakota 4. Sold to EAAC as VP-KHK

G-AGKJ c/n 14660. Dakota 4. Sold to Aden Airways as
VR-AAD

G-AGKK c/n 14655. Dakota 4

G-AGKL c/n 14662. Dakota 4. Sold as F-OADA

G-AGKM c/n 14986. Dakota 4. Dbr El Adem 8.4.45

G-AGKN c/n 14984. Dakota 4. Crashed nr Toulon,
France 14.7.48

G-AGMZ c/n 14978. Dakota 4. Sold to Aden Airways as
VR-AAE

G-AGNA c/n 14967. Dakota 4. Dbr Basra, Iraq 1.5.45

G-AGNB c/n 15274. Dakota 4. Sold to Aden Airways as
VR-AAF

G-AGNC c/n 15283. Dakota 4. Sold to Societe Indo-
Chinoise as F-OAFR

G-AGND c/n 15280. Dakota 4. Sold to Bahamas Airways.

G-AGNE c/n 15276. Dakota 4. Sold to EAAC as VP-
KHM.

G-AGNF c/n 15534. Dakota 4. Sold to Union of Burma
Airways as XY-ACM

G-AGNG c/n 15552. Dakota 4. Sold as CF-GVZ

G-AGNK c/n 15540. Dakota 4.

G-AGZC

G-AGZE

Douglas DC-7C

G-AOIA c/n 45111. Delivered 23.10.56. Sold to F.B. Ayer
and Associates as N90803 25.5.64

G-AOIB c/n 45112. Delivered 16.11.56. Sold to F.B. Ayer
and Associates as N90802 25.3.64

G-AOIC c/n 45113. Delivered 27.11.56. Sold to F.B. Ayer
and Associates as N90801 13.2.64

G-AOID c/n 45114. Delivered 24.11.56. Sold to F.B.Ayer
and Associates as N90778 31.5.63

G-AOIE c/n 45115. Delivered 14.12.56. Sold to
Caledonian Airways (Prestwick) Ltd 29.4.64

G-AOIF c/n 45116. Delivered 29.12.56. Sold to F.B. Ayer
and Associates as N90804 6.64

G-AOIG c/n 45117. Delivered 29.12.56. Sold to F.B.

Ayer and Associates as N90773 4.63

G-AOIH c/n 45118. Delivered 14.1.57. Sold to F.B. Ayer
and Associates as N90774 11.5.63

G-AOII c/n 45119. Delivered 29.1.57. Converted to DC-
7CF 12.60. Sold as OY-KNE 3.65

G-AOIJ c/n 45120. Delivered 18.4.57. Converted to DC-
7CF 11.60. Sold as N16465 15.5.65

Fiat G.12

HK940

Focke-Wulf FW200B Condor

G-AGAY c/n 2894. ex DDL. Seized 4.40. To RAF/Air
Transport Auxiliary. Dbr 18.1.42

Handley Page Halifax C Mk 8

6007M c/n 1320. ex PP236. Dbr as such 6.46. To BOAC
Training School, White Waltham 9.7.46

PP325 c/n 1387. Loaned to BOAC 10.45. Dbr
Aldermaston 8.7.46

G-AHYH c/n 1334. ex PP261. Loaned to BOAC by Air
Ministry 24.9.46–20.10.47

G-AHYI c/n 1373. ex PP311. Loaned to BOAC by Air
Ministry 24.9.46–10.7.47

G-AIAN c/n 1344. ex PP271. Loaned to BOAC by Air
Ministry 2.9.46–4.47

G-AIAO c/n 1345. ex PP272. Loaned to BOAC by Air
Ministry 2.9.46–4.47

G-AIAP c/n 1354. ex PP281. Loaned to BOAC by Air
Ministry 2.9.46–4.47

PP326/G-AIAR c/n 1388. Loaned to BOAC by Air
Ministry as PP326 10.45. Re-regd as G-AIAR 2.9.46.
Returned to Air Ministry 4.6.47

PP327/G-AIAS c/n 1389. Loaned to BOAC by Air
Ministry as PP327 10.45. Re-regd as G-AIAS 2.9.46.
Returned to Air Ministry 11.4.47

G-AIID c/n 1379. ex PP317. Loaned to BOAC by Air
Ministry 24.9.46–4.47

Handley Page Halton

G-AHDL c/n SH.23C 'Fitzroy'. Delivered 25.3.47. Sold to
Aviation Traders Ltd 2.7.48

G-AHDM c/n SH.20C 'Falmouth'. Delivered 7.46. Sold
to Aviation Traders Ltd 2.7.48

G-AHDN c/n SH.24C 'Flamborough'. Delivered 3.48.
Sold to Aviation Traders Ltd 2.7.48

G-AHDO c/n SH.29C 'Forfar'. Delivered 8.47. Sold to
Aviation Traders Ltd 2.7.48

G-AHDP c/n SH.25C 'Fleetwood'. Delivered 7.47. Sold
to Aviation Traders Ltd 2.7.48

G-AHDR c/n SH.26C 'Foreland'. Delivered 7.47. Sold to
E.M. Sutton 3.6.49

G-AHDS c/n SH.22C 'Fremantle'. Delivered 8.46. Sold to
Aviation Traders Ltd 2.7.48

G-AHDT c/n SH.27C 'Fife'. Delivered 6.47. Sold to
Aviation Traders Ltd 2.7.48

G-AHDU c/n SH.18C 'Falkirk'. Prototype Halton.
Delivered 7.46. Sold to Aviation Traders Ltd 2.7.48

G-AHDV c/n SH.21C 'Finistere'. Delivered 8.46. Sold to
Aviation Traders Ltd 2.7.48

G-AHDW c/n SH.19C 'Falaise'. Delivered 7.46. Sold to
    Aviation Traders Ltd 2.7.48
G-AHDX c/n SH.28C 'Folkestone'. Delivered 6.47. Sold
    to Aviation Traders Ltd 2.7.48

Handley Page HP.81 Hermes
G-AGUB c/n HP.74/1. Hermes II. Leased to BOAC by
    MoS 9.5.49–49.

HANDLEY PAGE **Hermes IV**
(N.B. All Hermes IV c/ns were prefixed HP.81/)
G-ALDA c/n 2 'Hecuba'. Loaned by Handley Page for
    tropical trials 5.5.51-23.5.51
G-ALDB c/n 3 'Hebe'. Loaned by Handley Page for
    tropical trials 22.2.50–6.4.50
G-ALDC c/n 4 'Hermione'. Delivered 25.2.50. Leased to
    Airwork Ltd 17.6.52. Cnvtd to srs IVA. Sold to
    Airwork Ltd 31.12.56
G-ALDD c/n 5 'Horatius'. Delivered 14.3.50. Cnvtd to srs
    IVA. Sold to Skyways Ltd 28.2.55
G-ALDE c/n 6 'Hanno'. Delivered 15.3.50. Cnvtd to srs
    IVA. Sold to LAC 14.9.54
G-ALDF c/n 7 'Hadrian'. Delivered 24.3.50. Leased to
    Airwork Ltd 27.2.52. Crashed nr Sicily 25.8.52 while
    on lease
G-ALDG c/n 8 'Horsa'. Delivered 29.3.50. Leased to
    Airwork Ltd 54. Cnvtd to srs IVA 2.55. Sold to
    Airwork Ltd 25.7.57
G-ALDH c/n 9 'Heracles'. Delivered 31.3.50. Cnvtd to
    srs IVA. Sold to Skyways Ltd 1.7.55
G-ALDI c/n 10 'Hannibal'. Delivered 5.7.50. Sold to
    Britavia Ltd 19.6.54
G-ALDJ c/n 11 'Hengist'. Delivered 10.7.50. Sold to
    Britavia Ltd 22.5.54
G-ALDK c/n 12 'Helena'. Delivered 12.7.50. Sold to
    Britavia Ltd 3.6.54
G-ALDL c/n 13 'Hector'. Delivered 6.3.51. Cnvtd to srs
    IVA. Sold to Skyways Ltd 9.5.55
G-ALDM c/n 14 'Hero'. Delivered 17.7.50. Cnvtd to srs
    IVA. Sold to African Air Safaris 29.5.56
G-ALDN c/n 15 'Horus'. Delivered 21.7.50. Dbr in
    forced landing in Sahara 26.5.52
G-ALDO c/n 16 'Heron'. Delivered 20.7.50. Leased to
    Airwork Ltd 1952. Cnvtd to srs IVA 12.56. Cnvtd
    back to srs IV 3.57. Sold to Airwork Ltd 9.57
G-ALDP c/n 17 'Homer'. Delivered 27.8.50. Sold to
    Britavia Ltd 28.6.54
G-ALDR c/n 18 'Herodotus'. Delivered 1.9.50. Cnvtd to
    srs IVA. Sold to Skyways Ltd 12.4.55
G-ALDS c/n 19 'Hesperides'. Delivered 8.9.50. Cnvtd to
    srs IVA. Sold to Skyways Ltd 24.2.55
G-ALDT c/n 20 'Hestia'. Delivered 15.9.50. Cnvtd to srs
    IVA. Sold to Skyways Ltd 24.2.55
G-ALDU c/n 21 'Halcyone'. Delivered 14.10.50. Cnvtd
    to srs IVA. Sold to Britavia Ltd 27.5.54
G-ALDV c/n 22 'Hera'. Delivered 5.10.50. Cnvtd to srs
    IVA. Sold to Skyways Ltd 24.2.55
G-ALDW c/n 23 'Helios'. Delivered 2.11.50. Cnvtd to srs
    IVA. Sold to Skyways Ltd 24.2.55

G-ALDX c/n 24 'Hyperion'. Delivered 14.12.50. Cnvtd to
    srs IVA. Sold to Britavia Ltd 31.5.54
G-ALDY c/n 25 'Honor'. Delivered 19.1.51. Cnvtd to srs
    IVA. Sold to Skyways Ltd 24.2.55

Junkers Ju52/3M
HK919 and HK920.Used by BOAC at Heliopolis, Cairo,
    for transport/communications

Junkers Ju88D
HK959. Used by BOAC at Heliopolis, Cairo, for
    transport/communications

Lockheed Electra
G-AEPR c/n 1083. Destroyed Egypt 14.4.44
G-AFCS c/n 1025. Crashed Almaza 19.11.43
G-AFGR c/n 1740. Crashed El Fasher, Sudan, 19.1.41
G-AFKD c/n 1484. Crashed nr Loch Lomond 22.4.40
G-AFZZ c/n 1493. Crashed Bucharest 24.7.40
G-AGAA c/n 1492. Crashed deliberately Bucharest
    24.7.40

Lockheed 14H Super Electra
G-AGAV c/n 1425. ex SP-LMK. Escaped from Poland.
    Leased from LOT. Loaned to ATA 2.40-6.41.
    Scrapped 3.44
G-AGBG c/n 1421. ex SP-BNF. Escaped from Poland.
    Leased from LOT. Returned to Polish Government.

Lockheed 414 Hudson II
T9367. Loaned from RCAF for training at Baltimore

Lockheed 414 Hudson III
G-AGDC c/n 2585. Returned to RAF 45
G-AGDF c/n 3772. Ditched 23.6.42
G-AGDK c/n 3757. Returned to RAF 45
G-AGDO ex AE581. Returned to RAF 45

Lockheed Hudson V
G-AGCE c/n 2789. Found unsuitable. Returned to RAF
    8.41

Lockheed Hudson VI
EW884/888/926/943/958/960/971
FK391/397/454/456/459/478/486/580/618
All above seconded to BOAC with crews from 163
    Squadron, Western Desert 12.9.42. Returned to RAF
    19.7.43

Lockheed 18 Lodestar
G-AGBO c/n 2018. To RAF 42/43
G-AGBP c/n 2024. To RAF 42/43
G-AGBR c/n 2070
G-AGBS c/n 2071
G-AGBT c/n 2076
G-AGBU c/n 2090
G-AGBV c/n 2091
G-AGBW c/n 2094. Written off 6.3.41
G-AGBX c/n 2095

All above purchased new from Lockheed 3.41. Most of
the survivors sold to EAAC approx 3.48
G-AGCL c/n 2092. Civil registration not used
G-AGCM c/n 2093
G-AGCN c/n 2020
G-AGCO c/n 2021
G-AGCP c/n 2022
G-AGCR c/n 2072. Written off 13.5.42
G-AGCS c/n 2031. Civil registration not used.
G-AGCT c/n 2001. Exchanged for G-AGIG with RAF
G-AGCU c/n 2068
G-AGCV c/n 2042
G-AGCW c/n 1956. Exchanged for G-AGJN with RAF
G-AGCX c/n 2012. Exchanged for G-AGJH with RAF
G-AGCY c/n 2077
G-AGCZ c/n 2023. Written off Egypt 23.2.43
G-AGDD c/n 2087
G-AGDE c/n 2086. Crashed nr Leuchars 17.12.43
G-AGEH c/n 2147
G-AGEI c/n 2084
G-AGEJ c/n 2085. Ditched 4.4.43
G-AGIG ex EW980
G-AGIH c/n 2619. Written off 29.8.44
G-AGII c/n 2492
G-AGIJ c/n 2593
G-AGIK c/n 2594
G-AGIL ex HK855
G-AGIM ex EW977
G-AGIN ex EW979
G-AGJH ex EW982
G-AGLG c/n 2615
G-AGLH c/n 2616
G-AGLI c/n 2620. Ditched 2.5.45

Lockheed L-049 Constellation
G-AHEJ c/n 1975 'Bristol'. Delivered 26.4.46. Cnvtd to L-
049D 10.52. Cnvtd to L-049E 5.5. Sold to Capital
Airlines as N2740A 26.5.55
G-AHEK c/n 1976 'Berwick'. Delivered 21.5.46. Cnvtd to
L-049D 52. Cnvtd to L-049E 7.53. Sold to Capital
Airlines as N2737A 27.2.55
G-AHEL c/n 1977 'Bangor'. Delivered 24.6.46. Cnvtd to
L-049D 52. Cnvtd to L-049E 7.53. Sold to Capital
Airlines as N2736A 28.1.55
G-AHEM c/n 1978 'Balmoral'. Delivered 22.5.46. Cnvtd
to L-049D 52. Cnvtd to L-049E 7.53. Sold to Capital
Airlines as N2735A 11.10.55
G-AHEN c/n 1980 'Baltimore'. Delivered 29.5.46. Dbr
Filton 8.1.51
G-AKCE c/n 1971 'Bedford'. Purchased 12.8.47. Cnvtd to
L-049D 10.52. Cnvtd to L-049E 5.53. Sold to Capital
Airlines as N2741A 27.6.55

Lockheed L-049E Constellation
G-AMUP c/n 2051 'Boston'. Purchased 9.1.53. Sold to
Capital Airlines as N2738A 27.3.55
G-AMUR c/n 2065 'Barnstaple'. Purchased 9.1.53. Sold
to Capital Airlines as N2739A 26.4.55

Lockheed L-749 Constellation
G-ALAK c/n 2548 'Brentford'. Purchased 13.6.48. Cnvtd
to L-749A. Wfu and stored London Airport 9.57.
Leased to Skyways Ltd. 6.59. Sold to Skyways Ltd.
22.6.62
G-ALAL c/n 2549 'Banbury'. Purchased 15.6.48. Cnvtd
to L-749A. Leased to Skyways Ltd 7.59. Sold to
Skyways Ltd 13.6.62
G-ALAM c/n 2554 'Belfast'. Purchased 6.48. Cnvtd to
L-749A.Crashed Singapore 13.3.54
G-ALAN c/n 2555 'Beaufort'. Purchased 15.6.48. Leased
to QANTAS 30.7.48-4.50. Cnvtd to L-749A. Wfu
and stored London Airport 9.57. Sold to Pacific
Northern Airlines 3.59
G-ALAO c/n 2566 'Braemar'. Purchased 22.6.48.
Cnvtd to L-749A 1.56. Sold to Capitol Airways
26.9.58

Lockheed L-749A Constellation
G-ANNT c/n 2671 'Buckingham'. Purchased 23.9.54.
Wfu and stored London Airport. Sold to Capitol
Airways 25.3.58
G-ANTF c/n 2504 'Berkeley'. Purchased 23.7.54. Sold to
The Babb Company Inc 9.12.57
G-ANTG c/n 2505 'Bournemouth'. Purchased 18.8.54.
Sold to Pacific Northern Airlines 30.11.58
G-ANUP c/n 2562 'Branksome'. Purchased 15.2.55.
Wfu and stored London Airport 9.57. Leased to
Skyways Ltd 9.59-4.62. Sold to Aero Transport
10.5.63
G-ANUR c/n 2565 'Basildon'. Purchased 26.2.55. Leased
to Skyways Ltd 7.59. Sold to Skyways Ltd 2.7.62
G-ANUV c/n 2551 'Blantyre'. Purchased 26.6.55. Wfu
and stored London Airport 2.57. Sold to The Babb
Company Inc 2.58.
G-ANUX c/n 2556 'Bala'. Purchased 3.12.54. Wfu and
stored London Airport 2.57. Sold to Pacific Northern
Airlines 6.5.57
G-ANUY c/n 2557 'Beaulieu'. Purchased 28.1.55. Wfu
and stored London Airport 3.57. Sold to The Babb
Company Inc 5.59
G-ANUZ c/n 2559 'Belvedere'. Purchased 28.2.55. Wfu
and stored London Airport 1.58. Sold to The Babb
Company Inc 14.3.58
G-ANVA c/n 2564 'Blakeley'. Purchased 22.5.55. Wfu
and stored London Airport 2.57. Sold to The Babb
Company Inc 29.4.59
G-ANVB c/n 2589 'Blackrod'. Purchased 25.3.55. Wfu
and stored London Airport. Sold to The Babb
Company Inc 7.3.58
G-ANVD c/n 2544 'Beverley'. Purchased 26.4.55. Wfu
and stored London Airport 3.57. Sold to The Babb
Company Inc 26.5.59

Miles M.11A Whitney Straight
HK853. Used by BOAC at Heliopolis, Cairo for
transport/communications

Savoia-Marchetti S.79

AX702. Used by BOAC at Heliopolis, Cairo for transport/communications

Short S.21

G-ADHK c/n S797 'Maia'. Upper component of 'Maia/Mercury' composite. Transferred from Imperial Airways on takeover 1.4.40. Written off Poole 12.4.51

Short S.23 Empire Flying-boat

(All examples transferred from Imperial Airways on takeover 1.4.40)

G-ADHL c/n S795 'Canopus'. Wfu 27.8.40

G-ADHM c/n S804 'Caledonia'. Wfu 22.3.47

G-ADUV c/n S813 'Cambria'. Wfu 13.1.47

G-ADUW c/n S814 'Castor'. Wfu 4.2.47

G-ADUX c/n S815 'Cassiopeia'. Written off Sabang, Singapore 29.12.41

G-ADVB c/n S819 'Corsair'. Wfu 20.1.47

G-AETV c/n S838 'Coriolanus'. Transferred to Qantas 12.8.42

G-AETX c/n S840 'Ceres'. Written off Durban 1.12.42

G-AETY c/n S841 'Clio'. Impressed into RAF as AX659 27.10.40

G-AETZ c/n S842 'Circe'. Shot down en route Jave to Broome, Australia 28.2.42

G-AEUB c/n S844 'Camilla'. Transferred to Qantas 12.8.42

G-AEUC c/n S845 'Corinna'. Destroyed by bombing, Broome, Australia 3.3.42

G-AEUD c/n S846 'Cordelia'. Impressed into RAF as AX660 9.7.40

G-AEUE c/n S847 'Cameronian'. Wfu 12.1.47

G-AEUF c/n S848 'Corinthian'. Written off Port Darwin 22.3.42

G-AEUH c/n S850 'Corio'. ex VH-ABD of QANTAS. Shot down off Koepang, Timor 30.1.42

G-AEUI c/n S851 'Coorong'. ex VH-ABE of QANTAS.Wfu 10.2.47

G-AFBJ c/n S876 'Carpentaria'. ex VH-ABA of QANTAS. Wfu 19.1.47

G-AFBL c/n S878 'Cooee'. ex VH-ABF of QANTAS. Wfu 11.46

Short S.30 Empire Flying-Boat

G-AFCT c/n S879 'Champion'. C of A granted 27.10.38. Wfu 16.3.47

G-AFCX c/n S883 'Clyde'. C of A granted 29.3.39. Written off Lisbon 15.2.41

G-AFCZ c/n S885 'Clare'. ex ZK-AMB of TEAL. Written off nr Bathurst 14.9.42

G-AFKZ c/n S1003 'Cathay'. C of A granted 26.2.40. Wfu 9.3.47

Short S.33 Empire Flying-Boat

G-AFPZ c/n S1025 'Clifton'. C of A granted 20.4.40. Impressed into RAAF as A18-14 12.3.42

G-AFRA c/n S1026 'Cleopatra'. C of A granted 8.5.40.

Wfu 4.11.46

G-AFRB c/n S1027. Not completed. Civil registration not used.

Short S.26 'G' Class Flying Boat

G-AFCI c/n S871 'Golden Hind'. Delivered 2.7.41. Sold 10.10.47

G-AFCK c/n S873 'Golden Horn'. Delivered to BOAC 'for inspection' 23.6.41. Returned to RAF 30.8.41. Re-delivered to BOAC 12.41. Written off Lisbon 9.1.43

Short S.25 Sunderland III 'Hythe' Class

G-AGER 'Hadfield'. ex JM660. Delivered 8.1.43. Sold to Aquila Airways 4.8.48

G-AGES. ex JM661. Delivered 15.1.43. Written off County Kerry 28.7.43

G-AGET. ex JM662. Delivered 16.1.43. Written off Calcutta 15.2.46

G-AGEU 'Hampshire'. ex JM663. Delivered 21.1.43. Sold to Aquila Airways 19.1.49

G-AGEV 'Hailsham'. ex JM664. Delivered 29.1.43. Written off Poole 4.3.46

G-AGEW 'Hanwell'. ex JM665. Delivered 29.1.43. Written off Sourabaya 5.9.48

G-AGHV 'Hamble'. ex JM722. Delivered 21.8.43. Written off 9.3.46

G-AGHW 'Hamilton'. ex ML725. Delivered 27.8.43. Written off Isle of Wight 19.11.47

G-AGHX 'Harlech'. ex ML726. Delivered 2.9.43. Renamed 'Harlequin'. Wfu 12.5.48

G-AGHY 'Hastings'. ex ML727. Delivered 3.9.43. Renamed 'Hawkesbury'. Sold to Aquila Airways 19.1.49

G-AGIA 'Haslemere'. ex ML728. Delivered 8.9.43. Sold to Aquila Airways 23.7.48

G-AGIB. ex ML729. Delivered 15.9.43. Written off 130 miles S of Tobruk 5/6.11.43

G-AGJJ 'Henley'. ex ML751. Delivered 13.1.44. Sold to Aquila Airways 5.2.49

G-AGJK 'Howard'. ex ML752. Delivered 21.1.44. Sold to Aquila Airways 24.3.49

G-AGJL 'Hobart'. ex ML753. Delivered 23.1.44. Sold to Aquila Airways 24.3.49

G-AGJM 'Hythe'. ex ML754. Delivered 2.2.44. Sold to Aquila Airways 17.2.49

G-AGJN 'Hudson'. ex ML755. Delivered 3.2.44. Sold to Aquila Airways 25.2.49

G-AGJO 'Humber'. ex ML756. Delivered 3.2.44. Written off Hythe 21.2.49

G-AGKV 'Huntingdon'. ex ML786. Delivered 12.7.44. Sold to Short Bros 30.12.48

G-AGKW 'Hereford'. ex ML787. Delivered 25.7.44. Renamed 'Hotspur'. Sold to Short Bros 30.12.48

G-AGKX 'Himalaya'. ex ML788. Delivered 27.7.44. Cnvtd to Sandringham 1. Sold to Aquila Airways 28.5.49

G-AGKY 'Hungerford'. ex ML789. Delivered 28.7.44. Sold to Aquila Airways 10.1.49

G-AGKZ 'Harwich'. ex ML790. Delivered 3.8.44. Wfu 20.1.49

G-AGLA 'Hunter'. ex ML791. Delivered 11.8.44. Sold to
Aquila Airways 10.1.49

Short S.25 Sunderland Mk 5

G-AHEO 'Halstead'. ex JM716. Delivered 2.3.45. Sold to
Aquila Airways 23.7.48

G-AHER 'Helmsdale'. ex PP142. Regd 20.3.46. Sold to
Aquila Airways 22.10.49

G-AHJR. ex SZ584. Loaned by the RAF for cargo use
only 27.6.46–15.4.48.

Short S.25 Sandringham 1

G-AGKX 'Himalaya'. Cnvtd from Sunderland III. Sold to
Aquila Airways 28.5.49

Short S.25 Sandringham V 'Plymouth' Class

(All leased to BOAC by MCA)

G-AHYY c/n SH31C 'Portsmouth'. ex ML838. Delivered
6.3.47. Wfu 8.6.49

G-AHYZ c/n SH35X . ex ML784. Not delivered.
Destroyed by fire during conversion 18.1.47

G-AHZA c/n SH34C 'Penzance'. ex ML783. Delivered
22.4.47. Wfu 31.8.49

G-AHZB c/n SH38C 'Portland'. ex NJ171. Delivered
26.4.47. Crashed Bahrain Marine Air Base 22.8.47

G-AHZC c/n SH39C 'Pembroke'. ex NJ253.Delivered
17.5.47. Wfu 17.6.52

G-AHZD c/n SH40C 'Portmarnock'. ex NJ257. Delivered
28.5.47. Wfu 13.8.49

G-AHZE c/n SH36C 'Portsea', ex ML818. Delivered
17.6.47. Wfu 4.9.49

G-AHZF c/n SH41C 'Poole'. ex NJ188. Delivered
11.7.47. Wfu 25.8.49

G-AHZG c/n SH37C 'Pevensey'. ex ML828. Delivered
23.9.47. Wfu 3.9.49

G-AJMZ c/n SH56C 'Perth'. ex JM681. Delivered
19.12.47. Wfu 25.8.49

Short S.25 Sandringham VII 'Bermuda' Class

G-AKCO c/n SH57C 'St George'. ex JM719. Delivered
18.3.48. Wfu 22.8.49

G-AKCP c/n SH58C 'St David'. ex EJ172. Delivered
15.4.48. Wfu 11.9.49

G-AKCR c/n SH59C 'St Andrew'. ex ML840. Delivered
1.5.48. Wfu 5.9.49

Short S.45 Seaford 1

G-AGWU c/n S.1293. ex NJ201. Loaned for evaluation
11.45-2.46

Short S.45 Solent 2

G-AHIL c/n S1300 'Salisbury'. Delivered 17.6.48. Cnvtd
to Solent 3. Wfu 29.9.50

G-AHIM c/n S1301 'Scarborough'. C of A 10.11.47. Wfu
26.12.49

G-AHIN c/n S1302 'Southampton'. C of A 22.4.48.
Cnvtd to Solent 3. Wfu 6.11.50

G-AHIO c/n S1303 'Somerset'. Delivered 19.5.49. Cnvtd
to Solent 3. Wfu 14.11.50

G-AHIR c/n S1304 'Sark'. C of A 4.5.48. Wfu 24.12.49

G-AHIS c/n S1305 'Scapa'. C of A 8.7.48. Cnvtd to
Solent 3. Renamed 'City of York' Wfu 26.9.50

G-AHIT c/n S1306 'Severn'. Delivered 30.4.48. Wfu
22.11.49

G-AHIU c/n S1307 'Solway'. C of A 2.3.48. Wfu 20.8.49

G-AHIV c/n S1308 'Salcombe'. C of A 18.2.48. Wfu
15.9.50

G-AHIW c/n S1309 'Stornoway'. Delivered 25.3.48. Wfu
22.10.49

G-AHIX c/n S1310 'Sussex'. C of A 20.10.48. Cnvtd to
Solent 3. Renamed 'City of Edinburgh'. Crashed nr
Southampton 1.2.50

G-AHIY c/n S1311 'Southsea'. C of A 25.11.48. Cnvtd to
Solent 3. Wfu 27.9.50

Short S.45 Solent 3

G-AKNO c/n S1294 'City of London'. C of A 1.4.49. Sold
as VH-TOA 20.12.50

G-AKNP c/n S1295 'City of Cardiff'. C of A 19.3.49. Sold
as VH-TOB 30.3.51

G-AKNR c/n S1296 'City of Belfast'. C of A 27.4.49. Sold
as ZK-AMQ 4.7.51

G-AKNS c/n S1297 'City of Liverpool'. C of A 24.4.49.
Sold as WM759 7.11.50

G-AKNT (c/n S1298) and G-AKNU (c/n S1299)..Not
delivered, Civil registrations not used

Vickers 415 Wellington 1C

BAW1-4. Loaned from South African Air Force 8.42-7.43

Vickers 456 Warwick C.1

G-AGEX to G- AGFK inclusive (ex RAF BV243-BV256
inclusive). All allocated to BOAC as freighters, but
did not gain C of As

Vickers 473 Warwick GR.V

G-AGLD c/n 3033. ex PN703. Used by BOAC
Development Flight at Hurn for trials 8.44–10.45

Vickers VC-10

G-ARVA c/n 804. Delivered 8.12.64. Sold to Nigerian
Airways as 5N-ABD 29.9.69

G-ARVB c/n 805. Delivered 6.2.65

G-ARVC c/n 806. Delivered 1.10.64

G-ARVE c/n 807. Delivered 1.10.64

G-ARVF c/n 808. Delivered 4.9.64

G-ARVG c/n 809. Delivered 17.6.64

G-ARVH c/n 810. Delivered 2.7.64

G-ARVI c/n 811. Delivered 22.4.64. Sold to Gulf Air as
A40-VI 10.3.74

G-ARVJ c/n 812. Delivered 21.4.64

G-ARVK c/n 813. Delivered 16.6.64

G-ARVL c/n 814. Delivered 16.6.64

G-ARVM c/n 815. Delivered 22.7.64

All above except G-ARVA and G-ARVI transferred to
British Airways on merger

G-ARVN to G-ARVP inclusive (c/ns 816 to 818
inclusive). Order cancelled

Vickers Super VC-10

G-ASGA c/n 851. Delivered 31.12.65

G-ASGB c/n 852. Delivered 30.4.65

G-ASGC c/n 853. Delivered 27.3.65

G-ASGD c/n 854. Delivered 27.3.65

G-ASGE c/n 855. Delivered 27.3.65

G-ASGF c/n 856. Delivered 2.4.65

G-ASGG c/n 857. Delivered 21.6.67

G-ASGH c/n 858. Delivered 4.11.65

G-ASGI c/n 859. Delivered 12.2.66

G-ASGJ c/n 860. Delivered 3.3.67

G-ASGK c/n 861. Delivered 27.10.67

G-ASGL c/n 862. Delivered 25.1.68

G-ASGM c/n 863. Delivered 9.4.68

G-ASGN c/n 864. Delivered 7.5.68. Destroyed by
    terrorists, Dawson Field, Jordan 12.9.70

G-ASGO c/n 865. Delivered 28.9.68. Destroyed by fire,
    Schipol Airport, Amsterdam 4.3.74

G-ASGP c/n 866. Delivered 6.12.68

G-ASGR c/n 867. Delivered 31.5.69

All above except G-ASGN and G-ASGO transferred to
    British Airways on merger

G-ASGS to G-ASHE inclusive (c/ns 868 to 880 inclusive).
    Order cancelled

Sources of Reference

The following publications (some, alas, out of print) and websites have been consulted in the preparation of this book, and are highly recommended to anyone with an interest in the history of commercial aviation.

Further Reading

The Annals of British and Commonwealth Air Transport. John Stroud. Putnams. 1962

Of Comets and Queens. Basil Smallpeice. Airlife. 1981.

Mosquito Portfolio. Stuart Howe. Ian Allan Ltd. 1984.

Mosquito: The Illustrated History. Philip J. Birtles. ISBN 07509 2327X.

British Commercial Aircraft: Sixty Years in Pictures. Paul Ellis. Janes Publishing Co. 1980

British Airways: Its History, Aircraft and Liveries. Keith Gaskell. Airlife. 1999.

The Lockheed Constellation. M.J. Hardy. David and Charles. 1973.

Classic Civil Aircraft 3-De Havilland Comet. Philip J. Birtles. Ian Allan Ltd. 1990.

The Avro York. Donald Hannah. Profile Publications.

In Cobham's Company. Colin Cruddas.

Atlantic Bridge. Air Ministry for Ministry of Information. HMSO. 1945.

Atlantic Air Ferry 50th Anniversary – Prestwick Airport 1940-1945. Sponsored by British Aerospace Commercial Aircraft. 1995.

Three Decades a Pilot: The Third Generation. Wilfred Emm. Spellmount Ltd. 1992.

Ian Allan ABC of Airports and Airlines 1948. (1998 reprint). Owen G. Thetford. Ian Allan Ltd.

Piston Engine Airliner Production List. A.B. Eastwood and J. Roach. The Aviation Hobby Shop. 1996.

Concorde: The Inside Story. Brian Trubshaw. Sutton Publishing Ltd. 2000

Jet Airliners of the World 1996. Air-Britain (Historians) Ltd. 1996.

History of BOAC. Winston Bray. British Airways. (In-house document. Unpublished).

The Illustrated Encyclopaedia of Propellor Airliners. Editor in Chief Bill Gunston. Windward.1980.

The Short Sunderland. Chaz Bowyer. Aston Publications. 1989.

Sixty Glorious Years. Arthur Pearcey. Airlife. 1995.

Douglas Propliners DC-1 - DC-7. Arthur Pearcey. Airlife. 1995.

Merchant Airmen-The Air Ministry Account of British Civil Aviation 1939-1944. HMSO. 1946.

The Flying Boats at Poole (pamphlet). Poole Maritime Trust.

Magazine Articles etc.

Bradshaw's International Air Guide. 15 Feb–14 Mar 1952 edition.
'Speedbird Service'. Brian Sullivan. Aeroplane Monthly. 1995.
'Hunting for Horus'. Tony Harmsworth. Aeroplane Monthly. April 2002.
'From the City of Cardiff to the Isle of Tahiti article'. Edward J. Davies. Propliner. 1990.
'The Halifax in Airline Service-Part 5'. Tony Merton Jones. Propliner. Autumn 1995.
'BOAC at War-Parts 1-5'. Peter Moss. Aeroplane Monthly. 1975.
Various editions of *Travel Trade Gazette.*
Various BOAC and BSAA timetables.
ICAO Accident Digests. G–ALYP, G–ALYY, G–ALYZ.
Various issues of *Plane Facts: The Magazine of the BOAC Flight Operations Department.*
Various issues of BOAC Review and BOAC News.
Various issues of: *Air-Britain Digest, Air-Britain Archive, Flypast, Air Pictorial, Aeroplane Monthly, Propliner.*

Websites

Royal Air Force Lyneham www.lyneham.raf.mod.uk
BBC News Online http://news.bbc.co.uk
Museum of Berkshire Aviation http://fly.to.MuseumofBerkshireAviation
A Little VC10derness http://fly.to/VC10
Aviation Safety Network http://aviation–safety.net
NICAP www.dabsol.co.uk
De Havilland Comet (Marc Schaeffer) http://surf.to/comet
De Havilland Comet (David Young) www.dlyoung.freeserve.co.uk/DH106/COMET
Airliners.Net www.airliners.net
Air-Britain. www.air-britain.com
Mike Charlton's Postcard Site www.maglas.freeserve.co.uk
The A.J. Jackson Photographic Collection www.ajjcollection.co.uk

Index

If you are interested in purchasing other books published by Tempus,
or in case you have difficulty finding any Tempus books in your local bookshop,
you can also place orders directly through our website

www.tempus-publishing.com